SISTERS IN ARMS

OSPREY
PUBLISHING

DEDICATION

To Andy and my daughters of the river,
Thames and Isis

JULIE WHEELWRIGHT

SISTERS IN ARMS

FEMALE WARRIORS FROM ANTIQUITY TO THE NEW MILLENNIUM

OSPREY PUBLISHING
Bloomsbury Publishing Plc
PO Box 883, Oxford, OX1 9PL, UK
1385 Broadway, 5th Floor, New York, NY 10018, USA
E-mail: info@ospreypublishing.com
www.ospreypublishing.com

OSPREY is a trademark of Osprey Publishing Ltd

This edition first published in Great Britain in 2020

This volume is based on material originally published as *Amazons and Military Maids* (1989).
Updated, expanded and revised for this new publication.

A catalogue record for this book is available from the British Library.

ISBN: HB 978 1 4728 3800 1; eBook 978 1 4728 3801 8; ePDF 978 1 4728 3802 5;
XML 978 1 4728 3799 8

20 21 22 23 24   10 9 8 7 6 5 4 3 2 1

Index by Zoe Ross

Typeset by Deanta Global Publishing Services, Chennai, India
Printed and bound in Great Britain by CPI (Group) UK Ltd, Croydon CR0 4YY

Osprey Publishing supports the Woodland Trust, the UK's leading woodland conservation charity.

To find out more about our authors and books visit **www.ospreypublishing.com**. Here you will
find extracts, author interviews, details of forthcoming events and the option to sign up for our
newsletter.

Contents

Acknowledgements

Behind every book is a team of people who have enabled its production. The idea to revisit my first book, *Amazons and Military Maids: Women Who Dressed As Men in Pursuit of Life, Liberty and Happiness*, published in 1989, came from Lisa Thomas, my editor at Osprey. So I owe a debt of gratitude to Lisa, who suggested there might be not only more to say on the subject of women in the military, and those who passed as men to enter its ranks, but that thirty years from the original, it might need a fresh approach. Although I have been writing on various aspects of women at war for the past decades, this book provided me with an opportunity to rethink my original ideas, to update and expand upon my research, and to ask new questions.

I'd also like to thank Marcus Cowper and Gemma Gardner at Osprey for their support, patience and professionalism. Jamilah Ahmed and Barbara Levy at the Barbara Levy Literary Agency were instrumental in launching this project. I'm also grateful to my colleagues in the English department at City, University of London, Patricia Moran, Lisa O'Donnell, Karen Seago, Minna Vuohelainen, and Caroline Sipos. Thanks to Liz Robertson at The Imperial War Museum London and Katy Jackson at the National Army Museum for providing opportunities to discuss my work in progress.

A number of archivists and historians generously shared their expertise. Dorothy Sheridan pointed me in the direction of the 'Colonel Barker' material at Mass Observation. Warren Sinclair provided archival material on Isabel Gunn; Julian Putkowski and

Julian Walker shared references on the First World War; and Dianne Dugaw was generous in providing references to eighteenth-century warrior heroines. I'd also like to thank Cynthia Enloe for her early inspiration and gendered analysis of the military, and historians Rudolf Dekker, Fraser Easton, Rene Gremaux, Louise Miller, Peter Moore, George Robb and Jane Schultz for sharing references and comments. Hannah Peake, Catherine Mayer, Sarah Waters and Kate Worsley generously provided their thoughts on contemporary and historical debates about sex and gender. I am grateful to several translators who were able to provide English texts from primary sources: Eva Antonijevic, Louise Askew, Henk van Kerkewijk, and Mira Harding. Arthur and Nan Baker welcomed me into their home to delve into the archives of their relative Flora Sandes, and provided me with lasting memories of her.

Maria Scherbov was a delight to work with, providing case studies of contemporary Russian servicewomen, translations of interviews and her cogent analysis. I am also grateful to Sarah Melcher, who gave me her thoughts on women playing male roles in historical re-enactment societies; and to documentary film maker Pepita Ferrari, who sadly passed away last year, for her generosity in sharing information about Sarah Emma Edmonds.

As ever, I am indebted to my family for their enormous support. My sister, Penny Wheelwright, the Canadian film director and producer, enabled us to revisit Isabel Gunn's story as a docu-drama, *The Orkney Lad: The Story of Isabel Gunn* in 2003. My daughters, Thames and Isis, remain my inspiration for speaking to future generations of powerful women. And my husband, Andy, makes everything possible.

Julie Wheelwright
London, 2019

Introduction

Under a cobalt summer sky, I arrived at the Plains of Abraham in Quebec City, the grassy expanse where British troops conquered the city in a pivotal battle of the Seven Years' War that would lead to the collapse of New France. It was 2004 and I was researching a biography about my eighteenth-century ancestor Esther Wheelwright, so was curious to witness a re-enactment of how they might have fought British and French colonial troops and militias on 13 September 1759. Above the fray I found the camp followers – mainly women, who, in early modern armies, provided the military's essential auxiliary services. Among tents, tipis, wooden stools and open fires, bonneted women drifted in petticoats and skirts, minding children, stirring iron pots or chatting as they sewed. While the menfolk cleaned muskets and adjusted uniforms, the women prepared real lunches for real children, much in the way that the historic military wives had. Or so I thought.

Amid the re-enactors preparing for battle, I discovered women in military uniform as soldiers, officers, drummers and fife players. I approached a figure dressed in the white breeches, green jacket and broad felt hat of the King's Rangers, a New England militia. Sarah Melcher, an American IT consultant, spoke eloquently about her adopted historic character. Chauncey Goodrich was a farm boy, born in 1740, who enlisted with the King's Rangers and fought in the Revolutionary War, and Sarah made clear that she was portraying a boy in the army. I was intrigued.

As Sarah talked about her life as Chauncey, I realized how strikingly her experiences reflected the historic cases of passing female combatants who were the subject of my 1989 book, *Amazons and Military Maids: Women who Dressed as Men in Pursuit of Life, Liberty and Happiness.* Listening, I recalled the early modern soldier Christian Davies, the British marine Hannah Snell, the French Girondist soldiers, sisters Félicité and Théophile de Fernig, the Russian cavalry officer Nadezhda Durova who fought against Napoleon, the American Civil War soldiers Sarah Emma Edmonds, Sarah Rosetta Wakeman and Loreta Velazquez, the Russian soldier of the Tsar's army Maria Bochkareva, and many more. Sarah herself was inspired to join the King's Rangers as Chauncey after reading about Deborah Sampson who fought as Robert Shurtliff during the American Revolutionary War. Whether one applauds or deplores their presence or their actions, they prove that women have always participated in wars, often volunteering for the same reason men do: to protect their country and their comrades.

Sarah shared with Sampson her motives for enlisting. While most female members of the King's Rangers re-enactment society stayed in camp, Sarah was drawn to the 'more active, running around kind of life' so became Chauncey. Her need to prove herself 'doubly to the men', to win their respect echoed the precious few reflections that history's female warriors left behind. 'When we're out there in camp or on the battlefield, the men know they can trust me. They know that I'll do the right thing and that I'll go the distance,' she says. The historic record offers scanty but illuminating details on attitudes towards the work itself which, for Sarah, was hard, involving maintenance of musket and kit, and long marches in a heavy wool uniform, all without the luxury of bathing. 'You've got to be able to get dirty, grubby and sweaty and not worry about it,' she says, recounting the awkwardness of keeping up her physical disguise, especially during her menstrual cycle. To support her male identity, among other things, she always carries a shaving kit. 'It still gets ugly. Many of the re-enacting men tend to be very conservative and that includes their perspective on how women should behave. Strong women doing what I was doing are often frowned upon. The women sewing and cooking are a lot less threatening.'

While historic female warriors rarely explain how, living amidst men, they would cope with such bodily functions as menstruation, they seem possessed of an intense pragmatism. More frequently, these women comment on their relationships with their comrades who, as Sarah found, might treat them like 'a little brother', and with whom a romance in her male persona was unthinkable. In more contemporary scenarios, where female combatants operated openly and even commanded mixed-gender units, their authority might be challenged. Although Sarah has won her fellow Rangers' acceptance, she says they still 'don't want to take orders from a female voice – no they don't – some of them don't mind but my major doesn't want the men taking orders from a woman.' Such resistance, Sarah thought, back in 2004, might prevent her from becoming an officer 'even though I might be one of the most competent soldiers there. I knew the drill and we were sharp and we were good.' When we spoke again in 2019, she had become a sergeant in her French and Indian unit, but said the men still 'didn't like strong women and I ended up getting complaints about what a bitch I was.' Her constant presence at events like the 1759 re-enactment, however, has inspired other women to take up their muskets, join cannon crews and adopt male roles. Even the past, it seems, cannot remain static.

———

Sarah reminded me of the hundreds of known, and countless unknown women who participated in combat, but whose stories were trivialized, reduced to sexual anecdotes, ignored or deliberately silenced. As military historian Linda Grant De Pauw so eloquently explains: 'Women have always and everywhere been inextricably involved in war. This thesis is simple and is supported by an abundance of evidence, but because it has profound, complex, and emotionally charged implications, the roles of women in war are hidden from history.' De Pauw, and many other contemporary historians have observed that when women become combatants their role is rationalized as exceptional. They threaten the social order because if girls can qualify as both mothers and warriors, what is the unique place for boys? This has historically led politicians, military authorities and public policy analysts to define concepts of 'battle' and 'combat' to keep women away from front-line fighting while letting them do the work of soldiers.[1] Such arguments form consistent patterns through the women's stories explored here which contribute to a collective feminist project of exposing and understanding female structural oppression.

The following book builds on my original research for *Amazons and Military Maids* as I attempt to bring these women out from history's shadows to explain the circumstances in which they enlisted and their motives for leaving their homes, families and ordered lives, to chronicle their experience and understand how it transformed them before they were forced by circumstances, or chose, to end their military careers. The return to Civvy Street for these warriors was often especially isolating and impoverished even though later generations might regard them as heroic figures, inspiring female readers' own rebellion against patriarchy's structures. The passing women warriors represented an alternative view of female physical and mental capabilities and showed up inequalities both of class and between the sexes which appalled some and excited others. They force us to consider basic questions about human nature and how women, in straitened circumstances, have found imaginative and courageous ways to transgress boundaries placed upon them.

While researching these lives in 2018 has provided me with a feast of new sources, there remains a paucity of writing from the women themselves, whether they were disguised or not. Memoirs, until the twentieth century, remain rare and those published in earlier historic periods were often ghost-written or contain fictional elements and conform to literary tropes which suggest the most unreliable of narrators. The insights they offer on attitudes towards bodies, sexual identities and sexual practices are necessarily limited. Those texts that have survived, however, demonstrate a remarkable consistency in women's experience, societal attitudes towards them, and their shared struggles.

Although the woman warrior is a universal phenomenon, my focus has been on European and North American conflicts where, until the early twentieth century, the context in which they entered the military can be roughly assembled into three categories. One belongs to military companions or wives who were already present on a ship or on campaign when fighting erupted and they took action. A second group disguised themselves as men to enlist, with or without a lover, husband or official complicity. And there is a final category where women were granted exceptional permission to enlist as individuals either within all-male regiments or in all-female or even mixed-gender units. I have also included cases of passing women who operated as sailors on merchant ships since they reveal much about the experience of quasi-military operations of the early modern period. The influence of the female warriors on popular culture, especially on female readers and audiences, is explored as a means through which women express their desire for the masculine privilege of participation in civil life and political decision-making.

Later chapters explore debates around women's admission into the armed services from the Second World War to the new millennium when they were recruited in unprecedented numbers to fight in global conflicts. The women who enlisted, or were conscripted, shared with their foremothers the challenges for acceptance or for equal pay, or of rumours about their sexuality as some endured sexual harassment or rape. For some the experience was utterly transformative, but despite proving their capabilities in warfare, women's participation did not automatically open up military occupations for future generations. Even while women have gained entry into combat specialisms across the globe, that ancient struggle continues. As Teresa Fazio, a former US Marine, concludes: 'The question, then, is not whether women can be effective combat troops but whether a hypermasculine military culture can adjust.'[2]

War rewards rather than sanctions women for behaving in ways deemed to be masculine. The servicewomen here, I argue, participate more for the benefits of masculine performance and less obviously from a sense of self-identification as human males. Military units, especially, require a homogeneity that is reflected in their dress, appearance and codes of behaviour; in combat, they depend upon each other for their survival and must act as one.

My critical framing is of gender, rather than of biological sex, and through this I explore historic sex-based patterns of oppression and harmful stereotypes. To make a meaningful assessment of an individual's internal conflict would require access to a subject's internal thoughts, which are largely beyond reach. This, of course, remains an area for further research and holds the possibility for innovative approaches. Readers of the passing women's stories have, however, understood them as transgressors whose actions reveal the constant tensions around definitions of gender. There is a paucity of sources for detailed, individual experiences of gender dysphoria, defined as 'a strong discomfort at the sexed aspects of physiognomy, even to the point of feeling "born into the wrong body"'.[3] In absence of such evidence, I have used female pronouns to refer to biological female adults where it accords with public presentation of their gender and male pronouns when referring to their male personas and identities.

In updating this book, I have considered the possible inheritors of the historic women warriors as a question to which there are many potential answers, but focus on the women in auxiliary services and combat roles from the 1930s to the new millennium. Since the publication of *Amazons and Military Maids*, I have written about American and British servicewomen in the Gulf Wars, and about the female fighters I met in Sudan and Eritrea. Their complex and emotionally charged struggles offered insight into the larger battles for equality taking place for women within civil society. This is now a massive and well-researched topic, in which a new generation of military women have contributed their own memoirs, academic studies, reportage and histories. I chose to concentrate the final chapters on historical continuities and discontinuities in the experiences of servicewomen in Britain, the United States, the Soviet Union and Russia where previous generations of sisters in arms both inspire and offer cautionary tales. Like any history, this is a work-in-progress, and my humble contribution to a longer, deeper and wider conversation.

Chapter 1

The Persistence of a Phenomenon

Victor Barker, a tall figure with neatly cropped dark hair, faintly streaked with grey, and a ruddy complexion, strode down the path towards St Peter's church, known as Brighton's Cathedral, on a frost-licked November morning in 1923 to marry Elfrida Haward. The bride's parents witnessed Reverend Laurence Hard conduct the proceedings as the bride wed a groom she would later describe as 'extraordinarily handsome, beautifully dressed, with perfect manners and tremendous, compelling charm'.[1] After the ceremony Elfrida and 'Bill', as Barker was known, departed for a modest wedding breakfast at Brighton's Grand Hotel where the couple had taken rooms.[2]

Six years later, now living as Captain Leslie Ivor Victor Gauntlett Bligh Barker, Elfrida's husband was arrested for contempt of court in connection with bankruptcy proceedings and put down for trial at London's Old Bailey Court.[3] On 28 February 1929, Barker was taken from the Regent Palace Hotel to Brixton Prison where medical officer Francis Herbert Brisby conducted a routine examination on the newly admitted prisoner. Although stripped down to trousers and singlet, Barker refused to remove anything else. When the doctor chided the prisoner, 'Why, are you a woman?' Barker asked whether Brisby could 'take my word for it that I am alright'. Brisby refused, gently. A long pause followed before Barker 'finally said that "he" had a confession to make that "he" was a woman', confirming

Brisby's suspicions. Soon, the prisoner was committed to Holloway Gaol for women to spend the night in hospital, recovering from a 'nervous reaction' to her arrest.[4]

After Brisby's discovery and the revelation that Barker was, in fact, Valerie Arkell-Smith, she faced an additional charge of perjury in connection with her marriage to Haward. During the subsequent trial, the prosecution grappled with the complexities of a woman who had successfully masqueraded as a man for six years, convincing even public officials that he had served as a messing officer in the British Expeditionary Force on the Western Front and claiming to have received the Distinguished Service Order.[5] When 'Colonel Barker' (she used many titles and names) was found guilty before an astonished court, the judge declared the case 'of an unprecedented and very peculiar nature' and sentenced her to nine months at Holloway.

The tabloid press had a field day. Features about the 'Colonel' were splashed across front pages with headlines that promised startling details about a 'Woman's Strange Life as Man', and, from Elfrida's perspective, life as a 'Duped Wife of Bogus DSO'. The public interest was so intense that the court doors were locked before the morning sessions to prevent overcrowding; all available seats were occupied and 'many fashionably dressed women stood in the gangways and between the seats.'[6] Prosecutor Sir Ernest Wild[7] probed deep into the Colonel's life for the dramatic disclosure that two years before the wedding in Brighton, Arkell-Smith had been tried in London – as a man – for possessing a forged firearms certificate. The Colonel, eyes swathed in bandages, had been guided into court on the arm of a friend who explained *sotto voce* that Victor suffered from stress-induced 'hysterical blindness', a legacy of the war. On 14 July 1927 Judge Llewellyn Atherley-Jones, who was known to be sympathetic to men charged with consensual homosexual offences, found Victor Barker, 'a retired army officer', not guilty of possessing falsified documents.[8]

Mr Freke Palmer, the Colonel's defending counsel in 1929, explained to the court what he saw as the larger matters at stake.[9] 'There has been a great deal of publicity in this matter,' he said, 'because a woman has been bold enough and has succeeded in earning her living as a man when she found that she could not do it as a woman. It seems to shock some people but there is no law against it.'[10]

Arkell-Smith's adopted martial identity opened doors into a masculine world; a brief acting career; management of a boxing club and later a dog kennel, a dairy farm and an orchard; riding with the Tedworth Hunt; playing cricket for a village team; the purchase of an antique and second-hand furniture business and a café. Valerie had, in reality, served her country during the war, not as an officer but as a nurse with the Voluntary Aid Detachment and, from August 1918, as a driver with the newly formed Women's Royal Air Force. Like so many women of her generation, however, she longed for action, as she would later recall, 'As the news of the fighting overseas came through, I felt an urge to do something more vigorous.'[11] While the veterans of the VAD and the WRAF, and thousands of other women workers, were dismissed from the labour force after the war, by posing as a retired officer, the Colonel had a better chance of securing a post. 'Although there was something mysterious about the new reception clerk,' an official at the Regent Palace Hotel told the court, 'we accepted him as what he pretended to be, an ex-army officer down on his luck.'[12] The court needed little persuading that it was all so much easier for Valerie Arkell-Smith as an officer and a gentleman.

Press reports, however, made no connection between the Colonel's relationship with Elfrida Haward and the lesbian love depicted in Radclyffe Hall's novel *The Well of Loneliness* which had been a major story only a few months earlier. On 9 November 1928 a court declared the novel – the first in Britain to explicitly describe a lesbian relationship – obscene and banned it six weeks after publication. Hall found the Colonel's case upsetting and feared that the trial gave the cause of same-sex relationships the very worst publicity. In male guise, the Colonel may have acted as Elfrida's dream man, but after four years of marriage, during which he flirted openly with other women, he deserted her for a 'red-headed woman ... [who] seemed to be able to make Bill do anything she wanted.'[13] Hall feared that 'Bill's' caddish behaviour would reflect badly on lesbians arguing for social acceptance. As she wrote to her friend and agent Audrey Heath: 'I would like to see [Colonel Barker] drawn and quartered ... A mad pervert of the most undesirable type ... and then after having married the woman if she doesn't go and desert her.'[14] Both the novelist and the bogus officer may have shared an interest in women claiming male social privileges but their methods were diametrically opposed: Valerie Arkell-Smith continued to live as a man and enjoy lesbian relationships even after release from prison, while Hall never presented herself as anything but 'a woman with a masculine psyche'.[15]

The Colonel Barker trial was heard less than a decade after Lieutenant-Colonel Moore-Brabazon MP's endorsement of an amendment to the Criminal Law Amendment Bill that would have added a new offence of gross indecency between women. The Conservative MP had advocated that in dealing with lesbians, parliament should consider the options of the death penalty, of incarceration 'as lunatics', or of continuing its strategy of deliberate silence.[16] Despite the very public nature of Bill and Elfrida's relationship, some press reports portrayed the Colonel with surprising sympathy. Arkell-Smith was seen, unlike Hall, as idiosyncratic, merely imitating male behaviour rather than appropriating it to promote sexual freedom and women's equality within that most masculine of spheres, the military. While some journalists may have struggled to understand Arkell-Smith's relationships, images of women in men's clothing and transgressive sexuality were widely circulated in mainstream popular culture including magazines such as *Ally Sloper's Half Holiday*, *London Life*, *Modern Society* and *Photo Bits*.[17]

In the tabloid version, Haward was the innocent who never realized her husband was 'anything but a man' until the trial. In early press interviews Haward said she met Colonel Barker, a tall, good-looking and charming officer, in her father's chemist shop in Littlehampton, Sussex. However, later in court, she confessed to knowing Arkell-Smith first as Mrs Pearce-Crouch, mother of two, who came into the shop dressed in a Women's Land Army uniform of trousers and an open-necked shirt. Haward protested that their earlier friendship, and her knowledge of Barker's biological sex, was irrelevant to their subsequent romance: 'Because she courted me as a man, I believed she was a man.'[18] Moreover, Arkell-Smith told her 'there could be no normal relations' because of an abdominal injury 'Bill' had suffered during the war. Arkell-Smith even managed to convince Haward's father that she was really Sir Victor Barker, baronet. It was explained to Elfrida and her father that Arkell-Smith's mother had always wanted a daughter and when Sir Victor senior died (the title was invented), she insisted on dressing her son as a girl. On the strength of this elaborate fantasy, Elfrida accepted the Colonel's proposal to which Mr Haward agreed.

The following day's testimony of the already sensational trial revealed yet another twist. Haward admitted that the couple had only married after her father had discovered them living together in Brighton's Grand Hotel in 1923. At this point in Haward's testimony, Sir Ernest, who had famously backed Moore-Brabazon's 1921 'gross indecency' amendment, focused his attention on the nature of the couple's relationship. He asked Elfrida if she had lived at the Grand with Barker, 'apparently as husband and wife?'

'Yes,' replied Elfrida.
'Did you sleep in the same room and bed?' he queried.
'Yes,' replied Elfrida who began to show signs of fainting as Wild pressed on.
'When did you discover she was a woman?'
'Not until I read about it in the newspapers.'[19]

In her extreme anxiety and, to preserve her reputation and avoid public vilification, Elfrida committed perjury. But Sir Ernest took up his cudgels, announcing that more upsetting than the possible motives for two women wanting to marry was their deception to innocent parties. In his summary he thundered: 'If [Colonel Barker] had wanted to marry another woman she could have gone through a ceremony in a register office. There is no justification for her abusing the church.'[20] To the prosecution, Valerie Arkell-Smith's lack of discretion was her greatest crime. Instead of furtively cross-dressing, she had flaunted the 'Colonel' before British society, choosing ever grander and riskier sights against which to test her new-found male persona. 'As the weeks slipped by,' she wrote of her transition from wife and mother to officer, 'I began to experience a sense of exhilaration at the knowledge I was getting away with it.'[21] She was shameless.

There was more. The *Sketch* reported that Arkell-Smith had successfully used her officer's guise to deceive Colonel R. Neave, who had witnessed her 1918 wedding to Australian officer Harold Arkell-Smith. When Colonel Neave had encountered Valerie as the 'Colonel', his knowledge of military manoeuvres had persuaded Colonel Neave to help organize a Fellowship of the Mons dinner at London's Adelphi restaurant. 'It is perhaps the biggest and most complex hoax the West End has ever known,' Neave said of her exploits, 'and I was completely deceived by "Colonel" Barker.'[22] The *Daily Express* portrayed Barker as a romantic figure who 'received a man's welcome among men, smoked, drank, worked and played as a man with men'.[23] For Arkell-Smith's astonishing ability to successfully pass as a man among men, reporters could only praise her. But in court, Arkell-Smith's piteous tears at the sight of Haward suggested, according to the *Express*, that she 'broke down and showed that she was, indeed, a woman'.[24] She descended into pathos, a figure bordering on collapse during the trial and when asked to stand murmured, 'Oh God, I cannot.' After she was charged, 'with tears streaming down her face and leaning heavily on two policemen, she was almost carried through a side door to another room'.[25]

Arkell-Smith played the eccentric and divorced herself from campaigns for sexual freedom or gender equality, claiming that her male disguise arose from financial necessity. Making a living, as Victor, or Bill or Colonel Barker was simply easier and more satisfying, and the Recorder of London, the Old Bailey's senior circuit judge, accepted this explanation. While Sir Ernest believed the defendant's short cut to economic security was unique, he remained concerned about its long-term effect on Britain's women. 'You are an unprincipled, mendacious and unscrupulous adventuress,' he told Arkell-Smith during her sentencing. 'You have profaned the House of God, you have outraged the decencies of Nature and you have broken the Laws of man ... You have set an evil example, which, were you to go unpunished, others might follow.'[26]

His vociferous condemnation reflected a broader societal fear that was current in the decades following the First World War when New Women were protesting, through individual and collective action, against oppressive gender conventions. With Hall's trial and public debates about whether women's war work in 'masculine' jobs had rendered them unfit for domesticity, the cross-dresser became a potent symbol. Typical was a *Daily Sketch* cartoon that depicted a pinch-faced woman wearing a suit and tie questioning a blimpish male politician during the 1929 election. 'Do you believe in sex equality?' she asks. He snaps back: 'Certainly, but leave us the neckties.'[27] Male power still resided in the masculine symbols of ties, trousers, cropped haircuts and, of course, an officer's uniform.

Wild was wrong in thinking of the Colonel's case as an anomaly.[28] Rather, Valerie Arkell-Smith's decision to adopt a military guise was rooted in a long tradition of passing women in uniform. The warrior heroine would have been recognizable to 1930s readers of the British newspaper accounts about the trial. The woman who swaps her skirts for a uniform played the role of the bold escapee, a prankster who adopted the most masculine of male professions for her own personal liberty. 'Behind the change from woman to man,' Arkell-Smith wrote in 1956, 'I would be able to screen myself against all the tortures, miseries and difficulties of the past and work out my own salvation.'[29] The marriage to Elfrida legitimized their relationship, and had its parallels in the lives of female-husbands and women in uniform who were standard fare in British tabloid newspapers throughout the century.[30]

In the post-war period, the avid readers of the Colonel's travails would be familiar with other women during the Great War, and in early historic periods, who wore military uniforms and enlisted to fight in military campaigns. They were also figures of erotic fantasies where the wearing of trousers and shouldering of weapons operated as the ultimate disruption of the gendered order.[31] Contrary to Wild's belief, women had been breaking the laws of men and outraging the decencies of nature since antiquity. Colonel Barker represented a continuity of such traditions rather than the revolution that Wild and his contemporaries so feared.

Chapter 2

The Founding Myth of the Amazons

*'I spoke to you of Amazons before ... but I could give you many
examples of women on our own ships who did men's service and
were exceptionally brave. Of these I could tell many amusing
stories only they would take up too much paper. I could also
tell you how I myself discovered women in soldier's clothing in
our armies and made them change their dress. During my days
in the army a girl in the cavalry was caught plundering and
suffered herself to be hung without her sex known. This sergeant
on duty told me; he had her undressed after she had died and felt
sorry about it. And are such women not also Amazons?'[1]*
NICOLAAS WITSEN, 1641–1717

The seventeenth-century mayor of Amsterdam, amateur geographer
and cartographer Nicolaas Witsen, took a keen interest in maritime
affairs, an inevitable consequence of his scientific journeys to
remote regions such as Morocco, the Levant and even Moscow
where he served as ambassador in 1665. As a cosmopolitan, he
could communicate in Arabic, Chinese, Turkish and Persian, often
commenting on the habits of people whose languages he studied.[2]
In Witsen's memoir, he writes of his Greek friends whose literature
may have inspired his comparison between the female combatants
of the Anglo-Dutch Wars and the mythic warrior women of
antiquity, the Amazons.

While stories of women at arms are as old as warfare itself, tales of a female tribe who sliced off their breasts to facilitate their bows, rejected or mutilated male babies and chose their partners from among their enslaved captives have proved the most enduring.[3] The ancient Greeks immortalized these superior female beings, who led their own armies to engage Heracles and other mythic heroes in combat. Popular among the Greeks, these stories offered an aspirational vision of equality between the sexes that was 'rumoured to exist in a faraway land called Scythia, the Amazon homeland'.[4] It was the Greeks' fear and fascination with these figures who represented a universal desire to reconcile the differences between men and women that ensured their survival in oral and written narratives passed down through the centuries. They were, in a sense, the founding mothers of the mythic female combatants.

Although earlier scholars dismissed the Amazons as a classic Greek fantasy, recent archaeological discoveries have confirmed their physical existence from battle-scarred female skeletons buried with weapons, found among the nomads of the Scythian steppes of Eurasia.[5] The 'Amazons' were actually women of Scythian society who lived amongst their men and were raised as equals, wore the same practical clothes as boys, and learned to shoot arrows and to ride. Even as mothers, they continued to share the same rugged outdoor life as their men. According to historian Adrienne Mayor, adventures of these women warriors – expert horsewomen who used defensive weapons, and were known to lead military campaigns – were mythologized in ancient cultures from the Mediterranean to the Great Wall of China.[6]

The Greeks wove their Amazonian stories from details culled from household slaves, from travelling merchants and from their encounters with the Scythians themselves. Although the tales were often garbled by mistranslation, the Greeks chose to imagine these women as worthy human adversaries for their heroes.[7] The mythmaking continued into the twentieth century until archaeologists such as Renate Rolle began to question the sex of skeletons buried in Scythian grave mounds (*kurgans*) in Ukraine. The possessions buried with the bodies included female items such as spindles and mirrors and also knives, swords and arrows, assumed by earlier archaeologists to be exclusively male objects. In an astonishing find at a Scythian dig along the Dnieper estuary in southern Ukraine, Rolle discovered female skeletons with weapons in six of the fifty-three graves.[8] Altogether, more than 1,000 tombs of ancient Scythians and related tribes have now been evacuated across the Eurasian steppes from Bulgaria to Mongolia with some cemetery populations revealing females in up to 37 per cent of burials.[9] In the same way that contemporary historians have verified the existence of hundreds of female warriors in later European conflicts, these recent archaeological discoveries have provided documented evidence of the Scythian women who inspired the Amazonian figures of Greek myths, art (they are depicted on more than 1,000 ancient Greek vases) and classical histories, geographies, ethnographies and other writings.[10] Mayor's compelling work on the relationship between the history of the Scythian women and the Greek Amazonian myths reveals how plausible historical accounts of women as combatants and military leaders were later 'transformed into something more sensational', obscuring the reality of those female lives and achievements.[11]

These ancient stories of autonomous women warriors who behaved as the equals of men spread far beyond the geographical boundaries of Western Europe to encompass cultures in the Caucasus, the Near East, Central Asia and China.[12] The exploits of women combatants, based on fragmentary details, continued to feature in narratives about the wars that changed the shape of Europe between the fall of Rome and the end of the eighteenth century. Throughout this grand sweep of history, the female warrior's story, whether expressed as a raucous tale, told in a ballad, performed on stage or appearing in print, inspired other women to undertake their own acts of rebellion by dressing as men and heading off to war.

Following the Dark Ages, scattered references to 'Amazonian' women both as military leaders and as combatants surface in reports of battles over territory and religious belief. Details of the most famous of the women warriors of the Middle Ages can be found in the writings of Saxo Grammaticus, a thirteenth-century chronicler of the Norse Wars. He writes of those who dressed as men and 'devoted every waking moment to the pursuit of war'.[13] Equally well known were bands of Viking pirates composed of Saxon, Goth and Swedish women who 'offered war, not kisses, and went about the business of arms, not amours', rejecting the loom for the lance and assailing men with spears.[14]

Women's presence in later medieval military campaigns led the writer Christine De Pizan to observe in her tract *Treasure of the City of the Ladies* (c.1405), that 'if [a noble widow's] land is attacked by foreign enemies – as frequently happens after the death of a prince with underage children – it will be necessary for her to make and conduct war'.[15] De Pizan, who is credited with writing the first feminist statement, collected examples of women who had mastered the arts of war. Later, she followed keenly the exploits of Jeanne d'Arc to whom she composed a stirring poem, written immediately after the coronation of King Charles at Reims. In praising the Maid's triumphs in raising the siege of Orléans, De Pizan argued that 'because she is only "a little girl of sixteen"', Jeanne had accomplished more than such towering classical heroes as Moses, Joshua, Gideon, Hector and Achilles.[16] According to historian Anne Llewellyn Barstow, De Pizan celebrated Jeanne for attempting to encompass 'both the masculine, invincible warrior and the diminutive but potent young maid'.[17] Like many warrior women who would follow her example, the nobility of Jeanne's cause, and her piety, would excuse its masculine expression.

Jeanne d'Arc, who led the French armies against the English in 1429–30 during the Lancastrian phase of the Hundred Years' War, remained a potent and controversial figure. An impoverished peasant girl, Jeanne claimed that holy spirits had instructed her to wear male clothing, to find a sword hidden behind an altar, and, with the Dauphin's support, to lead his soldiers in driving the English out of France.[18] Her success in liberating Orléans and other decisive military victories in May 1429 won her comparisons with Alexander the Great and with Caesar.[19] The following month Jeanne led the French troops again and in July 1429 accompanied

Charles to his coronation. Despite resounding achievements, throughout the following year, at Compiègne in May 1430 she was wounded, captured and turned over to her political enemies, the Burgundians.[20] Jeanne was tried and condemned for heresy as a military leader, and for the abomination of wearing men's clothing: she was burned at the stake in 1431 and canonized as a virgin saint in 1920.[21] As will be explored later in this volume, she regained significance in the twentieth century as an iconic figure for European women's suffrage movements whose followers compared Jeanne with the female combatants of the First World War.

From the late sixteenth to the end of the eighteenth century there are records of hundreds of women soldiers and sailors passing as men, many of them known to their recruiters, to the men they served alongside and to their commanding officers. In Germany, the Netherlands and England, fresh recruits were in high demand to fill ranks and fight wars erupting across the continent. Against the background of women's individual entry into the military, there were well-known cases in England of women passing as men for very different reasons.[22] Historians Judith Bennett and Shannon McSheffrey found thirteen reported cases, in civil and ecclesiastical records, of female cross-dressing in London before 1603. Passing allowed women to facilitate sexual liaisons, a practice that church and state condemned as examples of sexual misrule.

Recently, historian Mark Stoyle has uncovered evidence of both passing women and those in quasi-masculine attire who served in the armies of the King and parliament during the English Civil War.[23] He identifies five women who took up arms between 1642 and 1646. Among them was 'a poore loving Wench', mentioned in an anonymous letter written from King Charles I's camp which comments that 'Nan Ball ... was taken in mans cloathes, waiting upon her beloved Lieutenant' in the monarch's army near York, 'and by a foolish accident [was] betrayed and carried before the Earle of Lindsey'.[24] She was brought to a senior member of the royalist camp who demanded an explanation for her presence and although she escaped a severe punishment, was promptly expelled.

If caught a second time, she would have been 'whipped like [a] common strumpet'.[25]

While Nan Ball's motive for enlisting – to follow her lover – appeared conventional, Dorothy Leeke, a young gentlewoman, was swept up in the conflict when her mistress, Lady Sydenham, resolved to follow *her* husband. Such royal camp followers, while not disguised, may have adapted to military conditions pragmatically by pulling on men's breeches and other warm clothes more flexible and comfortable than dresses and stays. By June 1643 the prevalence of passing women in his army led King Charles to propose that: 'no woman presume to counterfeit her sex by wearing mens apparall under payne of the severest punishment.'[26] Like many of his contemporaries, Charles presumed that any woman who entered his army wearing trousers was a sex worker. However, Stoyle suggests that the king later reworked his proclamation, perhaps fearing that it might draw attention to women in his ranks (and give his enemies ammunition to mock him). Or there may have been practical difficulties in barring female warriors. Whatever his reasoning, the final version deleted references to the passing women whose presence aroused moral condemnation.[27] Ironically, the leaders of the New Model Army from whom Charles feared ridicule also included women within its ranks as foot-soldiers (infantry) and as troopers.[28]

The wider context for women's participation as soldiers in early modern Europe were the well-known cases of passing women who featured in pamphlets or popular ballads as examples of 'sexual misrule' and were a staple of seventeenth-century English dramas. According to one estimate of the more than 300 plays performed in London between 1600 and 1700, eighty-nine included roles in which female actors dressed as men.[29] The 'roaring girls' of the English stage disrupted the social order that required each gender to maintain its proper function through appropriate dress and appearance. The women warriors were symbols, albeit fleeting, of threatening female aggression, further evidence that the world was topsy-turvy during this turbulent period.[30] At their story's end, the female protagonist usually returned to her appropriate role, ultimately reinforcing the importance and stability of sexual difference. A century would pass before the woman warrior became a popular and familiar heroine.

Although there is mounting evidence of women passing in a range of occupations and trades, the best-documented cases are drawn from the military.[31] The long years of war in the eighteenth century when naval press gangs were active along British coastal towns produced more than 100 female warriors in more than 1,000 variants of Anglo-American ballads.[32] Although cases have been discovered from Denmark to Spain and Italy during this period, passing women seem to have been concentrated in England, Germany and the Netherlands where historians Rudolf Dekker and Lotte van de Pol found 119 cases, many of whom were soldiers or sailors.[33] The Amazons of antiquity remained a touchstone, despite the numbers of popular and home-grown contemporary stories which suggest that female warriors flourished in the Netherlands before waning in the nineteenth century. Throughout the Napoleonic Wars, they would resurface in dozens of recorded cases in continental European countries, and in England.[34]

Russian women also recognized their historical links to the Scythians who, according to legend, originated in the south Russian steppes and were immortalized in epic songs, *byliny*, as fierce maidens who engage in combat before settling back into domesticity.[35] The most famous Russian woman to engage in the fight against Napoleon's forces, however, inverted the legend by fleeing from her family's estate into a Cossack regiment. Nadezhda Durova was enormously influential for later generations of women fighters in Russia, for those campaigning for women's rights in the mid-nineteenth century and even for female combatants in the Red Army.

Like many earlier female warriors, Durova came from a military family. Her father was a hussar officer, quartered in Kiev, and until she reached the age of five, his orderly, Astakhov, acted as Nadezhda's nanny. She remembered how he would 'carr[y] me around all day, taking me into the squadron stables and sitting me on the horses, giving me a pistol to play with, and brandishing his sabre while

I clapped my hands and laughed'.[36] Later, her father presented her with a spirited horse, Alcides, and a Cossack-style uniform, defying his wife's attempts to tame their daughter's 'knightly spirit'. But by the age of eighteen, her marriage was arranged to a civil servant, Vasilij Chernov, and she gave birth to a son two years later. She feared a future of drudgery, caring for an ailing father, a child and her younger siblings, and this propelled her into action. So in September 1806 Durova cropped her thick, dark curls, dressed in her childhood costume of 'Cossack apparel' and, astride Alcides, joined a passing troop marching towards Lithuania.[37] She proved herself in battle against Napoleon's army before winning a commission in Tsar Alexander I's hussars' campaign; she served in three different regiments and saw action at the battle of Borodino before retiring.[38] While Durova's exploits were publicized through a memoir in Aleksandr Pushkin's magazine *Contemporary* in 1836,[39] evidence was emerging of other women in Austria, France, Germany and Prussia taking up their country's cause, during wars where 'probably every major battle … left women sprawled among the casualties'.[40] Durova's writing was known among Russia's educated class and at the outbreak of the First World War it inspired women to petition the Tsar to join the army. A number who wished to fight cited Durova in their petitions, such as Elena Iost who wrote to the military authorities on 28 May 1916, 'I will be so bold as to remind your Imperial Highness that already a hundred years ago a certain young woman, officer N. Durova, served in the ranks of our glorious army and participated in the battles of the campaigns of 1812.'[41]

And if women were unable to take up arms, they might dream about joining their fathers or brothers in battle. Fredrika Bremer, later known as the 'Swedish Jane Austen'[42] and the namesake for her country's first women's rights organization,[43] dreamed of enlisting in the fight against Napoleon's force. While living at Arsta, her family's country estate near Stockholm in 1813, Fredrika aspired to become a soldier after a group of officers from the Crown Prince Bernadette's Södermanland Regiment were billeted there. 'She wept bitterly for not having been born a man,' wrote her sister Charlotte, 'so that she could have joined her countrymen against the general disturber of the peace and oppressor of nations; she wanted to fight for her native country; longed to distinguish herself to win renown and glory.'[44] That desire to participate in warfare as an expression of active citizenship, and its connection with political engagement for women's rights, are powerful themes that surface frequently in the female warrior's story.

English women, meanwhile, were also mobilizing to take up arms against Napoleon's forces. Hearing rumours of an invasion, in 1803 the women of Neath petitioned Henry Addington, first Viscount of Sidmouth, for permission to defend themselves and their children:

> There are in this town about 200 women who have been used to hard labour all the days of our lives such as working in coal-pits, on the high roads, tilling the ground, etc. If you would grant us arms, that is light pikes … we do assure you that we could in a short time learn our exercise.[45]

When Addington rejected the women's plea, that, 'we are not trifling with you but serious in our proposal', in Devon and Cornwall they took matters into their own hands, dressing in military uniform to defend ports from the French and Spanish. Wrapped in red cloaks, they stood at the headlands in military formation to swell the appearance of the defence and frighten the enemy.[46]

The stories of female warriors and heroic wives illustrate their vital role in warfare. Although not officially recognized, they served aboard ships, worked in cannon crews, nursed the wounded and even gave birth at sea. They sailed with the 'first rates' during the Napoleonic Wars and performed a variety of jobs during large-scale operations. Women were equally vital in early modern armies as they foraged for food and other goods, sold meats and wines, laundered and sewed, and sold sex for money.[47] Their presence at Britain's largest military battles in the eighteenth and nineteenth centuries was well documented by officers and serving men. Sergeant-Major Edward Cotton's account of the battle of Waterloo in 1815 mentions those who died on the field, including a female officer of the French Hussars:

> Many women were found amongst the slain although not of the same class as the [French] Heroine alluded to. As is common in the camp, the camp followers wore male attire, with nearly as martial a bearing as the soldiers and some were even mounted and rode astride.[48]

Their function was organized, and received official recognition, only in the mid-nineteenth century. By then, three-quarters of Britain's infantry were stationed overseas and the decline of soldiers' employment in civilian service, alongside the construction of large-scale buildings, further removed them from public view. The establishment of barracks, in which they were now housed, excluded soldiers' relatives, along with sutlers, laundresses, seamstresses and other service providers. For the first time, sexual and marital relations were brought under the military's direct control. As the army became increasingly professional and bureaucratic, regiments assumed control over all aspects of a soldier's life as it became an increasingly male environment.[49]

Alongside changing ideals of femininity were practical changes in women's roles within the British military, which was being reorganized to conform more fully to Victorian concepts of marriage and family responsibility.[50] A dramatic rewriting of women's military history subsequently took place in the late nineteenth century, when female soldiers and sailors were either erased from official narratives or reduced to amusing anecdotes. The female soldiers hailed as heroines, albeit exceptions, a century earlier were now portrayed in popular histories as amusing freaks of nature and their stories regarded as examples of 'coarseness and triviality'.[51]

Throughout the nineteenth century, collections of stories about some of these famous female warriors appeared on booksellers' lists and peppered the pages of antiquarian magazines. Collected editions of their life-histories were still being produced by the century's end, albeit sanitized to conform to Victorian sensibilities. The Amazonian heroine appeared to go underground, attracting audiences into British music-halls where the lass in breeches swaggered in a caricature of masculinity. Pleasure Gardens provided another outlet for this powerful fantasy. At these venues in working-class neighbourhoods of London such as Vauxhall and Bermondsey, women could rent male costumes at the door or arrive in naval or army uniforms; here they had licence to rough-house with their male companions and to smoke and drink at the bar.[52] Newspapers regularly reported their appearance throughout the century.

There was little need to convince audiences or readers that women could withstand the hardships of the ship, army camp or campaign marches. A report in 1813 from a London newspaper, the *Weekly Dispatch*, illustrates women's involvement in the rough and tumble of masculine culture in that violent period. On a quiet Sunday morning in early October 1813, a crowd gathered in a South London field to witness 'a kind of pitched battle' between boxers Mary Flaharty and Peggy Carey for the prize of £17 10s. Although Carey won after the final round, 'both ladies were much punished and Mary was taken away senseless in a tilbury [cart]'.[53] That women of the early nineteenth century not only boxed but rode horses, hunted, played cricket and participated in other physically demanding sports lent credibility to female warriors. Whether they were farm labourers, fisherwomen or factory hands, women were engaged in work that demanded brawn and endurance, all of which were documented in the vivid descriptions and carefully composed photographs of a Victorian civil servant.

Arthur J. Munby led a double life, escaping from the dullness of his desk job in the Ecclesiastical Commissioner's office to wander London's streets, recording his exchanges with working women, and those who dressed in men's clothes. He subscribed to a press cutting service for reports of passing women whom he often interviewed. Typical was Munby's entry for 18 February 1866, when he met Helen, alias Richard Bruce, in Stroud, Gloucestershire after her female identity had been exposed. Bruce had begun his adventure with another passing woman who ran errands from

St Paul's churchyard in London and, in the seven years he had lived as a man, had known many others. Among them was a girl sailor from Downham Market, Norfolk, and an Aberdonian who served as an ordinary seaman but after discovery found another job, in male disguise, at the Gateshead Iron Works. Bruce met his Scottish friend in a pub where they disclosed their mutual secrets and became firm friends. And only a week before Bruce's arrest, as if to prove how prolific such cases were, the Ipswich police picked up 'a lass tramping West her way in sailor's clothes'.[54]

But if the Victorians found the female soldier and sailor too gritty and working class to warrant much attention beyond the risqué, this figure received a burst of fresh interest and prestige during the Great War. Magazines and newspapers in the United Kingdom and abroad often featured photos and reports of women fighting on the front lines, disguised as men or serving in Russia's all-female battalions. As historian Julian Walker's study of British satirical magazines reveals, they featured cartoons and stories about female soldiers and women in uniform which were 'highly sexualized, and exploitative, particularly exploiting the war environment for sexual titillation: e.g. they carry narratives of historical female soldiers, cartoons of sexualized women in uniforms, women wearing uniforms as lingerie'.[55] Walker observes, however, that in the magazine published as *Ally Soper's Half Holiday*, *Photo Bits* and *Modern Society*, whose titles had an estimated two to three million readers, the women in uniform were rarely disguised. Rather, along with a titillating enthusiasm, these warriors appeared in exaggerated female form with curvy hips, large breasts and tiny feet encased in heels.

The debate about whether women were fit for combat, and its potential impact on relations between the sexes, was lively on both sides of the Atlantic. As Dr Dudley Sergeant, a physical expert at Harvard University, told a journalist in 1917: 'The average, normal woman ... is biologically more of a barbarian.'[56] If their aggressive potential were unleashed, male commentators feared it would create a monstrous regiment of women. In Britain, as able-bodied men vacated jobs in industry for the Western Front, women filled their places and so the female combatant came to symbolize the ultimate breakdown in the gendered order. If women could now defend their countries by taking up arms, went a popular argument, they would soon be agitating for the right to political power. Indeed, as we'll see later in this volume, there were powerful links between narratives of the female combatants of the First World War and women's suffrage.

The following chapters will address questions which will focus on the Amazons' long legacy as we explore the practical methods and psychological processes that enabled women to cope with the female warriors' paradox; how did they transform and adapt to their male roles, how did they continue their disguise, what happened when they were discovered, how did their comrades respond, what became of them afterwards and how were they remembered? In wars men would assert their role as patriarchs at a time when gender differences were heightened and divisions of labour were blurred. Men became defenders of nations, protectors of their metaphorical and actual women and children. When the female warriors found themselves in battle, their circumstances were very different. As a collection, they offer an alternative view of military history, one which acknowledges their significant contribution and insights into the business of warfare itself.

Chapter 3

Enlisting

'On the first day of May, 1759, about six o'clock in the morning, I set off; and when I had got out of town into the fields, I pulled off my cloaths, and put on mens, leaving my own in a hedge, some in one place and some in another … a gentleman came up to me, and asked me if I would go to sea? for, said he, it is fine weather now at sea; if you go I will get you a good master on board the Sandwich.'

MARY LACY, 1773

Why would a woman risk her home, reputation, job and even her future to enlist as a soldier, or take to the high seas, and how did she get away with it? The answers to these questions are as varied as the circumstances of war. But we do know that many women longed to travel, to flee poverty, an abusive husband or a future filled with drudgery. Sometimes they came from military families where male relatives or friends enabled their disguise, or, if they came from a wealthy family, enjoyed special dispensation from their military commanders. They often came from labouring communities where women were confident of their bodily strength as they worked side by side with men so when their fathers or brothers went 'for a soldier', or were pressed into service, they realized they could cope with the hardship of a military life and relished its rewards.

In the early modern period, army and naval recruiters, fishers and even farmers in the Netherlands advised impoverished young women to become sailors or to pass as men in other occupations in a long-established tradition. An innkeeper advised Francina Gunnigh, travelling alone through France in 1811, to sell her clothes and buy a man's suit for protection. Unfortunately, she was caught a few days later by a French Gendarme and, without any identification, arrested as a deserter and quickly enrolled in the army corps at Cherbourg.[2] As Gunnigh's story illustrates, recruiters, concerned with rounding up required numbers, paid little attention to a man's capacity for duty. During periods of acute labour shortages, if a young lad was adequately performing his duties, dismissal on the basis of gender might create more problems than it solved.[3] As Europe was convulsed with military conflicts, the navy and army posed risks but offered substantial financial rewards for these passing women of the labouring classes. Many learned a trade or took up an apprenticeship which provided them with employment if they survived to enjoy their retirement.

One of the rare examples of a passing woman sailor from an eighteenth-century navy who penned her own story is Mary Lacy, author of *The Female Shipwright* (1773). Lacy was born in Wickham, Kent in 1740 to parents who were 'poor, and forced to work very hard for their bread',[4] and became a domestic servant at the age of twelve. But after working in a series of houses, she describes an epiphany when 'a thought came into my head to dress myself in men's apparel and set off by myself'.[5] Lacy's transformation began when she rooted through the bedroom of her master's brother for 'an old frock [coat], an old pair of breeches, an old pair of pumps, and an old pair of stockings, all of which did very well'.[6] Thus equipped, and with her father's hat, she left her employer's house at dawn for the busy naval dockyards at Chatham and, en route, met a helpful gentleman who directed her to inquire aboard the *Sandwich*. The Royal Navy, before the outbreak of the Seven Years' War, when England feared a French invasion, was desperate for recruits.

Then came a second fortuitous meeting. When the tide came up, Lacy ventured out along the muddy shore, and hailed a passing boat, asking if its sailors were going aboard the *Sandwich*. When she told the men she wanted to meet the gunner, they laughed but offered the 'brave boy' a lift; cleverly, Lacy avoided the recruiting officer and asked the gunner for work, introducing herself as William Chandler. The ship's carpenter, Richard Baker, offered an apprenticeship and took his new charge back across the water to his home where Mrs Baker outfitted the 'boy'. Lacy was thrilled to receive a 'clean shirt, a pair of stockings, a pair of shoes, a coat and waistcoat, a checked handkerchief, a red nightcap for me to wear at sea: I was also to have my hair cut off when I went on board.'[7] Finally, admiring the pleasing feel and look of her clothes, Lacy considered 'that I was a sailor, every inch of me'.[8]

Although Lacy had fled impetuously the dull work and poor pay of her master's home, she began to realize that by training as a ship's carpenter her life would improve immeasurably. Almost a century after Lacy left for the high seas, Mary Anne Arnold chose the navy as her route to escape poverty. Her working life began at the age of ten, following the death of her father, when she ran errands, laboured on a farm and worked in a rope-making factory in Sheerness, Kent, but always earned a pittance. Her resentment grew when she realized that her brothers, who were sailors in the Royal Navy, were better fed, more highly valued and 'in every way in a superior condition to her'. A boy lent Arnold his old jacket, trousers and a shirt 'for a lark' which she promised to return. To her great joy and her friend's dismay, however, she was hired as a cabin boy aboard the *Williams* – a Sutherland coal ship docked in Sheerness harbour.[9]

Lacy's suggestion that her metamorphosis was spontaneous seems less credible than Arnold's realisation that being male led to better pay and better food. At the other end of the British Isles, Isabel Gunn, a farm labourer, may have been inspired by her elder brother George to adopt a male guise and sign on with the mercantile Hudson's Bay fur trading company (HBC). George had returned to Orphir parish, Orkney in 1799 after the HBC failed to renew his contract; they dismissed him as, 'a Good

Servant tho' weak', thus starving his family of much-needed income.[10] Perhaps George's stories of canoeing down the inland passage and the riches of the Nor' West prompted Isabel in 1806 to seek her own adventure at a time when press gangs for the Royal Navy, hungry for recruits in the fight against Napoleon's forces, had depleted the islands of men. Whatever her motives, she crossed the island to the HBC recruiting office at Kirkwall, enlisting as John Fubister and sailing aboard the *Prince of Wales* for Moose Factory on James Bay.[11]

It seems that Isabel Gunn, like so many passing women of this period, was illiterate since she signed her company contract with an 'x', and in that gap of self-expression, unreliable narrators fleshed out the details of her years in the Nor' West. Stories of female soldiers and sailors were often filtered through romantic ideals so that the heroine's motives were read as a powerful commitment to her man. Lacy, however, in writing her own story, detailed both the hardships and rewards of work. Her disguise enabled her to apprentice as a shipwright, a trade closed to women, and she describes the ship's life in vivid detail along with the poignancy of obstacles – rheumatism, bullying, fear of being discovered – she overcame to gain her qualification. With these skills she escaped domestic servitude, gained her independence, and pursued relationships with women.

Lacy could look back to the warrior heroines of the Nine Years' War and, in particular, to Christian Cavenaugh, variously known as Christopher Welsh, Mother Ross, and most commonly, Christian Davies, an Irish publican born in 1667 who became known as the era's most famous 'bold, lower-class woman on the make'.[12] As her biographer (possibly the journalist and writer Daniel Defoe), describes, her inclinations towards a military life were evident from childhood when she enjoyed 'manly employments', 'took great pleasure to draw and snap the pistols' and understood that her 'inclinations … were always masculine'.[13] Later she inherited a pub from a relative and married her employee Richard Welsh, with whom she had three children. When he vanished suddenly, then wrote to her months later that he had been press-ganged into the army, she decided to find him. Like many such heroines, her transformation is strikingly understated.[14]

> I cut off my hair and dressed me in a suit of my husband's having had the precaution to quilt the waistcoat to preserve my breasts from hurt which were not large enough to betray my sex and putting on the wig and hat I had prepared I went out and bought me a silver-hilted sword and some Holland shirts [made of fine bleached linen].[15]

Eighteenth-century readers of stories about these warrior heroines seemed to accept that working women could convincingly and easily imitate male behaviour.[16] In Christian's case, the physical masquerade even included reference to an imitation penis. If readers were puzzled about 'how a woman could so long perform a certain natural operation without being discovered', she revealed her secret. It was 'a silver tube painted over, and fastened about her with leather straps', and recognizable to a contemporary reader as a device that men suffering from venereal disease might use if urination was painful. It was an item she inherited from Captain Bordeaux, a French officer. Her biography claimed that Bordeaux and Christian's father fled the family home one night for their troop that was headed for the Boyne to support King James II's forces. In an ironic twist, after Bordeaux was fatally wounded, it was discovered that the French officer was female and the 'silver tube' suggestive of a female urinating device.[17]

For the warrior woman, the uniform opened a gateway into male culture that might also elevate her social status, since items of dress – from the wearing of wigs, gloves and sabres to the practice of 'hat honour'[18] – encoded class. Female warrior ballads and stories abounded with parents, lovers, siblings and friends completely deceived by such cunning disguises. Employers seem as blind and gullible as widowed mothers about these masquerades and uncaring guardians routinely dressed girls as boys to hire out their charges at better rates. As adults, the passing women appear secure in such roles where the heroines exploit their 'masculine freedom' with a vengeance.

Courageous wives and daunting daughters

No wonder then that women were eager to join the fray by enlisting. The broader context of women's military participation in the eighteenth century reveals examples of whole groups who agitated to form all-female guards. Prudence Wright organized one such gang at Pepperell, Massachusetts, during the American Revolutionary War, to defend their families by taking up arms in 1775. Unlike Christian or the mysterious Captain Bordeaux, these women openly dressed in men's clothing while on patrol, some armed with muskets and others with farm implements such as pitchforks.[19] They were determined to partake in the conflict and, familiar with the rank-and-file drill of the male militia, learned to march smartly on their missions.[20]

Contemporary armies in Britain and North America often included women and children who were attached to regiments; an example of returns from the British army in America in 1779–80 records a ratio of one woman to every ten men.[21] This data reveals that accounts kept track of how funds were spent to feed, clothe and house soldiers *and* their dependants. When a regiment was on campaign, the local military commander determined the number of wives allowed to accompany their husbands; married couples tented together with women performing duties that ranged from nursing the wounded to foraging and cooking food, laundering, and mending uniforms and linen.[22] The women who took up arms appear in vivid accounts of the British Army's actions in Quebec and New England. Thomas Anburey, who served under General John Burgoyne in the battle of Saratoga, describes in a letter written from Cambridge, Massachusetts, on 9 December 1777, how a soldier's wife reacted after a quarrel with an elderly American guard at the British barracks on Prospect Hill. While soldiers' wives were allowed to move about the camp, one day the American sentinel refused to allow this 'true campaigner' to pass.

[A] great altercation ensued, in which the lady displayed much of the Billingsgate oratory, when the old man was so irritated as to present his firelock; the woman immediately ran up, snatched it from him, knocked him down, and striding over the prostrate hero, in the exultation of triumph, profusely besprinkled him, not with Olympian dew, but that which is esteemed as emollient to the complexion – and 'faith, something more natural – nor did she quit her post, till a file of sturdy ragamuffins marched valiantly to his relief, dispossessed the Amazon, and enabled the knight of the grisly caxon to look fierce, and reshoulder his musquet.[23]

A century after the Dutch geographer Nicolaas Witsen referred to women at arms as 'Amazons', Anburey applied it to army wives who were unwittingly and unofficially engaged in conflict.

Another Amazonian wife appears in the correspondence of Sir Francis-Carr Clerke, General Burgoyne's aide-de-camp. He described in a letter to his friend Lord Polwarth, on 13 July 1776, her confrontation with rebel soldiers at Trois Rivières, Quebec. Forgetting the Greeks' details of unsexed or overly masculine warriors, Sir Francis portrays Middleton's wife as first shaming, and then rounding up enemy soldiers as an extension of her domestic duties.

The wife of Middleton Soldier in the 47th Regiment quite alone took & disarmed six Provincial Soldiers, & was the means of two more being taken also. The Circumstances are thus, which [she] related to General Burgoyne in my Presence. She said she went to a House about a quarter of a Mile from the River near the Wood, for some Milk to carry to her Husband the 8th of June during the Engagement. That on opening the Door she saw six Rebel Soldiers armed, that this *daunted* her a little, however she took Courage, & rated them saying, 'Ay'nt ye ashamed of yourselves ye villains to be fighting against Your King & Countrymen' that they looked *sheepish*, therefore she said, you are all Prisoners give me your Arms, that two more remained at the Outside of the back Door, which she was more afraid of than all the rest, that however standing between them, & their Arms, she called to some Sailors at the River Side, to whom she delivered the Prisoners, & who presently took the other two.

This is exactly true, & she is, contrary to what you wou'd imagine her, a very modest, decent well looking Woman.[24]

During the American Revolutionary War, while military wives and family members appear in official records and passing women are rare, the case of Phoebe Hessel, born in London in 1713, suggests that, as with Middleton's spouse, the line from civilian to soldier might be easily crossed. Although contemporary accounts are contradictory, one version claims that Hessel's father, a drummer attached to the King's regiment in Flanders, pressed her into service as a child. To keep his daughter with him after his wife's death, he dressed Phoebe as a boy and taught her to play the fife to ensure swift admission into the regiment.[25] While the scenario of daughter-into-son is a popular trope in contemporary female warriors' stories, nineteenth-century accounts suggest that Phoebe enlisted in the 5th Regiment of Foot in 1728 to follow a private soldier, Samuel Golding. In this version the love-sick Phoebe follows her man to the West Indies and Gibraltar.[26] Another story suggests that Phoebe met her future husband *after* enlisting, fighting alongside him until they were wounded in the battle of Fontenoy in 1745.[27]

Not every passing woman entered the military by choice, of course. Eighteenth-century accounts often claim that unscrupulous husbands or greedy guardians forced women into their male roles. This operates as an explanation for the fictionalized story of Mary Anne Talbot, one of Britain's most celebrated sailors, who claimed that a corrupt officer pressed her into service as a foot-boy. Although recent historians have cast doubt on the authenticity of Talbot's 1804 autobiography, it reveals a popular plot and one which contemporary readers found both entertaining and convincing.[28] In reality, although Talbot claimed to be suffering from unhealed war injuries when interviewed at London's Middlesex Hospital by *The Times* on 4 November 1799, there is no evidence that she ever enlisted. Instead, this domestic servant seemed to have absorbed the current vogue for female warriors. Mary Anne the sailor made for better copy than Mary Anne the domestic servant.

Robert Kirby, Talbot's employer and a publisher of popular stories, narrated her story in his collection, *Kirby's Wonderful and Scientific Museum; or, Magazine of Remarkable and Eccentric Characters*, and, in 1809, *The Life and Surprising Adventures of Mary Anne Talbot in the name of John Taylor, a Natural Daughter of the Late Earl Talbot*. Mary Anne Talbot was a well-known London character and Kirby recast her as the illegitimate daughter of William Talbot, Baron of Hensol, who dispatched her to abusive guardians after her mother's death. The last of these was an army captain, Essex Bowen of the 82nd Regiment of Foot,[29] who seduced her and, when posted to the West Indies, forced her to accompany him as John Taylor, a servant. Although a number of discrepancies in dates and events suggest that this was more fiction than fact, a male abuser was often cited as the catalyst for the warrior heroine.

When sailor Marianne Rebecca Johnson was brought before the Lord Mayor of London at Mansion House in 1807, she claimed parental exploitation led her to the high seas. A Bishop's Gate bricklayer had discovered her sheltering from a downpour, shivering with cold, weeping bitterly and generally 'in a forlorn and distressed condition'.[30] The daughter of a seaman killed in a naval action against the French, she had been raised by a cruel stepfather who forced her mother to enlist on a man-of-war. After serving seven years on different ships, Marianne's mother was fatally wounded in the British capture of Copenhagen in 1807. In a letter written before her death, Marianne's mother claimed that she 'preferred the hardships of her situation to returning to her friends [and] the risk of meeting her unnatural husband'.[31] Meanwhile, the stepfather forced Marianne into an apprenticeship on a Sutherland coal ship, disguised as a boy. The stepfather had threatened murder if she divulged her secret, and she showed the court where he had assaulted her with an iron poker, leaving a scar below her left ear. Marianne had worked aboard the *Mayflower* for four years without detection but one morning when she missed morning call because of illness, she was flogged. Soon after, she fled.[32]

The credibility of Johnson's account of enforced labour is corroborated by accounts recorded, and mythologized, in eighteenth- and nineteenth-century ballads and chapbooks where young women pass as cabin boys or foot-boys. A popular ballad, *The Handsome Cabin Boy*, plays upon the presumption of the girls-as-boys' sexual availability. Most naval captains kept their lovers or wives aboard ship quite openly and so such subterfuge was hardly necessary. As early as the seventeenth century, Admiral John Mennes, comptroller of the British Royal Navy, complained that ships 'are pestered with women … There are as many petticoats as breeches', adding that women often remained on vessels for weeks at a time.[33] By the early nineteenth century little had changed, as Vice-Admiral Horatio Nelson complained to Admiral John Jervis in 1801, 'I hope there will be orders to complete our complement, and the ship to be paid on Saturday. On Sunday we shall get rid of all the women, dogs, and pigeons.'[34] And Admiral Edward Pellew, Viscount Exmouth, observed that during the bombardment of Algiers on 27 August 1816, 'British women served at the same guns with their husbands, and during a contest of many hours, never shrank from danger, but animated all around them.'[35] Most women at sea came from the British Isles, Germany and the Netherlands during the late sixteenth to nineteenth centuries when navy recruiters were active in seaports. The degree of their participation in battles varied, with many acting as camp followers, for whom joining the military was an alternative to the sex trade.[36]

Women who accompanied their men to sea fell into a limbo between official approval and tolerance, and criminal behaviour. At an extreme were Britain's famous female pirates, Mary Read and Anne Bonny, whose story illustrates how the struggle for survival, or a desire for love, adventure, opportunity or financial reward might form complex motives for passing on the high seas.[37] Much mythologized, they left a rare record of their experience when tried for 'Piracies, Felonies, and Robberies … on the High Sea', at the High Court of Admiralty in Jamaica in 1720.[38]

Anne Bonny[39] would later become known as much for her daring with a cutlass as her relationship with Captain Jack Rackham, aka pirate Calico Jack. Both she and Mary Read were the illegitimate daughters of working-class mothers who raised them as boys for pragmatic reasons. Anne Bonny, born around 1700 in Kinsale, Ireland, was the offspring of Mary Brennan, a maid servant, and her employer, a married solicitor in Cork. To disguise the identity of his daughter – who was known locally to be Brennan's child – he 'put [Anne] into breeches as a boy, pretending it was a relation's child he was to breed up as his clerk'.[40] When his wife discovered the ruse, father, maid and daughter sailed for the American colony of Carolina where he purchased a plantation. When her mother passed away, Anne became the housekeeper but, without her father's consent, 'married a young fellow who belonged to the sea, and was not worth a groat [four pence]' and departed for Providence Island, off the coast of Nicaragua.[41] Known as a haven for pirates, it was there that Anne met Calico Jack who, 'making courtship to her', persuaded her to become a pirate 'in man's clothes'.[42] After a brief interlude in Cuba, where she bore his child, she joined his ship where she encountered, also in disguise, Mary Read.

This second female pirate's history bore remarkable similarities to Bonny's. Captain Johnson in *A General History of the Pirates*, describes Mary Read's English mother as so 'young and airy' that, when abandoned by her sailor husband, she fell pregnant by another man.[43] When Mary's elder (and legitimate) brother died a few months after his sister's birth, her mother swapped their identities so that her former mother-in-law would continue paying for her grandson. When the grandmother died and the money stopped, Mary's mother was 'obliged to put her daughter out to wait on a French lady as a foot-boy, being now thirteen years of age'.[44] With her male identity well established, Mary served aboard a man-of-war during the War of Spanish Succession (1701–14) and, once trained, joined an infantry regiment in Flanders. Disappointed when she failed to receive an officer's commission ('they being generally bought and sold'), she enlisted with a cavalry regiment.[45] During the winter campaign she fell in love with a Flemish soldier and 'found a way of letting him discover her sex, without appearing to have done with design'. At the end of the campaign, they married.[46]

When Mary's husband died – a tragedy that coincided with the Treaty of Utrecht which ended the war – the pub they had established near the Dutch city of Breda lost its clientele. Without any other means of support, and widowed in a foreign country, she 'took a resolution of seeking her fortune another way; and … ships herself on board a vessel bound for the West Indies'.[47] Unfortunately for Mary, English pirates seized and plundered the ship but kept her, the only English sailor, on board; when King William III announced a pardon of pirates who voluntarily surrendered themselves, Mary was among them. The peace, however, was short-lived as the crew's funds ran dry so Mary became a privateer for Captain Woodes Rogers, governor of the Island of Providence. The crew later mutinied against their commanders and turned to plundering any passing vessel for profit and, as if inevitable, they joined Captain Rackham's ship.[48]

Whether Anne Bonny or Mary Read chose to risk their lives aboard a crowded, dangerous vessel, as the heroic female figures of popular imagination suggest, they relished their piratic escape. Life at sea or in camp might prove, for many women, the lesser of various evils. Whatever difficulties life in male guise posed, the stories seem to recognize that, for women with few alternatives, the rewards of enlisting for a foreign adventure appeared tantalizing. Not only were there tangible benefits but the heroines were often depicted as runaways from social shame, violence or poverty.

While European women of the eighteenth century were sailing on the high seas, reports surfaced in official documents and news reports of those who served as soldiers in North American colonial conflicts. Intriguing though scanty are the details of two women who attempted to enlist with British regiments in the American Revolutionary War. A London newspaper in December 1775 reported from Newcastle that a 'good-looking girl about twenty-seven years old, dressed in mens cloaths', had attempted to sign on with Frazer's Highland Regiment. 'Her sex, however, was soon after discovered. She said the cause of this act was from a quarrel with her father, whose cloaths she had absconded in: and not withstanding her sex, she would have no objection to the army, as she thought the exercise not superior to her abilities. She was, however, discharged.'[49] While the Newcastle woman revealed convincing motives for her passing, a report in Rivington's *New York Loyal Gazette* of 25 September 1779 conforms to conventional warrior heroine narratives; she was following her lover.[50]

The first obstacle a woman might encounter in joining the British Army was the required physical exam, however cursory, and the common practice that soldiers slept naked 'in order to save their linen'.[51] Newspaper accounts of passing women being discovered suggest that even after slipping into the ranks, a disguise could be difficult to maintain without your comrades' support. Women in the Continental Army may have had an easier time, according to historian Alfred F. Young, since a recruit need only show up: 'there was no physical examination and no request for proof of age, residence or citizenship'.[52] This relaxed attitude enabled Deborah Sampson, the famous female soldier of the American Revolution, to serve for seventeenth months, between the British surrender at Yorktown and the final signing of the treaty. Her first attempt at enlisting as a Continental Army soldier, using the name Timothy Thayer, came in the early spring of 1782; Baptist Church records in her hometown of Middleborough, Massachusetts refer to 'Deborah Samson', 'who last spring was accused of Dressing in mans Clothes and inlisting [sic] as a soldier in the army'.[53]

While staying with Captain Leonard and his family, Deborah borrowed his son Samuel's clothes and, after enlisting, spent her bounty money at a tavern in nearby Four Corners, where Timothy Thayer, 'called for spirituous liquors, got excited and behaved herself in a noisy and indecent manner'. Deborah, however, escaped detection and went back to Captain Leonard's home, the next morning, returning 'to her female employments as if nothing had happened'.[54] Weeks later when Middlesborough's newly enlisted soldiers were due to join their regiment, Thayer was missing. Evidence pointed to Deborah as the culprit and, after repaying the enlistment money, she left town for nearby Bellingham. There she enlisted on 20 May with the 4th Massachusetts Regiment and would serve as Robert Shurtliff.[55] Her many successful adventures in male clothes and her appreciation for trousers, which she realized were much more convenient than dresses, gave her the confidence to embark on her military career.

Sampson had an inkling of potential public disapproval, however, when members of Middlesborough's First Baptist Church, who had heard rumours of her revelry at the Four Corners tavern, took action. On 3 September 1782 the congregation found that, 'although she was not convicted, [she] was strongly suspected of being guilty and for some time before behaved very loose and unchristian like'.[56] The church members excommunicated their parishioner until she returned to Middlesborough to beg forgiveness for her bad behaviour.

By the time Deborah-as-Robert had signed up, however, the Revolutionary War had been dragging on for years and recruiting officers had resorted to enticing bounties. Financial incentives loomed large for many passing women and, given that they were often present in continental armies and navies during this period, the transition between military wife and combatant seems less surprising. The nineteenth-century chapbook *The Surprising Adventures of Almira Paul* provides a fictional illustration of how a widow might choose the military life over poverty.

Nathaniel Coverly, Jr., a Boston publisher, commissioned a hack writer to produce the unlikely tale of the eponymous Almira Paul, a Canadian mother who enlists after her husband William dies aboard the British privateer *Swallow* on 20 February 1812 and who serves in disguise aboard American, English and Algerian naval vessels before settling down to marry in Portsmouth. In this telling Almira leaves her children behind with her mother because, once widowed, she had no means to support her family. The story followed Coverly, Jr.'s earlier success of *The Female Marine or, The Adventures of Miss Lucy Brewer*[57] whose circumstances were more complex than Almira's. Lucy had been seduced by a false-hearted lover, fallen pregnant, and given birth to an illegitimate child before being forced to work in a brothel; she adopted male dress to escape these oppressive conditions and advised, 'youths of my sex never to listen to the voice of love, unless sanctioned by paternal approbation: and to resist the impulse of [a sexual] inclination when it runs counter to precepts of Religion and Virtue'.[58] The main customers for Coverly, Jr.'s pamphlets who would have delighted in these female swashbucklers were Boston's street population of sailors, sex workers, their customers and 'juveniles'.[59]

Although the date for the naval battle in *Almira Paul* is inaccurate, the *Swallow* did suffer an 'obstinate and sanguinary engagement' against the French Navy on 16 June in which six of the crew were killed. Ironically, an eye-witness aboard ship describes the death of Seaman Phelan 'who had his wife on board: she was stationed (as is usual when women are on board in time of battle) to assist the surgeon in the care of the wounded.' Phelan's wife also died in action, a double tragedy as 'the poor creature had been only three weeks delivered of a fine boy who was thus deprived of a father and a mother'.[60] The seamen, concerned about baby Tommy's survival, brought the infant a Maltese goat to supply him with fresh milk, a luxury originally purchased for the officers.[61] It is the sailors' concern for the little orphan, rather than the presence of Phelan's wife, giving birth during a naval battle, that earns the headline 'melancholy and interesting narrative'.[62]

So perhaps the plot of Almira's 1840 tract seemed familiar to readers; she leaves her two young children with her mother in the seaport of Halifax, Nova Scotia, dresses in her husband's suit and engages as a cook's mate aboard a cutter. Retracing her husband's footsteps, she later enlists with a Royal Navy ship that engages the USS *Constitution*. Anticipating questions about how a woman might maintain her disguise in the ship's close confines and with an all-male crew, Almira divulges that she wore a close-fitting vest and kept a spare change of women's clothes close at hand.[63] Elsa Jane Guerin, who may have been a composite of several women,[64] began her purported sailor's career in circumstances similar to Paul's. After being widowed, she was left destitute with two small children, considered her options and decided to take the name of Charley, 'dress myself in male attire and seek for a living in this disguise among the avenues which are so religiously closed to my sex.'[65] Guerin would revert to female clothing on visits home to her children but was soon bored with female life and 'could not wholly eradicate many of the tastes which I had acquired during my life as one of the stronger sex.' Elsa inhabited Charley again to wander through St Louis, Missouri 'in any and all places that my curiosity led me'.[66] Comparing male and female clothes she found 'the change from the cumbersome, unhealthy attire of women to the more convenient, healthful habiliments of a man was in itself almost sufficient to compensate for its unwomanly character.'[67] In one version of Guerin's story, she travelled to the California gold fields and eventually enlisted in the Union Army as Charles Hatfield with a Wisconsin regiment. Another version places her with the Iowa Cavalry, and promoted to lieutenant.[68]

Nineteenth-century American newspaper reports and popular accounts of passing women often gave practical reasons for their disguise which, by then, readers would have recognized. But the rare autobiographies or memoirs written by the women themselves hint at more complex motives. Among them is Sarah Emma Edmonds, the most famous female combatant of the American Civil War, who published an 1864 account of her life as Franklin Thompson, who served for two years with the Union Army. Originally published as *Unsexed; or The Female Soldier*, a year later it appeared under the less controversial title of *Nurse and Spy in the Union Army*. While a publisher's introduction comments on Edmonds' use of disguises, ('it makes but little difference what costume she assumes while in the discharge of her duty'), throughout the memoir Edmonds suggests the 'unsexing' refers exclusively to her duties as a military nurse.[69]

But if Edmonds was coy about her male disguise then, she was more open about her motives for enlisting in Colonel Frederick Schneider's history of the Second Regiment of the Michigan Infantry:

> You have expressed a desire to know what led me to assume male attire. I will try to tell you. I think I was born into this world with some dormant antagonism toward men. I hope I have outgrown it immeasurably but my infant soul was impressed with a sense of my mother's wrongs before I ever saw the light and I probably drew from her breast with my daily food my love of independence and my hatred of male tyranny.[70]

But alongside her 'hatred of male tyranny' a favourite childhood heroine had inspired her to escape the drudgery of her life on a New Brunswick farm and to flee her father's volatile temper.

Edmonds became familiar with the notion of a female warrior, not through the grizzly exploits of Anne Bonny and Mary Read but the fictional pirate and blue stocking Fanny Campbell. The eponymous heroine of Captain Murray's 1815 novel, in a frontispiece etching, stands astride the wood-planked deck of her ship, gazing over a foreign sea. She grasps a black flag embossed with a skull and cross bones in her left hand and in her right sports a menacing sabre that arcs towards the deck. The captain's hips are hidden beneath a short but modest skirt, curls adorn her peacock-feathered hat and frame her delicate features. Her lips lift towards a smile.

This figure so appealed to teenaged Sarah that she ditched potato planting on the family farm in Prince William parish to read her novel on a spring day in 1854. Her mother's gift of *Fanny Campbell: or the Female Pirate Captain* offered her daughter an aspirational vision of womanhood which began with education. While Fanny's days were filled with writing poetry, composing music and reading, she was equally adept at rowing a boat, hunting animals or riding the state's wildest horse. 'Fanny Campbell was none of your modern belles, delicate and ready to faint at the first sight of a reptile,' wrote Murray. 'No, Fanny could ... do almost any brave and useful act.'[71]

At thirteen, Sarah was impressed that Fanny, by dressing in a sailor's jacket and breeches, and cutting off her luscious curls, could step 'into the freedom and glorious independence of masculinity'.[72] While Sarah scorned her heroine's mundane motive – the rescue of her lover William Lowell – Fanny's transcendence from female to male appeared touched with genius. Standing among the potato rows, Sarah experienced an epiphany that would chart the course of her life. 'All the latent energy of my nature was aroused and each exploit of the heroine thrilled me to my fingertips ... I was emancipated! and could never again be a *slave*.'[73] Sarah knew her body was as lean and muscular as her brother's since they worked alongside each other chopping wood, milking cows, planting and harvesting crops.[74] That evening, as she crossed the fields home, she plotted her adventure, astonished as this ingenious route to liberty opened to her.

Sarah had a powerful incentive to leave since she considered her father abusive, and the first step towards independence required money. While still in her teens, she left home to open a Moncton millinery store with her sister Mary Jane, which proved profitable.[75] But when her father demanded that she marry a local farmer against her wishes, Sarah knew she had to leave quickly. To pacify her father, she agreed to the engagement 'in obedience to orders' but after her nineteenth birthday, 'unceremoniously left for parts unknown', dressed as a man.[76]

While Edmond's memoir was vague about her reasons for moving from New Brunswick to Michigan, claiming she was undertaking missionary work, in reality she began her new life as Franklin Thompson, selling family bibles door-to-door for a publisher in Hartford, Connecticut.[77] Unsure whether her disguise was convincing, she travelled south, canvassing the good book only by night and sleeping in the woods by day. Once New Brunswick was far behind him, Frank sold bibles 'in earnest' and settled in Flint, Michigan, renting a room from Reverend Mr Joslin, a Methodist pastor whose parishioners boosted his sales. Frank spent his free time taking his lady friends on country rides in a stylish, horse-drawn buggy. Damon Stuart, who knew Sarah first as Frank, described him as, 'glib of tongue, thoroughly business-like, and [having] an open persuasive manner that was particularly attractive.'[78]

The regimental history describes how, about a year after leaving New Brunswick, Sarah made a brief visit home during which her family failed to recognize her when she joined them for supper. When she stepped into the barn and the animals greeted her, her mother 'look[ed] up through a mist of tears and asked my sister, "Fanny, don't you think this young man looks like your poor sister?"'[79] Her mother demanded proof of her daughter's identity and Sarah, fearing an encounter with her unforgiving father, soon left.

Frank Thompson proved a successful salesman, selling bibles throughout Nova Scotia, New Brunswick and Connecticut, and clearing $900 (about $18,000 today) in less than a year. On the road he enjoyed a gentleman's lifestyle: well-appointed guest houses, fine meals and 'came near marrying a pretty little girl who was bound I should not leave Nova Scotia without her.' Frank's new identity and class provided him with prosperity, ease and confidence: 'Oh how manly I felt; and what pride I took in proving (to my employers) that their confidence in me was not misplaced.'[80] But Frank was forced to abandon the 'pretty little girl' in Halifax for the lure of the West, returning to Michigan at the beginning of the American Civil War.

On 12 April 1861 Confederate forces fired upon Fort Sumter and President Abraham Lincoln, whose election brought to a head the issue of slavery in America, swiftly called for 75,000 recruits for the Union Army. Five days later Frank enlisted in a local militia unit, the Flint Union Greys, which was recruiting for the 2nd Michigan Volunteers and captained by his friend William Morse.[81] A town parade with an address from Morse saw off the Greys, who were ceremoniously presented with a bible, courtesy of the Methodist Episcopal church. The Flint ladies pinned a rosette on each boy inscribed with the slogan, 'The Union and The Constitution', and Reverend Joslin pronounced a benediction.[82]

As a Canadian Sarah could have returned home but instead prayed for advice.[83] As God seemed to approve the continuation of her disguise, she enlisted as a male field nurse for the Union Army. Her memoir, however, not only glosses over her passing but ignores Frank's previous existence. While *Nurse and Spy* presents her as a pious woman who takes up nursing and engages in espionage for the Union Army, later accounts, published long after the war, illuminate the paradoxes of her life as Frank.

Edmonds' memoir, one of only two written by female soldiers of the Civil War,[84] is equally vague about her escape from the arranged marriage in New Brunswick and the pleasures of living as Frank. Instead, *Nurse and Spy* has a polemic quality where Sarah's adventures are framed within a narrative of patriotic sacrifice rather than female liberation. Although the warrior heroine was well known from European and North American ballads and popular literature from the seventeenth century onwards, few articulated women's 'dormant antagonism' towards the opposite sex as openly as Edmonds.[85] Revelations about her earlier incarnation as Frank and her proto-feminist statements surfaced decades after the war when she spoke from the decidedly feminine perspective of wife and mother. But the published testimony of her enlistment, her motives and their later popular representations and misrepresentations shed much light on the woman warriors' experience.

What Edmonds seems to share with her fellow female combatants of the Civil War is her sense that 'the freedom and glorious independence of masculinity'[86] was within their grasp. Acquiring the totemic pair of trousers, a transformation involving a simple costume change, was her entry into male culture. Shorn of their long, flowing locks and no longer encumbered by stays, bodices, petticoats, skirts, hats or gloves, these women could move freely. In shirts and breeches they strode forward, capable of expressing themselves in novel ways. They shed feminine concerns about their appearance even if they remained anxious about the legitimacy of their masculine personae. Despite the horrific casualties of the Civil War, which claimed approximately 620,000 soldiers from combat, accident and starvation, Edmonds would remember the temporary liberty it offered her.

Although Edmonds remains the Union Army's best-documented case of a passing woman, there were an estimated 400 who participated on both sides during the conflict. Historians conclude that enlisting for these women – whatever their physical features – proved remarkably easy. 'All a woman needed to do was cut her hair short, don male clothing, pick an alias, and find the nearest recruiter, regiment, or army camp … Both men and women were free to become anyone they wished to be by simply moving to a place where no one knew them and creating a new persona.'[87] For a former house slave, Cathay Williams, enlisting with the US regular army in St Louis, Missouri on 15 November 1866 brought emancipation. Williams is the only documented African American woman to have joined the more than 186,000 'Buffalo' soldiers who served, 38,000 of whom were killed in action. As Williams would later explain, she joined with the assistance of friends, and served as a regimental cook for three years, 'to make my own living and not be dependent on relations or friends'.[88] She was assigned to the 38th US Infantry, a segregated African American unit.[89] Williams's experience of a cursory exam by an army surgeon before being found fit for duty was endorsed by Mary Livermore, a journalist and women's rights campaigner who wrote about her experiences with the United States Sanitary Commission. While Livermore provides no details, she claimed that women simply appeared in uniform and recruiters asked no further questions.[90]

The circumstances in which Loreta Janeta Velazquez, the daughter of Cuban immigrants who married an American army officer, joined the Confederate Southern Army contrasted with Edmonds's tale of forced marriage. Loreta writes in her memoir that after eloping with her fiancé William, they had three children, all of whom had died by 1860. Still grieving, she adopted her disguise as Harry T. Buford to enlist with the Independent Scouts, and confessed to being 'perfectly wild about war'. William discouraged his wife from following him to war in June 1861, so Velazquez headed for New Orleans, 'ready to start on my own campaign'.[91] That campaign was a reaction to the limits of being female as she explained: 'I wish I had been created a man instead of a woman. This is what is the matter with nearly all the women who go about complaining of the wrongs of their sex. But being a woman, I was bent on making the best of it.'[92]

This involved taking practical steps and the first was to fashion a coat, heavily padded with cotton along the back and under her arms to her hips, as her disguise which gave her a new-found confidence. As she wrote in, *The Woman in Battle: A Narrative of the Exploits, Adventures, and Travels of Madame Loreta Janeta Velazquez*, 'I lost all fear of being found out and learned to act, talk and almost to think like a man.'[93] Rather than expressing anxiety about her disguise, Velazquez restrained herself from snapping back when fellow officers made derogatory comments about her height.

Even if Velazquez's story was dramatized by her editor C. J. Worthington, it is ostensibly an authentic narrative account of her four years with the Confederate Army as both a spy and a soldier.[94] Since the 1980s historians of the Civil War have verified that far more women participated as combatants on both sides of the conflict than previously thought and have collectively documented some 240 cases.[95] As Livermore noted, few of these accounts were written down and most circulated as rumours:

> I am convinced that a larger number of women disguised themselves and enlisted in the service, for one cause or other, than was dreamed of ... Some startling histories of these military women were current in the gossip of army life; and extravagant and unreal as were many of the narrations, one always felt that they had a foundation in fact.[96]

Typical was a report that General Philip Sheridan, of the Army of the Potomac, received from Colonel Conrad of the 15th Missouri Infantry about the shocking behaviour of two women in his detachment. Conrad described how the female soldiers 'had given much annoyance by getting drunk and to some extent demoralizing his men'. The women had 'in some mysterious manner' enlisted as soldiers before their identity was revealed; they had become inebriated on a foraging expedition, fallen into a river and half-drowned, and were taken to the army surgeon. Although Sheridan found Conrad's story astonishing, the women were only dismissed because they had become 'disturbers of Conrad's peace of mind'.[97] In fact, General Sheridan encountered another female soldier, Ella Reno, who was a niece of Brigadier-General Jesse Reno, and served in both the 5th Kentucky Cavalry (US) and the 8th Michigan Infantry. Sheridan disparagingly recalled that with Ella's coarse masculine features 'she would readily have passed as a man'.[98]

Given the evidence that so many female combatants served in the Civil War, it seems significant that only later versions of Sarah Emma Edmonds' story questioned the ease of her recruitment. In response to an 1883 article in the Detroit *Post and Tribune*, Edmonds corrected a statement by her friend Damon Stuart, that the Greys initially rejected her because of her height. According to

Stuart, she was only accepted on a second attempt to enlist when many volunteers had dropped out after their initial three-month service.[99] In a newspaper article Delia Davis wrote long after Edmonds' death in 1898, she quotes Sarah as saying that despite her fear of discovery upon enlisting, the process was straightforward:

> Although volunteers in those days were not subject to the strict examination of our recent recruits, Frank felt rather nervous and apprehensive over this part of the programme, particularly when he noted how the man ahead of him in the line was treated. However, the examiner merely looked into the frank honest face, took hold of the firm, strong, but fair hand and asked, 'Well, what sort of a living has this hand earned?' With the dash native to her Frank replied, 'Well up to the present that hand has been chiefly engaged in getting an education.' And the examiner passed on.[100]

In later versions of the story Frank was described as a 'smart, handsome lad' who convinced recruiting officers that he was twenty, although he looked no more than seventeen. An article from the *Detroit News* reporting on the Second Michigan Infantry's reunion of 1885 describes how Frank sailed through a cursory physical examination 'by looking "his" examiner square in the eye and gripping his hand in a firm handshake.'[101]

Although Edmonds and Velazquez were rare as memoirists, fictional versions of Civil War heroines proved popular and suggested why, and how, women might slip into the ranks. Among them was Madeline Moore, who described her 'thrilling adventures' as an officer in the Kentucky Home Guards, published during the war as *The Lady Lieutenant* (1862). In a disguise that consisted of a 'small pair of whiskers and moustache' (a technique Velazquez also adopted) she fools not only her miserly aunt, 'a hypocritical blue stocking', but Frank, the lover she sets out to follow.[102] Madeline exclaims over her image as 'Albert' in a full-length mirror, 'I looked in the glass and must say I fell in love with myself – that is, I should have been apt to take a fancy to just such a youth as I appeared to be.'[103] So convincing is 'Albert' that Madeline enjoys a narcissistic moment as her own sexual object. However, in these nineteenth-century stories, such psychic transformations are transitory and performative: they enable her to win a battle, to find her lover, to wreak revenge, to complete a task or a journey. Even though Madeline proves herself courageous under fire, once she finds Frank, she adopts the more feminine role of nurse.

In every age, whatever the female warriors' motives, their narratives conform to certain gendered ideals, the most enduring of which is that of the longing lover. In twentieth-century Russia, a country in which the Scythian women first rode on horseback with their weapons, romantic stories of female soldiers were laced with male military glory. The most famous warrior of the First World War was Maria Leont' evna Bochkareva, who enlisted first with the Tsar's army before being awarded her own female battalion. Bochkareva's ill-fated 1st Russian Women's Battalion of Death (*zhenskii batalion smerty*) of about 2,000 women served under the direction of Alexander Kerensky's war ministry. The first Russian woman to command a military unit, Bochkareva qualified for this post after fighting on the Western Front in the 5th Corps, 7th Division, 28th Regiment of the Second Army and was decorated for rescuing many wounded soldiers from the field. She was never disguised but served as the regiment's only woman.[104]

Although Bochkareva, like Nadezhda Durova, had a father in the military, their childhoods were a study in contrasts. While Durova grew up on an estate in the foothills of the Ural mountains, Bochkareva, born in 1889 to a peasant family, was raised in poverty in Tomsk, Siberia; her father had been a sergeant in the Imperial Army during the Russo-Turkish War and was an abusive alcoholic. As a child, she received little education and left school to work before, at age fifteen, marrying Afanasi Bochkareva, who matched Maria's father in his brutal treatment of her. The couple moved away from Tomsk to work on a construction site where Maria rose rapidly to assistant foreman, a promotion that bolstered her confidence and income but outraged her husband. Fed up with Afanasi's treatment, she left to join her sister in Barnaul in western

Siberia and found work on a steamship before her husband appeared, demanding her return. Back in Tomsk, she found more appropriately feminine work in a bakery which enabled her to save enough money to leave him a second time.[105] Maria then returned to Barnaul, and there worked again as a construction foreman, winning her employer's praise for her efficiency; soon she had twenty-five men working under her and although she was regarded as a 'queer novelty', she appealed to their 'sense of fairness' to gain their cooperation. Her employer even acknowledged her right to that classic symbol of male status – a pair of trousers. As Maria recalled, he announced on site, 'Look at this *baba* [old woman]! She will have us men learning from her pretty soon. She should wear trousers.'[106]

But Afanasi stalked her again, demanding she return to Tomsk where, to her relief, he enlisted in the Tsar's army. Although she found a second partner, Yakov Buk, with whom she had a civil agreement in lieu of marriage, he proved just as disappointing. But when he was convicted of petty crimes, she followed him into exile where he drank heavily and became abusive.[107] While Yakov was delirious with fever in hospital, Maria escaped by cutting her hair and dressing in his clothes. By abandoning her female self, which had brought her so little happiness, she describes in her memoir, with the fervour of a religious convert, her desire to join the Tsar's army at the outbreak of Russia's war against Germany in 1914. She took the name Yashka, a diminutive of her husband's name, Yakov:

> My heart yearned to be there [on the East Prussian front], in the boiling cauldron of war, to be baptised by its fire and scorched by its lava. The spirit of sacrifice took possession of me. My country called to me. And an irresistible force from within pulled me …[108]

The language of her description, albeit provided in translation from the Russian and through the interpretation of her editor, the Russian-American journalist Isaac Don Levine, alludes to ideals of heroic military glory. The religious symbol of the cleansing fire suggests purification of Maria's past and, like a novice nun, she is 'called' to her military vocation. Bochkareva's presentation as an almost spiritual figure prompted a newspaper correspondent writing in July 1917 to fall back on a popular image: 'The woman that saved France was Joan of Arc – a peasant girl, Maria Botchkareva is her modern parallel.'[109]

However, to put Bochkareva's experience into context, Russia's Joan was among some 600–800 women of all social classes in Russia who volunteered for army service, and roughly 50,000–70,000 women who would serve in the Red Army during the Civil War.[110] Although early press reports described Bochkareva as a spiritually motivated patriot, in echoes of the classic warrior heroines, she faced rumours about her motives for enlisting. As if anticipating that Western readers might struggle to understand a woman fighting for the Motherland, Bochkareva cast her eagerness for the East Prussian front as a means to avenge Afanasi's death in battle.[111] Bochkareva never contradicted this story, says Levine, because she knew what the journalists wanted to hear and were willing to believe.

The story of the 1st Russian Women's Battalion, which Bochkareva initially recommended to President Rodzianko in answer to his problem of army morale (her female warriors would shame men into enlisting) made global news in 1917. Many journalists focused on the Battalion's commander, turning Bochkareva into a Russian and international celebrity. The unit was visited by such influential people as Princess Kikuatova, veteran revolutionary Ekaterina Breshko-Breshkovskaia and the women's suffrage campaigner Emmeline Pankhurst who inspected the Battalion in June 1917 with an entourage of British journalists.[112] In 1918, Florence Harriman, an American philanthropist and social reformer, sponsored Bochkareva's visit to the United States where she urged President Wilson, senators and congressmen to finance a military expedition to Russia.[113] Harriman also introduced Bochkareva to Levine who had been asked by her, and Pankhurst, to write the biography of 'the Russian Joan of Arc'.

Although Bochkareva entered the realm of politics, which was an extraordinary feat for a Siberian peasant woman, the press uncritically adopted her narrative of having the 'great pluck' to follow her husband to war.[114] This fantasy made acceptable Bochkareva's desire for the masculine adventure of war and ignored the abuse she had endured from her father and partners. Even American journalist Bessie Beatty who covered the Russian Civil War for *The San Francisco Bulletin*, and lived in the Battalion's barracks for ten days, repeated this rumour about Bochkareva as a wife on campaign.[115] Beatty's memoir articulates the paradox that war's organized violence liberated Bochkareva whom she quotes on learning that she could join the Tsar's army: 'I was so happy, so joyous, so transported ... It was the most blissful moment of my life.'[116] In reality, Bochkareva's first experiences in her all-male regiment, the 4th Company of the 25th Tomsk Reserve Battalion, had, initially, left her 'confused and somewhat bewildered, hardly able to recognize myself,' before the men came to accept her as 'a comrade and not a woman'.[117] In this alternate universe, she had to win the respect of her fellow soldiers, who became blind to her gender, before she felt the military ethos of comradeship freed her from sexual vulnerability.

When Beatty interviewed women of the 1st Russian Women's Battalion in their barracks, many used patriotic language to explain their reasons for enlisting. The former stenographers, dressmakers, servants, factory hands, university students, peasants and even bourgeois ladies described their motives: 'they believed that the honour and even the existence of Russia were at stake and nothing but a human sacrifice could save her.'[118] But Beatty interviewed others who joined because 'anything was better than the dreary drudgery and the drearier waiting of life as they lived it'.[119] A Japanese woman failed to explain her reasons because there were too many, while a fifteen-year-old Cossack girl enlisted after her father, two brothers, and her mother, a nurse, were killed in battle. '"What else is left for me?" she asked with a pathetic droop to her young, strong shoulders,' wrote Beatty.[120] While these Western female journalists dug beneath the surface to expose the context in which women were prepared to risk their lives and reputations in a national conflict, the Battalion's public message remained one of female love, personal sacrifice and patriotic duty.

Despite Bochkareva's desire for the authority, status, and financial rewards of her hard work on all-male construction sites in Siberia, Beatty noted her appeal to potential female recruits as nurses and auxiliaries. American journalist Louise Bryant, who was accompanied by her lover, John Reed, author of *Ten Days that Shook the World*, recorded Bochkareva's address as the battalion standard was consecrated on 21 June 1917 at Petrograd's St Isaak's Cathedral. Bryant witnessed Bochkareva spread her arms wide and, before the assembled crowd of potential recruits, boom in a deep voice, 'Come with us to dry the tears and heal the wounds of Russia. Protect her with your lives.' Bochkareva then turned to her 250 young female soldiers and said: 'We women are turning into tigresses to protect our children from a shameful yoke – to protect the freedom of our country.'[121] Bochkareva's appeal stuck to national and maternal sacrifice as the only acceptable grounds for women's involvement in warfare. Once her recruits were enlisted, Bochkareva enacted a regime of tough love, taking personal responsibility for the unit's 'moral integrity' and enforcing rigid rules governing their behaviour. Giggling was strictly forbidden and within two days of their signing on, she had dismissed more than eighty women for laughing too much and for frivolity; women were confined to barracks and minor breeches of discipline were punished with slaps across the face. In Petrograd only 300 made it through Bochkareva's training regime.[122]

Ironically, the Russian women soldiers' motives for enlisting bear more similarities than differences to those who disguised themselves to slip into all-male ranks. They too were often escaping the boredom of domestic life or felt compelled by the same sense of urgency to join a national, religious or political struggle or, in more brutal circumstances, to ensure their survival. But however they articulated their reasons for donning a uniform, once enlisted the experience of shedding their female selves and adopting a male persona appears almost universal.

Even though the Tsarist government had no consistent policy on female combatants, women's names appear frequently in Russian military records throughout the First World War. Many women joined their brothers or fathers when they had the opportunity, as they had done in eighteenth-century European wars, and more recently, in the Civil War.[123] Marina Yurlova, daughter of a Kuban Cossack colonel, followed in this ancient tradition when she stumbled into a military career in 1915. She had been harvesting sunflowers and potatoes the morning the Cossack troops left for the front and was shoved accidentally aboard a train packed with women from her village of Raevskaya near Krasnodar, a region bordering the Black Sea. The women were following their men, military volunteers, travelling south towards the war zone in Armenia and to fight the Turks. Marina assumed that her father was aboard so, although only fourteen years old, and bound for an unknown destination, she felt secure amongst the camp followers.[124] As she would later describe her experience:

> I am not exaggerating when I say that I felt no remorse and no fear. I was a Cossack. As with my companions, so with me it was a blind instinct to follow men to war. And beside that, to me – caught up in all this violence and carried helplessly along – here was an adventure, the sort of adventure I had always dreamed about ...[125]

Yurlova's military induction, however, proved haphazard. When the train reached its destination, a military camp in Armenia, her father was not among the recruits. Like any other adolescent might, Marina howled with misery when this stark reality dawned. Her weeping attracted the attention of 'a big Cossack' of the Reconnaissance Sotnia (100-horse squadron) of the 3rd Ekaterinodar, into which she would be adopted. Once befriended by Sergeant Kosloff, he outfitted Marina in army regulation trousers, khaki shirt, boots and a lamb's wool hat. As she put on her new uniform, Kosloff promised her: 'All right *synok* [sonny] ... before I die, I'll make a Cossack out of you.' In the camp Marina found that her new clothes 'made all the difference in the world'.[126]

Since Marina was so young, the men in the camp took an avuncular attitude with their latest recruit, giving her work and tolerating her presence. For two months, before the company moved onto the bare plateau of Armenia, she worked as a regimental groom. But thereafter, and once equipped with a sabre and with the elimination of her pigtails, she was finally initiated as a Cossack soldier. Then her company awaited their orders.

Yurlova's memoir describes her gradual transformation from mascot into a soldier whose presence depended on the army's lax attitude towards women in its ranks. In part, the officers' indifference stemmed from a recognition that among these peasant soldiers, women were equally capable of enduring war's physical privations. While Russian peasant men and women worked side by side in the fields, women like Maria Bochkareva had moved from labouring alongside men in the country's developing industries before enlisting. In fact, women's presence in the ranks was far from unusual. Historians of Russia's female combatants during the Civil War between the Reds and Whites have discovered that 'women fought in regular combat on every front (geographically this was the most dispersed land war in history since the Mongols), from Siberia to Crimea, from the Baltic to Central Asia'.[127] Women served in the *politodel*, the agency of political propaganda, an area in which the Revolutionary Communists outplayed their enemies.

By 1915 the British and American press were fascinated with all Russian women soldiers whether disguised or informally enlisted. New York's *Literary Digest* quoted the *London Graphic*'s report of about 400 women bearing arms in Russia, most in Siberian regiments. But rather than pointing out the relative disarray that enabled women to penetrate military ranks more easily, reports stressed Russian women's patriotism:

The sex of 50 [women] has been revealed by death or wounds. This number is quite remarkable when one considers the obstacles to be surmounted in eluding or circumventing the recruiting officials. For even in Russia women are not supposed to be soldiers. One can but feel that the passion of the Russian woman to fight side by side with their men is not only patriotic but symptomatic of a fine sense of comradeship.[128]

Such accounts entwined the ideals of female devotion to husband and country. Ignored in such popular articles were women's less socially acceptable reasons for enlisting – the desire or need for escape, the longing for independence, the excitement that a masculine identity appeared to offer. Undoubtedly women were susceptible to patriotic rhetoric and Russian women had followed their men into battle for centuries. As a former Red Army soldier told the English journalist Rosita Forbes: 'I had to go to the front. The whole of my village went. I didn't think about [whether I liked fighting]. I had to do it.'[129] Russian women were also moved to protect their homes and their children's futures and to ensure the future of their communities. Tatania Alexinsky, who was a medic on the Eastern Front in 1916, described meeting a female soldier on a train journey from Brest. 'A lady appeared before us: she was clad in soldier's uniform and wore a *papakha* [sheepskin hat] on her head: she was wounded and hobbled up on crutches.' The woman told Alexinsky that she had 'left her two children [with her mother in Poland] to go with her husband, an Army doctor, and her brother, a captain'. Disguised as a soldier, she had served the cause as an orderly in the trenches, and all three had been wounded with shrapnel shell.[130]

To the American and European press the Russian female soldiers appeared as novelties, while specialist suffrage magazines, and feminist campaigners, regarded them as icons of emancipation. As active participants in the war, they proved the argument about women's capacity for military action, especially for those who chafed against the limits of newly founded auxiliary services. The International Woman Suffrage Alliance magazine *Jus Suffragii* carried regular news items from Russia which detailed women's work as doctors, ambulance drivers, nurses, railway crews and munitions crews, often detailing their pay and working conditions. But the women soldiers received particular attention and as the war progressed the reports became more frequent.

An early account from November 1914 mentions that a linguist who was 'the wife of a Russian Army captain' had petitioned the Tsar to join her husband as an interpreter. When the request was denied, she enlisted anyway, dressed in a soldier's uniform, 'and cut off her beautiful hair'.[131] By the spring of 1915, the magazine reported that women in front-line regiments had become a regular occurrence. It describes how Alexandra Braiko, disguised as 'Alexander Daniloff', who had enlisted with two of her brothers at Vilna, had recently been wounded in Galicia.[132] A month later, another high school student, Kira Aleksandrovna Bashkirova, was receiving hospital treatment after participating in 'several very dangerous reconnaissance expeditions' in an infantry regiment as 'Nikolai Popoff'. Growing restless there, she enlisted again, this time with a corps of Siberian sharpshooters and was assigned to lead a group of cavalry scouts. 'In a night reconnaissance on December 20, she showed such exceptional bravery and daring that she was awarded the Order of St George of the IV class.'[133] When her sex was discovered, however, she was sent back to Vilna where she escaped the military authorities to enlist in the infantry, in which she was wounded.

The same month's issue of *Jus Suffragii* recounted a married couple of Moscow university students, who had enlisted in the same company as brothers. They endured hardships together as their regiment pursued the Austrian troops through the forests and marshes of Eastern Prussia, often marching up to forty miles a day. In defending the town of Czestochowa from German advance in August 1914, 'they found themselves in the trenches under continuous shrapnel fire for two whole days'. During a full-frontal attack the couple were both wounded, and the wife was rewarded with the St George Cross for her bravery.[134]

Women soldiers remained a feature in the magazine until the Revolution, and the establishment of the Women's Battalion in 1917. In February *Jus Suffragii* described the experience of another officer's wife, Olga Petrovna Habich, who had switched from nursing to serving in an artillery brigade, for which she received two St George medals; Elena Konstantinova Shutakaia, disguised as 'Leonid Shutski', was killed in action, while on 31 July sisters Turikova, Rauer and Shagin perished in an enemy aerial attack.[135] Early twentieth-century female combatants often emphasized their ideological or professional motives for volunteering to fight in conflicts where the casualty rates were high and the morale of conscripts low.[136] As eighteen-year-old Mariya Golubyova described her reasons for joining:

> I had no sensation except to rid my country of an enemy. There was no sentimentality.
>
> We were trying to kill them and they were trying to kill us – that is all. Any Russian girl or any American girl in the same position would have the same feeling.[137]

Lifting the veil of propaganda Bryant found many disillusioned young recruits in the Battalion. Some claimed they had enlisted for the wrong cause, seduced by Bochkareva's appeals. Anna Shub, a seventeen-year-old from Moghilev, left home after the Bolsheviks seized control in 1917 because, she thought, 'the poor soldiers of Russia were tired after fighting so many years and ... we ought to help them'. But she wanted to 'die of shame' when she realized that the Women's Battalion was intended to embarrass the men into fighting.[138] Another woman had joined, 'moved by a high resolve to die for the revolution', but was disappointed because, she felt, their comrades misunderstood the women's motives. 'We expected to be treated as heroes, but always we were treated with scorn ... The soldiers thought we were militarists and enemies of the revolution.'[139] Undeterred by their experiences, the women Bryant interviewed resolved to fight for the new Soviet government, but only in male battalions.

Historians A. E. Griesse and R. Stites mention that, whatever the women's personal motives, they were facilitated by particular historical and social circumstances in Russia during the First World War: 'The front was so vast and mobile (from Riga to the Carpathians to the Black Sea), the situation so desperate, and the scene so chaotic that resistance to the presence of women was perhaps considered not worthy of the time required.'[140]

In the United States, meanwhile, women's groups had been establishing their own international networks, lobbying for women's political and military involvement. A few months before

America entered the war in April 1917, Captain Lucius H. Higgins led a group of 120 khaki-clad uniformed women of the American Woman's League for Self Defense through their drill at the 9th Regimental Armory in New York.[141] Formed to teach women martial arts to defend their country, the League hired drill sergeants to instruct dentists, lawyers, surgeons, teachers and secretaries in 'everything that men are taught to train them for war'. Dressed in 'stunning khaki' they learned to shoot guns, bows and arrows, ride cavalry horses and drive cars.[142] Among the speakers at the Armory was suffragette Miss Anna Higgins who reassured the crowd about the benefits of a uniform:

> This is the age of the new woman. Get rid of your dresses. Dresses have been the curse and burden of women. Dresses belong to women of the last generation …
>
> Think no longer of husbands and sweethearts. Think about ditches and barb fences. Think of the work you will have to do when your husbands and sweethearts go to the front … It will be man's work and you can't do man's work in a dress.[143]

A competing and perhaps more serious organization was the Women's Section of the Navy League which held its first conference in November 1915, with more than 2,000 women in attendance. By 1916, its organizers had established the National Service School to provide women with essential wartime skills at privately funded training camps which proved popular with debutants and college students. The commandant was Miss Elizabeth Ellicott Poe, a journalist and relative of author Edgar Allan Poe whose celebrity connections guaranteed press attention and international contacts. The organization's representative, Grace Julia Parker Drummond, a Canadian philanthropist and suffragette, travelled through the United Kingdom for two months in 1916 on a fact-finding mission about mobilizing women for the war.[144]

Whether in Europe or North America, wartime press reports and memoirs of female combatants provided fleeting glimpses of women's rebellion against socially imposed restrictions. No doubt women reading these stories, or seeing Amazonian images on postcards or represented on stage, projected themselves into this masculine space with the enticements of adventure, heroism and a testing of their physical limits. Captain Flora Sandes, an English nurse who joined the Serbian Army to fight for the British Empire and her adopted country, confessed to such longings in her memoir:

> When a very small child I used to pray every night that I might wake up in the morning and find myself a boy ... Many years afterwards, when I had long realised that if you have the misfortune to be born a woman it is better to make the best of a bad job and not try to be a bad imitation of a man, I was suddenly pitchforked into the Serbian army and for seven years lived practically a man's life.[145]

Valerie Arkell-Smith described a similar reaction when war was declared. At age nineteen, 'for the first time there surged over me the wish that I had been born a man. I can recall the urge to do something. Realising that I could not go and fight, I decided to become a nurse.'[146] Flora Sandes, however, would realize this dream shared by many English women of her generation.

Sandes was the youngest daughter of Reverend Samuel Dickson Sandes and his wife, Sophia Julia, born in 1876 at Nether Poppleton, County of York. Even as a girl she was captivated by stories of travelling to far-flung places to satisfy her longing for broader horizons, captured by Irish poet Dora Sigerson Shorter in a passage which Sandes pasted carefully into her scrapbook:

> Oh to be a woman to be left to pique and pine
> When the winds are out and calling to this vagrant's heart
> of mine
> There is a danger in the waters – there's a joy where dangers be –
> Alas to be a woman with the nomad's heart in me
> Ochine! To be a woman only sighing on the shore
> With a soul that finds a passion for each long breaker's roar.[147]

Flora quenched her nomad's heart by purchasing a pair of pantaloons and taking solo camping holidays, sometimes with the family dog. Later, she spent a year working in Cairo as a typist, and in 1903 travelled to New York; from there she planned to 'type' her way across the globe, from city to city, country to country, with her friend Bessie Stear.[148] In 1905 Flora posed with her canine camping companion as an intrepid traveller for a press photo underneath a caption that read: 'This tent which weighs under three pounds has sheltered its owner Miss Sandes in many parts of the world from Surrey to the Rocky Mountains.'[149]

Family responsibilities caught up with her, however, when her sister-in-law Rose passed away and her brother Sam, then living on Texada Island off British Columbia's coast, asked her to accompany his five-year-old son, Dick, back to England. The family engaged the detective agency Pinkertons to track her down to a box factory where she was working. She travelled north to the remote mining town of Van Anda to collect her nephew, and while staying there an 'old timer' taught her to helm a boat and 'handle a fishing rod in the approved backwoodsman style'.[150] With Dick, she wandered down the Pacific Coast to Mexico, then into Central America, and up the East Coast to New York before sailing home.

After settling back into the family home in Thornton Heath, Surrey, Flora received a considerable legacy from a relative that allowed her to pursue her adventurous hobbies, even buying a second-hand French motor car.[151] So when Flora signed on with the First Aid Nursing Yeomanry (FANY; organized to provide military support services in the event of hostilities) soon after its founding by Edward Charles Baker in 1907, her skills were welcomed.[152] There she met the suffragist Mabel St Clair Stobart – who would go on to lead an all-female medical team in Serbia – who believed that women's war work would support their campaign for the vote.[153] The FANY, as they were known, trained in First Aid and Home Nursing and were required to pass, 'a course of Horsemanship, Veterinary Work, Signalling, and Camp Cookery'.[154] Flora's experience, and her success at fundraising for the breakaway organization the 'Women's Sick and Wounded Convoy Corps' (formed after Sandes, Stobart and others had become disillusioned with Baker's leadership), prepared her well for the coming conflict.

As Flora Sandes would later tell Australian audiences on a speaking tour in 1920, when she signed on as a nurse, bound for Serbia in August 1914, she had 'no more idea of going to war than any other lady now in the hall'.[155] Despite her organizational experience, the War Office had rejected Sandes as a nurse for the Voluntary Aid Detachment (VAD), the organization which nineteen-year-old Valerie Arkell-Smith had joined. The seven-woman unit hastily assembled by American Mabel Grouitch, wife of Slavko Grouitch, Serbia's Under-secretary of State for Foreign Affairs, was definitely Flora's second choice. She left London on a three-month contract on the morning of 12 August 1914 aboard the first boat to follow the British Expeditionary Force across the English Channel. She was thirty-eight years old.

It was a baptism of several kinds of fires; France was still mobilizing its troops, train routes and timetables were disrupted, platforms chaotic and crowded with soldiers on their way to the Western Front, and boats scarce. Flora's diary, however, suggests that these early days en route to Serbia seemed, at first, an extension of the rough travel and thrilling adventures she had experienced in North America. She even hints at flirtations with men, although she was careful to conceal their identity and details about these encounters were scant.

Among other less serious mishaps Flora noted that during a train trip down the Adriatic coast, 'a Miss Saunders lost her purse' and her friend Emily Simmonds, a surgical nurse known affectionately as 'Americano', 'lost her reputation – neither ever found again'. In Athens a war correspondent discretely identified in Flora's diary only as 'Mr X' sent the women a bouquet 'which nearly caused a battle'.[156] In the sultry air Americano and Flora drove through the streets of the Greek capital till about midnight, accompanied by Mr X and 'sundry others'. The nurses arrived safely in Serbia after thirty-six hours sitting on the deck of a Greek cattle ship in a raging thunderstorm from Piraeus to Salonika. From there their train wound the rugged Vardar valley to Kragujevatz.[157] But then the dizzying adventure came to a screeching halt. When Flora arrived, a telegram informed her that her father, the Reverend Samuel Sandes, had died on 23 August. Flora made no further notes in her diary until the middle of November.

There were extremely basic conditions in the First Reserve Hospital where Flora spent her first few months in Serbia. The seven English women were the only nurses, working with doctors and orderlies to tend more than 1,000 sick and wounded soldiers. They were casualties of the Serbs' efforts to drive the Austrian invasion back across the River Danube. Many patients journeyed more than three days in a bullock cart over rough terrain with only field dressings on their wounds. Those admitted to hospital were in a terrible condition.[158] After exhausting hours on duty, the nurses shared a single small room, where they ate their meals and alternated sleeping on straw mattresses, sharing one army blanket. The hospital was desperately short of medicine and other supplies so only the worst cases were treated under anaesthetic.

At the end of Flora's first contract, she returned to England while Americano sailed for New York, both to raise funds for the hospital. In only six weeks Sandes' campaign, publicized by the *Daily Mail*, had generated more than £2,000 (just over £14,000 today) and she journeyed back to Serbia in early 1915, sitting on packing cases weighing 120 tons, filled with precious medical supplies. When the cargo was safely delivered to Niš, Colonel Subotić, the vice-president of the Serbian Red Cross, asked the women to travel to Valjevo in northern Serbia which had been devastated by a typhus epidemic and was cut off. Sandes had read about the illness in the English press, and agreed to undertake this mission despite her qualms.[159] A town along the River Kolubara, nearly 200 miles north, Valjevo was also the front line of battle where Serb forces had resisted an Austrian invasion. The conflict left many casualties, and, according to Sandes, 50,000 prisoners and an outbreak of typhus fever.[160] An American doctor in Niš, also enlisted to fight the epidemic, predicted the women would die within a month if they didn't turn back.

After the British consul, Charles Greig, absolutely forbade them to go, the women resolved to press on.[161] Despite his protestations,

Greig handed Sandes a letter from the Foreign Minister, Sir Edward Grey, addressed to all nurses working in Serbia and explaining that their work was 'an inestimable benefit to the common cause'. The women would be important in carrying out Grey's pledge, made on 24 September, that Britain would assist Serbia 'without qualifications and without reserves', a statement he quickly watered down to '[support] in a political and not a military sense'. This left the Serbs without the promised troops and supplies upon which they had been relying. The British nurses would represent Britain's commitment which they aimed to fulfil.[162]

'So we chewed it over together,' Sandes wrote in her diary, 'and finally left for Valjevo on the 8pm train.'[163] They boarded, duty bolstering their courage, and headed into a region where fatalities from illness and injury hovered around 150 a day.[164] When Flora and Emily arrived at the train station on 20 February, they heard rumours that two American doctors, Albert Samuel Cooke and Barton McCosh Cookingham, were in a local hotel, suffering with typhus.[165] The medics were in grave danger since the mortality rate among those who contracted typhus was 70 per cent and more than 5,000 were afflicted with the disease. Sandes and Americano promptly left the station:

> We went at once and found that one doctor had died the day before[166] and been taken away and at the same time as they carried him out they brought in the coffin for his pal and laid it down beside his bed ready for him. He was lying there with his coffin beside him having completely given up all hope.[167]

Cookingham recovered but the epidemic's toll on medical staff at the Fourth Reserve Hospital where the women worked was enormous. Twenty-one doctors died in Valjevo in three weeks; and while Flora and Emily were stricken, they survived. Each evening meal became a celebration to the living as the staff fought to keep calm while the death rate soared. There were fourteen seated at the long wooden table when the women arrived, and over each place hung a large, black-edged funeral notice of its former occupant.

As Sandes noted in her diary: '[The hospital staff] won't let us go to bed early because they say you never know which will be your last night and why waste it in bed.'[168] At the end of a month only the Serbian doctor, one other man, and the two women remained.[169]

During her time in Valjevo, Flora's Serbo-Croatian improved, her commitment to the Serbian cause grew stronger and her medical responsibilities expanded. One day, as Flora was finishing an operation, Serbia's Chief Military Surgeon arrived for an inspection. He looked around the makeshift theatre and asked, 'Who's the surgeon here?' When Flora replied meekly that it was her, 'he just crossed himself three times and said, "Carry on, do the best you can, there's no one else to do it."'[170] On 1 March she had 'cut off a man's toes with a pair of scissors this afternoon', and, ominously, two days later, plucked her first louse, the typhus carrier, from her clothing.[171] Between 16 and 21 March she wrote, 'sick with typhus, kept no diary' and it was not until 2 April that she rose from her bed again.[172]

By the spring of 1915, the typhus epidemic had begun to wane and Emily and Flora became anxious to work where their skills were more urgently needed. That summer the women inquired about joining a regimental ambulance unit at the local military headquarters. As Flora explained, it was a position barred to women under ordinary circumstances because first-aid dressing stations were frequently shelled and nurses were required to live with the regiment. Flora's first attempts to secure an ambulance position were refused and so in August 1915 she returned to England, having noted, 'All is quiet, no sign of war, A[mericano] and I have decided to go home.'[173]

But the interlude was brief and on 18 October Flora returned to Serbia via Marseilles, Sardinia and Athens aboard the *Mossoul*. Dr Isabel Emslie Hutton, also destined for relief work in a Serbian hospital, befriended Sandes on a journey marked by its submarine chases and seasick crew. Dr Hutton described her companion as, 'a tall handsome woman with short grey hair and skirt'.[174] Sandes and the other foreign medics arrived at Salonika – 'a scatty mess of soldiers and officers of all nationalities' – in early November and at Prilep three weeks later.[175] After much negotiation, Flora was attached to the Ambulance of the 2nd Regiment, Morava Division of the Army of the New Territories as a dresser, a reward for her work in Valjevo. A commandant formally assigned her to the regiment while she nursed at Prilep's military hospital and, against the advice of Greig, the British consul, she accepted.

When Dr Hutton wrote about her Serbia experience, she recalled one intimate, late-night conversation with Flora Sandes aboard the *Mossoul*. Despite Flora's protestations that she had 'no intention of going for a soldier' when she left London in 1914, Dr Hutton was only mildly surprised at her friend's transformation from nurse into combatant. On that ship, so crowded with French soldiers that the women stole cushions from the smoking room to sleep on deck underneath the stars, Flora confessed her real ambition. When Dr Hutton saw Flora again in 1916, she noted in her diary:

> She has got what she wanted without much difficulty for I remember that on the *Mossoul* she told me that she had always wished to be a soldier and fight … she got caught in the retreat, however, shouldered a gun and was made a soldier … she looks well and in good spirits.[176]

Later Flora commented on the seemingly incongruous shift from healing the wounded to fighting alongside the enemy on the front line with the 2nd Regiment: 'Looking back I seem to have just naturally drifted, by successive stages, from nurse into soldier.'[177] The change may have been gradual but logical to the Serbs for several reasons: the military had a history of female combatants, and enlistment was often haphazard, Flora had rifle training, was an excellent horsewoman, and represented an Allied country. Rather than drifting, in reality, she placed herself deliberately close to the Serbs' front line where the Bulgarian forces were 'conducting "guerrilla warfare"'[178] and offered her services to the military hospital. She realized that it would soon be evacuated back to Salonika, so, when she heard that the 2nd Regiment's military ambulance was a few miles north, she enlisted with the Serb authorities' approval.[179]

Only six days after joining the regimental ambulance Flora treated the injured men of the 2nd and 14th Regiments of the Morava Division, writing in her diary that: 'the men seem bent on turning me into a soldier and I expect I'll find myself in the trenches next battle.'[180] As she explained to her eldest sister Sophia, in a letter dated the next day: 'I threw my lot in with the second regiment and they seem to think I've done something wonderful whereas ... I've done absolutely nothing except share their grub, ride their horses and they've adopted me as a kind of mascot.'[181]

The regiment ('a ludicrously small force'),[182] she noted, considered her riding and shooting skills more valuable 'than the fact that I'm supposed to be a nurse'.[183] Her nursing career, however, ended abruptly when the 2nd Regiment retreated into Albania, which was impassable to an ambulance. The Serbs' last battle before the Bulgarian invasion was fought at Babuna Pass but the enemy's superior numbers slowly drove back the Serb forces; the Germans and Austrians were pressing from the north and the Bulgarians from the east, and the south was blocked by neutral Greece. Serbian Field Marshal Radomir Putnik ordered a retreat through neutral Albania, but this carried terrible risks.[184]

Colonel Milić, her regimental commander, said it would be better for Serbia if she stayed, but better for Flora Sandes if she left. Dr Nikolitch warned Flora of the horrors ahead but admitted that she was a boon to morale as 'I represented England!'[185] She ceremoniously stripped the Red Cross badge from her arm while Colonel Milić laughed as he took the small brass figure '2' from his own epaulettes and fastened them to her shoulder straps.[186] Equipped with her violin, three cases of cigarettes, jars of jam and warm helmets (gifts for the soldiers), Flora Sandes, now the embodiment of Allied rescue, motored back to her regiment's camp. Along the way she breathed a sigh of relief: 'for me it [was] too good to be true, having fully expected to be ignominiously packed back to Salonique as a female encumbrance.'[187] She wrote a quick letter to her family and in half an hour disappeared into a howling blizzard, bound for Albania.

Flora's awareness of her unique status may explain her motives to stay and Colonel Milić's willingness to enlist her. Each night, the soldiers gathered round their campfire would ask Flora, 'when are the British coming to help us?' and she felt responsible for fulfilling their promise.[188] So she endured the terrible journey where an estimated 70,000 soldiers and 140,000 civilians froze, starved to death, died of disease or were killed by bandits between November 1915 and February 1916. Such shared hardship, commitment and knowledge supplied her with the credibility to campaign internationally for the Serbian cause.

The Serbian military may have made an exception for Flora, but more as a foreigner than a female combatant. She noted wryly how differently her comrades regarded a girl soldier, Milunka, who, according to Flora, was a seventeen-year-old peasant. They respected Milunka's extraordinary bravery in battle – she once crossed an open space swept by fire to fetch badly needed ammunition – but she was always in trouble. 'Being a peasant like the men', Flora observed, 'they did not treat her at all in the same way they treated me.'[189] When her regimental colonel punished Milunka for being absent without leave by making her sleep in a small tent away from her comrades, she retaliated by setting it ablaze.[190] Flora was set apart by her age, her education, her international contacts, and for risking her life for an adopted country.

Flora had already demonstrated a talent for fundraising and when she returned home on leave in 1916, fresh from the front line where she had lived with and fought alongside the Serbian soldiers, she spoke to audiences with convincing authority. The British press celebrated their native warrior, hailed this Red Cross nurse-turned-soldier as 'the Serbian Joan of Arc' whom cab drivers stopped in the streets, who dined with British generals and lunched with royals. Her 1927 autobiography was described in a *Times Literary Supplement* review as 'important to students of Balkan affairs and to those diplomats whose duty is to preserve the peace of the Near East.'[191]

Although Flora's motives for enlisting with the Serbian Army are complex, her military and diplomatic roles were not unique in the Balkans. Forty years earlier, another foreigner, the Dutch heiress

Jeanne Merkus, had enlisted in the Serbian ranks after participating in the anti-Ottoman rebellions in Herzegovina and Bosnia. Before her adventure in the South-Slav struggle for liberation, Merkus had lived through the Prussian siege of Paris and the Paris Commune where 'she must have grown familiar with females as political and military leaders'.[192] By mid-December 1875, Merkus had joined the all-male Herzegovinian insurgents, hoping to defeat the Muslim rulers and recapture the Holy Land from the Ottomans. She wore a uniform adapted from the local men's dress and joined other Western-European volunteers in supporting the Serb-led rebellion. On 10 March 1876, Austrian forces on Turkish territory captured Merkus along with her commander, and friend, the military leader Mihalio Ljubibratić, who was imprisoned in Linz while Merkus was freed and returned to Belgrade.[193]

Merkus rode into the Serbian city, a novelty for the French, German and Slavic journalists who wrote lavish descriptions of this Dutch woman astride a horse, wearing a Montenegrin cap over her curly blonde hair and a man's cape slung around her shoulders. Just as Flora would do years later, Merkus used her status as the 'Joan of Arc of Serbia' and 'the Amazon of Herzegovina' to negotiate a military role. She came under the command of Lieutenant-Colonel Gruja Miskovic who would later praise her as a 'shining example' of courage in action.[194] Merkus insisted her motives were religious: 'I did not wish to nurse wounded soldiers, but to help liberate Christian people, and also Christ's land from the sovereignty of the Turks,' she wrote in her memoir.[195] Although Merkus was not the only known female fighter during the war – the names of Stana Kovačević, Vukosava Nikolić, Draga Strainović and Marina Veličković appear in the contemporary press and eye-witness accounts of the Serbo-Turkish War – she was, uniquely, a foreigner who supplied the rebels with arms and whose international press coverage aided their cause.[196]

While there were a few documented cases of women passing in nineteenth-century Balkan conflicts, many more may have volunteered, and others longed to join the fight. A British medical student Alfred Wright who worked at a hospital during the Serbo-Turkish War in 1876 heard such a confession from Mademoiselle

Miloikovitch: 'I wish I were a man instead of a woman. I would enlist immediately.' Miloikovitch had witnessed atrocities in her village and wanted to take revenge on the perpetrators: 'it has been my cruel lot to see all this take place before my very eyes, and I care not what any one thinks, and I repeat it, – I long for vengeance, and I often think of going – woman as I am – to the front and firing a shot at our accursed enemies.'[197] When Alfred suggested that she volunteer as a nurse, she reminded him, 'I wish I were a man! Your greedy sex monopolised all the sensible occupations, and left us poor women nothing but nursing and needlework.'[198]

Despite her protestations about the boredom and irrelevance of 'nursing and needlework', the well-born Mademoiselle Miloikovitch expressed a popular motive for women enlisting in disguise. However, as a phenomenon, it became increasingly rare by the early twentieth century as European armies 'travelled light', and required physical exams for recruits.[199] By the First World War, while Flora Sandes, Maria Bochkareva and the soldiers of the 1st Russian Women's Battalion were celebrated for their battle courage, when an English woman passed briefly as a soldier on the Western Front in 1915, she was banned from writing about her experiences which seemed much more threatening to the social order.

Dorothy Lawrence, a nineteen-year-old English woman, attempted to further her journalistic aspirations by joining the Royal Engineers as a sapper in 1915. Lawrence, who had been a freelance journalist for the *Times* and *Nash's Pall Mall Magazine*, was living in Paris and was frustrated that newspaper editors rejected her offer to cover the Western Front. In her memoir, which she was finally able to publish in 1919, she recalls a typical comment: 'Do you suppose we're going to send a woman out there when even our own war correspondents can't get out for love or money?'[200] As she wrote in *Sapper Dorothy Lawrence* (1919) the editors' refusal galvanized her into a determination to prove them wrong:

I'll see what an ordinary English girl, without credentials or money can accomplish. If war correspondents cannot get out there, I'll see whether I cannot go one better than those big men with their cars, credentials, and money. I'll see what I can manage as a war-correspondent.[201]

To circumvent military regulations that banned civilians from the front, she initially volunteered for first aid with the War Office. When that failed, she attempted to enlist with the VAD; aged eighteen, she was judged too young.

Dorothy was eventually able to take advantage of the fact that trench warfare on the Western Front proved disorganized enough that she could slip into a newly formed tunnelling company composed of soldiers from other regiments. Her memoir observes that discipline was not rigidly enforced and, since engineers regularly moved from company to company, no one noticed a stranger in their midst. Other women describe how bureaucratic ineptitude might work in their favour. Australian author Louise Mack described her journey to witness the 'Boche' at the front in a 300-page account published by Mills and Boon in 1915; Lady Isabelle St John journeyed to Bethune, France that year looking for her son, missing in action, and found him; and an English nurse, Mary Wilkinson, received her pilot's certificate from the United Aero Club and volunteered for the Russian Army Service in 1916.[202] These accounts parallel those of the Russian women soldiers who appeared in the midst of battle and stayed until they were dismissed. The worse the conditions and the greater the need for recruits, the more likely it was that women, even in the twentieth century, would enter the conflict.

Dorothy's opportunity to head for the front came when she met two English soldiers at a café in Paris. They agreed to source a uniform and smuggle it into her apartment, piece by piece, wrapped in discreet brown paper while, in return, she guided them around the city's sites. Once her uniform was assembled, Dorothy bound her breasts with bandages to hide 'a robust figure' and padded her back with cotton wool and sacking. Despite resembling the Michelin Man, the outfit enabled her to drill and march as the Tommies had taught her.[203] Two friendly Scots policemen gave her a military haircut and she used a disinfectant, Condy's Fluid, to produce 'the requisite, manly bronzed complexion'.[204] As Private Denis Smith of the First Leicestershire Regiment, with a forged pass and a real identification disc, she headed to the front.

Dorothy Lawrence's exposure after just ten days puzzled the British military authorities. Even worse for her, however, her journalistic coup appeared as less than honourable and may explain the poor sales for her post-war account. Although Lawrence was unique in serving at the front, albeit for a few days, back at home accounts of passing women continued to appear in the press.

As Lawrence adopted her male persona to promote her career, a thirty-two-year-old woman who passed as 'Albert F.' and worked as a printer in a North London shop entered the war to protect her identity. Albert was 'earning very high wages even for a man' when the war broke out and, after five other printers in the shop had enlisted, he could not refuse military service without divulging his identity. Albert, described in a contemporary newspaper account as 'a slightly-built, fair-haired, and smooth-faced conscript dressed in a neat navy-blue suit, brown cap, and patent-leather boots',[205] appeared before the Mill Hill Medical Examining Board in August 1916. The sergeant was surprised when Albert produced a National Health Insurance form as proof of a cardiac condition and requested a private medical exam. The sergeant denied Albert's request and said later that he had no reason to question the conscript's gender. 'The voice was soft and rather gentle,' he said, 'but no notice was taken of that. Plenty of young fellows – and she looked like a young man of 24 – have effeminate voices, and when a great many men are being dealt with … individual characteristics are passed without comment.'[206]

London newspapers reported that the woman passing as Albert had been previously married in a northern seaport but that this relationship had ended after the couple's two children had died in infancy. (Other accounts claim that she was living with two dependent children in Hornsey by 1916.[207]) She moved into a nearby lodging house and met the woman who later became her 'wife'. Still fearing that her former husband might find her, she assumed a male identity, began a new life in North London and found a job. Albert's employer launched an appeal following his exposure, claiming: 'He was one of the best "workmen" at this particular job I have ever had – punctual, quick and with just the touch of imagination needed to make a success out of that particular line ... "he" was my right hand man.'[208] Albert was later invited back to the Mill Hill barracks where he shook hands with the colonel, who declared him 'a perfect little brick'.[209]

The idea that a woman would, and could, change her gender to earn a better living or enter the forces was picked up by Berta Ruck, a columnist in the *Illustrated Sunday Herald* – the newspaper that broke Albert F.'s story. Ruck invented a conversation between two women – 'of opposing types [but] full of character and independent ways' – discussing an unspecified news article about a passing woman and including a veiled reference to Chelsea Pensioners Christian Davies and Hannah Snell:

THE BRUNETTE: Another of them? Only lately I heard about that girl who ran away from home dressed as a boy to earn her living as a plumber's mate. Then there was that doctor 'man' in America. There was the woman who served in the ranks and became a Chelsea pensioner. Quite often these cases seem to crop up.

THE BLONDE: I suppose it's because as men, the women get better jobs and earn better money than they do as members of their own sex.[210]

Ruck's imagined dialogue acknowledged women's growing frustration with being paid less than men, especially during a period when they occupied jobs vacated by servicemen.[211] Such articles exposed the tensions about the rewards for women as they entered heavy industry, commerce and farming during the national emergency. Since the military was considered the ultimate exercise of masculinity, women's involvement as combatants, it was argued, might herald a true revolution of the sexes. In the US, the navy played on the popular notion of the New Woman as an emancipated and eager recruit after it entered the war in 1917.

A US Navy recruitment poster displayed a smiling young woman, with ringlets peeking out from beneath a standard issue rating's uniform, and pulling at a pair of invisible braces (an eerie update of Fanny Campbell), exclaiming: '*Gee!!* I wish I were *a man. I'd* join the Navy.' If this coquette appropriating a sailor's duty could not entice potential recruits to the nearest station, the poster urged: 'Be a Man and Do It.'[212] It carried the message – already advocated by the Women's Battalion of Death – that female fighters might shame men into enlisting.

The woman passing as Albert F., although a highly skilled printer and valued employee, was barred from her trade once her biological sex was revealed. However, financial security and a profession were only partial reasons for her disguise. Throughout her four years in London she was dogged by a fear that one day, somehow, her abusive husband would appear. In an interview she said that when the call-up notice came it was 'a godsend', explaining, '[I] felt that here was a chance, at any rate, of getting where my husband would never find me.'[213] But once her passing became a news story, she was forced to leave London for northern England and went into hiding.

Financial security, employment, patriotism, rejection of domesticity, a desire for fame or infamy, for a same-sex relationship, or to express a masculine identity, form a complex web of motives. There are no clear and simple answers to the question – why did she do it? The female warriors became the stuff of legends and even those who explained their reasons to willing interlocutors might find their stories shaped to fit contemporary narratives. Few women wrote their own stories and most left that task to historians, journalists, balladeers and popular storytellers. Each generation and place refashioned these heroines to fit the prevailing ideals of female love and male glory that arose during periods of war.

The life-histories of these women, as will be discussed in later chapters, are often a challenge to interpret. Whose voice is really telling the story, and for what purpose? The heroines who starred in the immensely popular eighteenth-century ballads about female warriors were rooted in historical realities but where did the fiction begin and end? Even Sarah Edmonds, who later became more forthcoming about her earlier existence as Frank Thompson, used romantic conventions to appeal to her readers. Flora Sandes wrote her first autobiography as a polemic for the Serbian cause and the second, in part, to supplement her military pension. If the 'facts' of these stories remain elusive, the myths are not. Fiction drew from popular narratives which in turn drew from fact in an endless loop. If Fanny Campbell, the inspiration for Sarah Edmonds' cross-dressing, was a creature of fiction, Anne Bonny and Mary Read were her real-life counterparts. Their persistence kept alive an alternative image of female heroism and convinced women that the masculine world was within their reach.

However her story was recast and rewritten, the female warrior still operated as a source of inspiration, hope and optimism for women seeking an escape from the poverty of their lives, from the boredom of waiting for a lover's return or from the oppression of their physical selves. In every historical period these heroines hinted at an alternative plot for their lives and suggested another ending to mundane, painful or predictable stories of acquiescence. The freedom they gained, however, was often paid for at a very high price. The next chapter explores what life on campaign or on the high seas involved for the women who kept their secrets hidden at all costs.

Chapter 4

Life Among the Men

*'Trousers make a wonderful difference in the outlook on life.
I know that dressed as a man I did not, as I do now I am
wearing a skirt again, feel hopeless and helpless … Today when
the whole world knows my secret I feel more a man than a
woman. I want to up and do those things that men do to earn a
living rather than to spend my days as a friendless woman.'*[1]
VALERIE ARKELL-SMITH, 1929

Generations of women who challenged dominant feminine ideals of passivity and weakness might have agreed with Valerie Arkell-Smith, alias Colonel Barker, that an active, independent life was best imagined on male terms. During the Great War, many women in auxiliary military roles dreamed of joining men in battle while music hall singers Bessie Bonehill, Hetty King, Dorothy Raynor, Ella Shields and Vesta Tilley trod the London boards in a variety of male uniforms.[2] Christabel Pankhurst, organizing secretary of the Women's Social and Political Union, littered her speeches with military metaphors, encouraging women to take direct action. Her mother Emmeline counted Maria Bochkareva as a friend, inspected her 1st Russian Women's Battalion of Death in 1917 and hosted her visit to Manchester that year. Caught up in the rhetoric of empire and Britain's need to defend her interests, some women believed that military participation would be rewarded with the vote and greater equality.[3] Arkell-Smith had served in the VAD and the WRAF, even ferrying horses to France to replace those killed or wounded in battle, but knew that as Colonel Barker she might become richer and more powerful, be afforded greater respect and be free to love women.

The early twentieth-century treatments of passing military women provide continuity with those of previous centuries who successfully made the transition into manhood. Colonel Barker's precursors – the chapbook and ballad heroines, theatrical performers, national mascots – made the male sphere appear exotic and enticing, and merely a costume change away. In reality and in fantasy, passing women employed a range of strategies both to reimagine themselves psychologically in the opposite gender and to make their disguise convincing. Critical to their passing was the approval of their comrades and their adoption, or imitation, of their masculine behaviour. Such friendships were never taken for granted since their lives depended on such support. Masculinity was a performance that required constant reinforcement, whether demonstrated through flirtations with other women, through mastery of skills or trade, through displaying bravery in battle or through a charming personality. It was often a lonely position for a woman, ever-vigilant in maintaining a disguise, deceiving the men upon whom she depended, and pondering the internal tensions of embodying dual identities.

Comradeship

Male relatives, many of whom were either serving or retired servicemen, or friends played a crucial role in either engineering a woman's enlistment or preserving her disguise. The passing women warriors, or those who enlisted informally, were dependent on their fellow comrades and often hyper-vigilant about maintaining their support. These men not only had the power to expose their identity but were necessary to the women's physical survival. For those who found themselves amongst ranks of men without such comradeship, their situation was much more precarious. These women persistently negotiated the boundaries of friendships, sexual exploitation and the pressure to sacrifice their safety for a common cause. And all of this took place often in the most intimate quarters and in extreme conditions.

The passing woman warrior inevitably became a keen observer of men as she created the reality of her male persona through her dress, behaviour and attitudes, and often by beguiling her comrades. In disguise she might endear herself by force of a flamboyant or eccentric personality, by emphasizing her youth, or by making herself indispensable through her skills or courage. She might charm her way into the other men's affections so that, even if discovered, her comrades could be trusted not to alert the officer or ship's captain with the power to banish her from their midst.

Hannah Snell was a master of such tactics although we have no real knowledge of whether her shipmates knew the true identity of their lowly cabin boy, James Gray. Aboard the *Swallow*, the ship that would feature in Almira Paul's story, whose crew provided the Maltese goat for the orphan Tommy, Hannah-as-James enlisted. There, she 'rendered herself so conspicuous both by her skill and intrepidity that she was allowed to be a very useful hand on board'.[4] James busied himself cooking, washing linen and mending shirts and whatever else might need repairing, earning him the title of 'Favourite amongst them all and was looked upon as the most handy Boy belonging to the Sloop'.[5] According to Snell's biographer, James challenged any sailor who hinted at his effeminacy to beat him at a task. When teased about his hairless chin 'with the disagreeable title of Miss Molly Gray', James smiled, swore, and worked 'to prove herself as good a man as any of them on board for any wager to be deposited in her master's hands.'[6] This combination of bravado and skill made James indispensable and quashed rumours about his sex.

One passing female sailor whose exceptional professionalism endeared her to the crew was William Brown. An Afro-Caribbean British sailor, she had been deserted by her husband before enlisting in the Royal Navy during the Napoleonic Wars around 1804. Brown became as famous for climbing the rigging as he was for '[his] partiality for prize-money and grog'.[7] Brown rose to captain of the foretop, a position requiring the utmost dexterity and strength, and during twelve years at sea took 'grog with her former messmates, with the greatest gaiety'.[8] Despite the passing sailor's achievements, however, when her identity was discovered as the *Queen Charlotte*'s crew were paid off in 1815, her estranged husband attempted to exercise his legal claim to her prize money.[9]

Another sailor who secured her place aboard ship through charm and friendship appears in W. H. Davies' account of working aboard a freight steamer in the 1890s, sailing from Baltimore, Maryland to England. He describes a sailor whose 'vitality of spirit seemed overflowing every minute of the day', almost a caricature of the jolly tar who entertained the crew by singing 'with surprising sweetness', deftly rolling cigarettes, spitting tobacco and swaggering about the dock.[10] A few weeks later, Davies met his friend Blackey, who had worked a cattle steamer back to England with the sweet-voiced sailor. Though Blackey worked side by side with the 'cattleman' for eleven days, when an accident forced his companion off the ship he discovered his friend was female. 'By his singing, laughing, and talking, he made a play of labour,' Blackey reported. 'Down in the forecastle at night he sang songs and in spite of our limited space, and the rolling of the ship he gave many a dance and ended by falling into his low bunk exhausted and laughing still.'[11] Though Blackey considered his friend 'a queer man' and Davies regarded the sailor as 'playing a part, all this cigarette smoking, chewing tobacco and swaggering', neither man suspected the nature of her sex.[12]

While many passing women exuded charm to maintain their disguise, Dr James Barry, born Margaret Anne Bulkley in 1795 to a merchant's family in Cork, who became the first woman to graduate from a British medical school in 1812, exuded ferocity. Biographers have suggested that Barry developed this fierce personality to mask fears of detection since he was remembered as arrogant and temperamental and, like the Baltimore cattleman, seemed almost a caricature of masculinity. While posted to South Africa as Britain's Colonial Medical Inspector, Dr Barry was rumoured to have challenged three men to duels, hunted, attended military parades, rode horses and cultivated a reputation with ladies. The memoir of military officer William Cattell describes the doctor's formidable reputation:

> [Barry] made love to a handsome Dutch girl of whom another officer (Mannering) was enamoured, and won her affection. They taunted Mannering who flung a tumbler of wine in his [Barry's] face. The duel followed in which Barry allowed himself to be slightly wounded. The next day he told Mannering he never really loved the girl, [and] the latter ultimately married.[13]

Dr Barry also made caustic remarks about women he found unattractive to his employer and friend, Lord Charles Somerset, governor of the Cape Colony. Barry's stinging insults about, and flirtations with women signalled his distance from their female world.[14]

The passing woman was also forced to confront the problem of sharing intimate physical spaces with their male comrades. The American revolutionary soldier Deborah Sampson, disguised as Robert Shurtliff, comments that he often slept with other men, usually officers, without concern. 'They as little suspected my sex as I suspected them of a disposition to violate its chastity, had I been willing to expose myself to them and act the wanton.'[15] Such an adventure involved many risks, including the consequences if she had been assaulted. She might then have been charged under colonial law which defined the criminal act of 'fornication' as sexual intercourse by any man with a single woman or women: during the Revolutionary War years women rather than men were routinely fined for such crimes.[16] The acceptance, continuing support and comradeship of other men were crucial to the female warrior's success.

One of the most fascinating records of a passing woman's friendship is revealed in the correspondence of American Civil War soldiers Sarah Emma Edmonds and Jerome Robbins. Throughout the war, Robbins kept a detailed diary of his experiences with the 2nd Michigan Infantry Regiment. On 30 October 1861 Robbins, then assistant surgeon, made his first reference to Frank Thompson with whom he worked at the regimental hospital at Camp Scott.

The friendship deepened over the following weeks as Robbins found Frank an entertaining conversationalist, 'a good noble-hearted fellow' and a keen intellectual companion.[17] Together they attended prayer meetings, took long walks and on 7 November Jerome noted that he 'arose greatly refreshed after a sound sleep in a couch with my friend Frank.'[18] Although bed sharing to affluent families in the nineteenth century had 'no implied meaning or sexual titillation associated with the activity', Robbins' passing mention suggests a growing intimacy.[19] The evening even prompted him to note that, 'The society of a friend so pleasant as Frank I hail with joy though foolish as it may seem a great mystery appears to be connected with him which it is impossible for me to fathom.'[20] Despite Robbins' deepening confusion, they grew closer, since they shared religious beliefs and work that kept them in constant and intimate contact. They often filled in for each other at the hospital or stayed up late to talk while on night duty.

Only two weeks later, after a 'long and interesting conversation' with Frank, Jerome returned to his quarters and wrote in his crabbed hand, 'my friend Frank is a female'.[21] Neither surprised nor outraged at a woman in the ranks Jerome expressed instead his profound sense of betrayal. A more than platonic love for his stalwart companion may have prompted Frank to reveal his true identity. When Jerome spoke about his fiancée, Anna Corey, Frank volunteered an explanation for his decision to leave New Brunswick in male guise and join the army. Since Frank Thompson's enlistment with the Union Greys on 17 April 1861, Jerome was probably the first person, after eight long months of subterfuge, to learn of his friend's secret.

Contrary to Sarah Edmonds' published accounts, Jerome Robbins' diary offers insights into why she left her home town; rather than because of her father's attempts to pair her off with an elderly farmer, Sarah may have left because of an ill-fated love affair with Thomas, a local merchant. 'My friend describes him as pleasing in manner and so won her heart as to cause the object of love to be nearly worshipped,' wrote Robbins. 'But a change came; her lover seemed cold, reserved, and exacting, which was too much for the nature of my friend.' The lovers separated, Sarah became ill with scarlet fever and, after several weeks languishing in bed, recovered and abruptly left Canada.[22] Sarah may have invented these details to please Jerome or she may have left the mysterious Thomas out of her published accounts to conform to a more conventional heroic narrative.

Whatever the truth, Sarah's story was consistent in having compelling reasons to seek a better life, as a man. Neither did Robbins have reason to embellish Sarah's account as he protected her confession from accidental discovery with care. He glued together the pages for this diary entry and wrote across the top, 'please allow these leaves to be closed until author's permission is given for their opening.' Jerome never again refers to their conversation and while he appears to have resented Frank's betrayal, he still regarded their friendship as 'one of the greatest events of my life'.[23]

Despite this assurance, however, Robbins found a replacement for an increasingly surly Frank. On 6 December his moody companion watched as Jerome 'had another long conversation with Russell in which he expressed to me the deepest friendship that even a brother could not.'[24] Two weeks later Jerome wrote of Frank: 'I am a little fearful our natures are not as congenial as at first supposed by me yet I feel he is the same friend.'[25] For the next few weeks the friendship appeared to deteriorate, Jerome noting that Frank 'acts strangely', and was 'very much out of humour'. He suggested that Frank might be jealous of Jerome's fiancée and wrote, 'Perhaps a knowledge on her part that there is one Michigan home that I do regard with especial affection creates her disagreeable manner.'[26] But when Frank was absent for a few days, Robbins admitted, 'I feel quite lonely without him.'[27]

By late December 1861 Frank had left Camp Scott for a nursing post at the Mansion House Hospital, Virginia, before moving to the General Hospital in Georgetown, and later acting as the regimental postmaster and letter carrier. According to Jerome, Frank had left because a cook and other men in the camp were constantly teasing him about his feminine appearance.[28] Despite these tensions, when the friends met again in Alexandria in 1862, they continued their evening walks, often discussing religion, nursed each other when sick, and swapped magazines and stories. One evening, when Jerome was out, Frank left a note between two pages of Robbins' journal saying that he had read it 'for spite'.[29] Such was their intimacy that Jerome seemed only mildly irritated by his friend's disregard for his privacy.

Frank enjoyed the company of other men, which Jerome mentions on 20 December 1861 when he had observed his friend with a 'Genl Reed [who] seems a fine fellow & is very fond of Frank'.[30] They repaired their friendship, however, and saw less of each other when Frank accepted his new nursing posts and job as a mail carrier. They exchanged warm letters but, by the spring of 1863, it became clear that Frank had developed an affection for a married man, Assistant Adjutant General James Reid of the 79th New York Volunteers. Here Robbins seems openly jealous and wrote on 4 April 1863 while nursing Frank through a bout of malaria: 'It is a sad reality to which we awaken when we learn that others are receiving the *devotion of one* [emphasis in original] from whom we can only claim friendships [sic] attention of which too we are deprived.'[31]

When Frank, after suffering from illness and the accumulated anxiety about the discovery of his true sex, finally deserted, Jerome was furious. On 17 April 1863 he searched for Frank and was surprised to hear that he hadn't been seen since the previous day. By 20 April 1863, Frank's desertion from the army near Lebanon, Kentucky was confirmed,[32] as Robbins wrote that his friend had taken the one o'clock train with Reid. Although Jerome knew Frank had planned to leave, he felt betrayed that it happened without warning.

Frank has deserted fro [sic] which I do not blame him. his was a strange history/he prepared me for his departure in part. yet I did not think it would be so premature. yet he did not prepare me. for his ingratitude and rotten disregard for the finer sensibilities of others. of all others whom I termed friends he was the last I dreamed capable of the petty business which was betrayed by his friend R [Reid] ... and while I own a slight disgust to such a character. I am excited to pity that poor humanity can be so weak as to repay kindness, interest and the warmest sympathy with deception. almost every attribute of a selfish heart.[33]

This was not, however, the end of their remarkable friendship, and their correspondence during the last two years of the war reveals Edmonds' continuing affection for Robbins. A month after leaving the army she wrote, as Sarah, from Washington, DC: 'Oh Jerome *I do miss you so much* [emphasis in original]. There is no person living whose presence would be so agreeable to me this afternoon.'[34] Sarah also mentions that she knew that Reid and Robbins had discussed her situation, prompting her to ask: 'I want you to write to me the import of [that conversation]. Will you please do so? [Reid] says he wants me to come and visit his wife who is very anxious to see me.'[35] Two years later Sarah remained an intimate, writing to Jerome from Camp Falmouth, Virginia: 'I daily realise that had I met you some years ago I might have been much happier now. But providence ordered it otherwise and I must be content.'[36]

It remains difficult to determine the nature of Sarah's relationship with Reid, but if she was in love with him, it must have been excruciating. Their intimacy could have jeopardized her disguise and her friendship with Jerome who, after all, was the keeper of her secret. Her affair with a married man would have violated her Christian principles and was probably the source of vicious rumours that she took pains to quell in her memoir. In *Nurse and Spy*, along with other accounts of her wartime experiences, she deserted because she was stricken with malaria but not before a request for leave was denied. However, as Jerome's diary suggests, her desertion may have been prompted when her relationship with Reid became uncomfortably public.[37]

Apparently Reid and Robbins were not the only men who knew of Sarah's secret. William Boston, also of the 2nd Michigan Regiment, wrote in his diary on 22 April 1863: 'Our brigade postmaster turns out to be a girl and has deserted when his lover Inspector Read [sic] and [General O. M.] Poe resigned.'[38] Several years later Poe was willing to testify that 'her sex was not suspected by me or anyone else in the regiment' although he alludes to her fear of detection as her reason for desertion.[39] Through their willingness to maintain Frank's cover, Sarah's comrades demonstrated extraordinary loyalty (in Poe's case supporting her pension application) and this suggests they accepted a woman in their ranks. Sarah may have been an exception but one who had 'proven' herself through her tireless hospital work and as a postmaster, a job which entailed carrying two or three bushels of post back and forth over fifty to sixty miles at a time.[40] When Sarah disclosed her identity to Robbins, he never considered turning her over to their commanding officer. It was only in later newspaper accounts and in the governmental hearings about her pension that questions arose about whether a woman belonged on the battlefield.[41]

Jerome Robbins' documentation of his relationship with Sarah Edmonds reveals the entanglements of living with a dual identity. Jerome struggles to make sense of his conflicted feelings for Sarah as a woman *and* as a fellow medic working in an all-male environment. He hints at deep emotions and a possible yearning for sexual contact when late night hospital duties and bed sharing presented opportunities for physical intimacy. Perhaps the reality of Robbins' fiancée and their shared religious beliefs enabled them to patrol such boundaries. Whatever the motivation, it seems curious that Sarah's passing caused so little comment or consternation among her comrades. Robbins' diary suggests that her desertion with Reid was far more wounding than the disclosure of her sex.

Flirting and female companions

While male friendships were central to the female warrior's tale, another constant, from the eighteenth century onwards, is her inversion of the male gaze. Instead of being the object of male heterosexual interest, she becomes the pursuer of other women, to satisfy her own desires, or as a means to consolidate her masculine persona. Women who expressed an interest in the passing soldier at a brothel or sought to woo a charming officer provided useful cover; or else, as Mary Lacy describes, a woman's affection might satisfy a genuine longing for female friendship or sexual contact, or provide the familiarity and intimacy so often absent in a military environment. But the female lover, who falls for the uniform rather than the person who occupies it, might also arouse the passing warrior's fear of detection and elicit a cruel rejection.

The belle of the eighteenth-century popular heroines was the Dublin publican Christian Davies aka Kit Cavenaugh. According to a widely read account of her exploits, an 'as-told-to' biography, Christian pursued and was chased by other women at a time when sexuality was linked to behaviour rather than our contemporary conception of identity. While on a winter campaign in the Netherlands, living as Christopher Welsh, a dragoon in the Scots Greys during the War of the Spanish Succession, she was assigned to repair dykes and dig ditches. There, as Christopher, she courted a burgher's daughter, drawing on her observations of men's flirtatious language and behaviour. In this account, although she was later contrite about such 'frolics' when the young woman fell in love with Christopher, during the course of the romance Christian demonstrated her extensive knowledge of courtship:

> As I had formerly had many fine things said to myself I was not at a loss in the amorous dialect; I ran over all the tender nonsense (which I look upon as the lover's heavy cannon, as it does the greatest harm with raw girls), employed on such attacks: I squeezed her hand whenever I could get an opportunity, sighed often in her company; looked foolishly and practiced upon her all the ridiculous airs which I had often laughed at, when they were used as snares against myself.[42]

Such romances and visits to local brothels ('houses of civil conversation') lent her disguise legitimacy. But the biographer's narrator noted that Christian was quick to state that her infatuation was merely platonic and that the object of her affection spurned her seducer. 'I own that this rejection gained my heart and taking her in my arms I told her that she had heightened the power of her charms by her virtue. I was now fond of the girl though mine, you know, could not go beyond a platonic love.'[43] Although Christian denies a sexual relationship, her readers would be fully aware of women's potential for lesbian coupling.

Christian later added to her reputation for philandering when a Dutch prostitute claimed that Christopher Welsh had fathered her child, a charge he failed to deny, adding fatherhood to Christian's list of masculine accomplishments. When Christopher's true identity was revealed a few years later, the soldier who had shared his bed for several months claimed that 'he never knew I was a woman or even suspected it'.[44] Susanna Cope, an eighteenth-century soldier, also 'played amongst several lasses who supposed her to be a man, and fell in love with her, by which means she got store of putting the bilk upon [deceiving] the maids, widows, and wives.'[45] Female soldiers were often portrayed in popular literature as happily exercising their new-found male power by exploiting love-sick women who were then blamed for their lack of propriety.

The female warriors often distinguished between misguided but virtuous woman who fell in love with them and evil seductresses. Hannah Snell as James Gray would experience her own female troubles long after first enlisting aboard the *Swallow* in 1748 under the command of Admiral Edward Boscawen whose forces consisted of ten naval ships and East India Company vessels. James Gray was among 2,000 soldiers, 800 of whom were marines, who formed the largest European expeditionary force to sail to Asia. The forces were on a mission to seize the island of Mauritius and the Indian coastal town of Pondicherry then held by the French.[46] The *Swallow*'s 100-strong crew weighed anchor on 1 November to battle heavy seas, reaching safe harbour at Lisbon a month later.

After such a lengthy sea-voyage James took advantage of the respite by visiting the Portuguese city along with his mate

Edwards Jefferies. To quieten the teasing about how James gratified a 'lustful appetite' he accompanied Jeffries to a brothel. James attracted the attention of a pretty Portuguese woman whom Edward had been eyeing and the sailors tossed a coin for her. James lost and, reputation restored, discretely left. But on returning to Portsmouth, a Miss Catherine fell in love with James, who returned her affection. Back aboard the *Swallow*, when James boasted of his new love, his mates approved and accepted their shipmate's excuse for avoiding the harbour brothels.[47]

While Snell's publisher Robert Walker may have invented or embellished the romance between Miss Catherine and James Gray (he more than doubled the sales figures of her original biography of 1750 when it was reprinted the same year[48]), it follows a pattern of female intimacy found in more authentic accounts. Mary Lacy, the domestic servant from Kent who worked as a shipwright for twelve years as William Chandler, had several girlfriends, flirted with many others, and was 'very intimate' with a woman named Sarah Chase.[49] Lacy describes physical female friendships which even aroused other men's jealousy, earning William Chandler the reputation as 'a man-and-half to a great many'.[50]

In 1760, while still a shipwright's apprentice, William was assigned aboard the 100-gun guardship *Royal Sovereign* stationed at Spithead, Portsmouth harbour. There he befriended the girlfriend of his messmate John Grant, who lived aboard ship:

> The young woman and I were very intimate, and as she was exceeding fond of me, we used to play together like young children ... Our messmates believed we were too familiar together, but neither of us regarded their surmises, and if they said anything to her, she told them that if anything like what they suspected had passed between us, the same should be practiced in the future.
>
> However, when John Grant became acquainted that she and I were so fond of each other's company, he began to be somewhat displeased. Nevertheless, he was afraid to take any notice of it lest his messmates should laugh at him. Yet though he seemed to

wink at it, he showered her with several tokens of his resentment by beating her and otherwise using her very ill, threatening to send her on shore.[51]

Lacy's reference to 'play[ing] together like young children' hints at intimate touching and she describes several other encounters with sailor's wives or domestic servants who find William Chandler attractive. While aboard the *Royal William* in 1763 where William was apprenticed to a carpenter, Alexander M'Clean, he would spend occasional nights on shore. One night Robert Dawkin, the boatswain, invited William home for supper where, after the meal, a maid 'lighted me up to her chamber [bedroom]' the only spare sleeping quarters. As Lacy described her experience: 'I must confess that if I had been a young man I could not have withstood the temptations which this young person laid in my way, for she was so fond of me that I was ever at her tongue's end.'[52] The fear of discovery, a theme that runs through the memoir, may also have prompted her to take the maid's advances beyond kissing.

Lacy describes many flirtations on these Portsmouth visits which ended in drunken parties. During one raucous evening, M'Clean's lover attempts to seduce his apprentice:

My mistress observing me, came and placed herself in my lap, stroking me down the face, telling the waterman [who had ferried the party from the ship to the harbour] what she would do for me, so that the people present could not forebear laughing to see her sit in such a young boy's lap as she thought I was.[53]

Lacy enjoyed women's company, accompanying them to dances, visiting 'lewd houses ... where I was obliged to be very free with the girls', and even reached an 'agreement' with Sarah Chase that 'neither of us should walk out with any other person without the mutual consent of each other'.[54] Although their monogamous relationship ended when an old family friend moved to Portsmouth and spread rumours which lead to Lacy's discovery, she recalls that 'My girl at Gosport [Sarah Chase] had heard it, but could not believe it.'[55]

Lacy and her girlfriends may have perceived their relationships as an extension of friendship and affection since sex was then defined as mutual masturbation, kissing and fondling, where couples spent long hours 'in mutual touching, but very little penile-vaginal penetration' to preserve the woman's virginity and to prevent unwanted pregnancy.[56] As the eighteenth century proceeded, erotic practices, including 'sapphism' and other categories of 'perverse' sexualities emerged. Many of the female warrior's memoirs, including Lacy's, conform to historian Susan Lanser's definition of the *sapphic picaresque* where heroines swap domestic confinement for physical 'mobility' and, on their adventures, whether disguised or not, experience erotic and affectionate same-sex relationships.[57] These heroines choose these intimate relations as a viable and satisfying alternative to heterosexuality.[58]

The American Revolutionary War soldier Deborah Sampson's biography devotes two and a half chapters to her romance with 'the nymph of Maryland' with whom Robert Shurtliff has a tearful parting before being discharged at West Point. The object of Robert's affection, to whom he became 'mutually and tenderly attached' in the summer of 1783, was a seventeen-year-old girl from a wealthy Baltimore family.[59] By then, according to Herman Mann's 1797 account, Robert had fought in the Continental Army for two years and met Miss P. while recovering from a long illness.[60] Even though appearing 'emaciated and pallid', Robert remained convincing as 'the young gallant soldier' and former aide-de-camp to Major-General John Paterson of the Continental Army. Deborah-as-Robert found her affection for Miss P. confusing and so she left Baltimore abruptly for a tour of duty in southern Virginia.[61] While travelling, Deborah resolved to fully disclose to her friend her true identity. 'If you receive these lines remember they come from one who sincerely loves you,' she wrote Miss P. while in a relapse of fever. 'But my amiable friend, forgive my imperfections and forget you ever had affection for one so unworthy of the name of *your own sex.*'[62]

When, still disguised as Robert Shurtliff, Deborah returned to Baltimore, 'an irresistible attraction drew me again to … Miss P.'

However, in a melodramatic twist of fate, the confessional letter posted from Virginia went astray and when they finally met Robert Shurtliff risked the friendship by revealing the truth.[63] While a romance between two women was neither unprecedented nor likely to inflict reputational damage in late eighteenth-century America, the improbable twist in Sampson's tale suggests that her publisher drew on other famous female warriors for inspiration.[64] Deborah's romance with Miss P. is shaped by the narrator Mann's distinction between 'platonick love' and an 'animal love' suggestive of an erotic encounter. Alfred Young's 2004 biography concludes that Deborah Sampson, who provided Mann with details of her experiences as Robert Shurtliff long after the war when she was married and a mother, probably suggested that women found her attractive in uniform.[65] But nothing more.

Young points out that Mann may have invented Deborah's romance with Miss P. even while he stressed its platonic nature in the memoir's first edition in 1797. While Sampson then appears as a woman who conformed to eighteenth-century values of same-sex sentimental love, this portrait was revised three decades later. That Mann in the 1802 edition introduced erotic elements into the saga involving Miss P. may reflect the rise of pornographic literature and a shift in contemporary attitudes about gender and sex.[66]

Passing woman had gone from being understood within a category of hermaphroditism where those who were attracted to other women were assumed to have enlarged clitorises but did not imitate male sexual behaviour by penetrating other female bodies, to possessing corrupted minds. Human sexuality, by definition, involved a penis.[67] By the nineteenth century women who were attracted to their own, rather than the opposite sex were believed to have deviant desires; no longer was erotic play between women regarded as innocent or mischievous.[68]

The paradox of identity

Memoirs by passing women and female combatants suggest an avoidance of intimate contact with either sex by the early twentieth century. Indeed, these combatants might even scold women for being too free with their favours as the aristocrat Kati Dadeshkeliani, disguised as Prince Djamal, did in her 1934 memoir. In 1915, under the protection of a family friend, Colonel Edik Khogandokov, the Prince was assigned to the 4th Squadron of a Tartar regiment known as the 'Savages' where he served as Khogandokov's aide-de-camp. Later, he was detailed to a front-line position and, traumatized by its brutality, returned to an ambulance company.[69]

During the Prince's military career his 'few adventures' were 'far from flattering, [and] caused me cruel embarrassment'.[70] Prince Djamal was rumoured to be the illegitimate son of Grand Duke Michael Alexandrovich, the regimental commander, which increased his attraction for any potential admirers. One evening, while stationed at Borszczow, a city near the front of Eastern Galicia, the Prince found a woman hiding in his carriage who 'insisted that I should take her to my apartment'.[71] During night duty at the ambulance hospital where the Prince was posted, a woman crept into his private quarters, 'in a state of *déshabille*, and with the manifest intention of sharing my bed'. After a brusque reminder to the intended seducer that she was a mother with a wounded husband in Crimea, the Prince 'took her by the shoulders and thrust her unceremoniously out of the room'.[72]

While in Petrograd, on leave from his Russian regiment in 1916, Prince Djamal and his sister attended a theatre performance where among his admirers was a celebrated singer with whom the Prince became friendly. But, according to Kati's memoir, the singer was soon 'entertaining too lively an affection for me … The knowledge was very painful to me as I both loved and respected her.'[73] Like Deborah Sampson, Princess Kati resisted disclosing the truth until she had no alternative. The infatuated singer later confessed to the Prince's sister that she was deeply in love with him 'because he is so reserved and so respectful', emphasizing the platonic nature of their relationship. When the Prince eventually broke down and confessed, 'Mademoiselle … my dear friend … you must forgive me … I am a woman', the astonished singer fainted away.[74] But even as Kati cut herself off from female friends to avoid exposure, her potential erotic attraction lent credibility to her disguise while rejecting any hint of lesbianism. If Prince Djamal had women swooning, he would have no difficulty passing with his regimental comrades. A soldier with the White Army during the Russian Civil War, who wrote a memoir under the name Lul Gardo, once woke up in a hayloft in the arms of a woman she had never seen before. 'I had not the heart to tell her that I was a woman and to witness her subsequent confusion,' she wrote. 'I preferred to let her think I didn't want her caresses.'[75]

Beyond issues of sexual preference and of sexual intimacy, the female combatants of these early twentieth-century conflicts experienced the contradictions of living amongst men most sharply when reminded of physical differences. It struck Marina Yurlova, after her enlistment as a soldier with a Cossack regiment of the Tsar's army in 1915, one night as she lay in bed, watching her fellow soldiers who grew raucous as they drank, played cards, and then stripped off their clothes to hunt for lice. Although dressing and undressing in front of the opposite sex was common among Russian peasants, the fifteen-year-old had never seen a man naked and watched the hunched figures, with their hairy, matted chests, in horror and fascination.[76] 'I lay curled up in my bunk,' she wrote of the scene, 'with an entirely new feeling: modesty.' She realized that despite her uniform, it was her female body and sexual innocence that separated her from these hulking men. Still a child, the realization was shocking and shaming, emotions which invoked a stark loneliness.

The stench of the men's unwashed bodies and feet, of their drying-foot wraps and shirts mixed with stale tobacco smoke, was so repulsive she ran outside, preferring the mud and rain. Later, she dreamed about Kosel, her mentor, as a goat, with 'four legs, and a great shaggy coat of fur', which was, however unintentional, a powerful sexual metaphor.[77] But as the weeks passed, and the regiment decamped for the front, she grew familiar with masculine smells and male bodies, prompting her to reflect, 'I was beginning to be a soldier.'[78] Posted to sentry duty was a further mark of their acceptance since it 'meant [the men] really considered me as one of them, or they wouldn't have trusted me with so much responsibility.'[79]

Once she became a soldier, Flora Sandes quickly grew comfortable with her comrades' physical presence, a necessary milestone. On her first night with the Serbian Army's 2nd Regiment, she pitched her tent away from the camp. But her need for warmth overrode her need for modesty so she bedded down with her comrades, often sleeping fully clothed next to her 'raggys' ('someone who sticks closer than a brother'), Sergeant Miladin and Sergeant-Major Mallesha. The trio shared their tobacco and food, and even their overcoats at night.[80] On long marches blankets were a luxury so during the winter soldiers were obliged to huddle together for warmth. Flora once fell asleep by herself one night and was woken when a machine-gun captain kicked her, with the warning: 'What are you thinking of, going to sleep like this by yourself, have you gone mad? You'll be frozen to death by morning.'[81] Flora moved over to a heap of male bodies and fell back into a deep, untroubled sleep.

While the threat of sexual assault was far from Maria Bochkareva's mind when she reported for duty with the 4th Company of the 25th Tomsk Reserve Battalion of the Tsar's army in 1914, she quickly realized the challenge of 'establishing proper relations' with her comrades. The men burst into laughter at the sight of her; a woman with clipped hair, wearing their uniform of heavy boots, foot rags, regulation trousers, blouse, a thick leather belt, epaulets and a cap, and shouldering a rifle. According to Bochkareva, 'the news of a woman recruit had preceded me at the barracks and my arrival there precipitated a riot of fun.'[82] The men tested the physical boundaries of their latest recruit, pinching, jostling and brushing up against her, as they slung their insults until the commander intervened.

In the barracks, the men were ordered to leave her alone but assumed she was 'a loose-moraled [sic] woman' who enlisted to carry on her 'illicit trade'.[83] The teasing grew increasingly sexual that night as Bochkareva recalls:

As soon as I made an effort to shut my eyes I would discover the arm of my neighbour on the left around my neck, and would restore it to its rightful owner with a crash. Watchful of his movements I offered an opportunity for my neighbour on the right to get too near me, and I would savagely kick him in the side. All night long my nerves were taut and my fists busy.[84]

Adding to her humiliation, the next morning Maria was so anxious to be punctual at roll call that she put her trousers on inside out, which provoked another storm of laughter.

Winning the regiment's respect was a gradual and difficult process but eventually Maria 'was tested by many additional trials and found to be a comrade and *not a woman* [my emphasis] by the men.'[85] Acceptance often involved, for the lone female combatant, refusing any concessions to her sex and demanding equal treatment. Bochkareva's experience within the Tsar's army reveals how women balanced aggression, considered a masculine quality, alongside the 'feminine' qualities of co-operation, obedience, submission, loyalty and selflessness.[86] So when her regimental train left Tomsk, Maria refused any special treatment, bunking down with the men rather than sitting in the officer's car which 'immensely pleased' her comrades. In return, she observed that they grew so indifferent to her sex that she could join their communal bathing without feeling self-conscious.[87] Like Flora Sandes and Marina Yurlova, her identity as a soldier was complete once her bodily differences became irrelevant.

While female warriors worked hard to adopt masculine qualities while purging themselves of their perceived vulnerabilities, Bochkareva experienced what was almost universal for women in the military in earlier centuries: acceptance as an honorary man. Conformity to masculine behaviour – bravery under fire, suppression of fear, demonstrations of physical strength and endurance under horrific conditions – was essential to the female soldier's survival.[88] The female warriors were also required to prioritize the group over the individual as they forged intimate bonds through experiences of camp and combat. As the political theorist Michael Walzer has argued, war is 'a rule-governed activity, a world of permissions and prohibitions – a moral world, therefore, in the midst of hell.'[89] The female soldiers found their comrades would test those rules of permissions and prohibitions, including behaviour involving sex workers.

Memoirs of early twentieth-century female soldiers often include episodes where they are pressured to participate in communal sexual activities such as brothel visits. Bochkareva regarded this as part of her military education 'to learn the soldier's life so that I can understand his soul better'.[90] The men bonded as they smoked, drank, played cards, wrestled, and danced with prostitutes in rare moments of pleasure. At a Siberian brothel, Bochkareva passed successfully but was spared a sexual encounter when an officer arrived and ordered her back to camp or face punishment for breaking the 8pm curfew.[91]

Thin and sunburnt, Flora Sandes easily passed as a man in her Serbian uniform and faced a similar dilemma while on leave, recovering from a leg wound in a hospital, in Bizerta, Tunisia. In the summer of 1917 she was among the Serbian convalescents, big, good-looking fellows who spent hours drinking in local cafes before returning to active service. One sultry evening Sandes accompanied her comrades to a local brothel where a young woman planted herself on Flora's knee, put an arm around her neck and commented: 'He doesn't look so stupid, but he's very shy.' Flora 'kept it up for awhile' but turned her cheek when the woman attempted to kiss her. The incident provided her with an insight into an unknown masculine world. Sergeant-Major Sandes was impressed the next day when, walking along the street, she and her friends passed the woman who refused to acknowledge them, 'not by a flicker of an eyelid'.[92]

This incident from Sandes' memoir was probably intended as a humorous anecdote that played on the ambiguity of her position, relieving it of sexual tension. In her officer's uniform, hailed as a wounded war hero, fighting for an important cause, Flora might regard herself as having no more in common with the woman sitting on her lap than her comrades. The passing women's narratives often suggest, however, that the price for becoming an honorary man was sexual erasure or 'a cancellation of the feminine'.[93] In this dynamic, the potentially disruptive power of the female body through sexual expression or motherhood is rendered neutral and made safe: the female warrior, whether passing or not, must perform militarily to be accepted and to maintain her status.[94]

But this balancing act was, and remained, fraught with complications. Flora Sandes' memoirs record several episodes where she experienced acute embarrassment and confusion over which gender role to perform. One such poignant moment occurred at an officer's party in Bizerta when she slipped into an evening dress. Sandes-in-a-frock was intended as a joke but it made her comrades very uncomfortable. '[My fellow soldiers] declared that they did not know how to talk to me when dressed like that,' she wrote, 'and implored me to get back into uniform at once, and be one of them again.'[95] Flora had visibly reminded them of her true identity which was incompatible with her status as a Serbian officer. To restore order after this awkward display, she hid her female body behind her uniform.

The rules for women warriors who occupied the space between genders – those who were not attempting to pass – were ill-defined and tortuously fluid. Flora Sandes' reflection on the evening dress in Bizerta prompted her to write, 'My chief difficulty was that I could never be quite sure when I was supposed to behave as a "lady" and a guest and when as a plain sergeant for sometimes I was treated as one and sometimes the other.'[96] At the New Year's Eve ball in Belgrade in 1919, while still a serving officer, Flora endured another excruciating moment when the Prince Regent Alexander asked her why she refused to dance. Sandes explained that she would rather not dance with the women, nor they with her, and in uniform, she could only do the kolo (the Serbian national dance) with the men. 'If you won't find a partner for yourself I am going to find one for you,' laughed the Prince. A few minutes later he approached her friend, Dr Katherine MacPhail, a Scottish medic who had worked with Flora on the Salonique front and now directed her own children's hospital in Belgrade. 'I've got a partner for you for the next waltz, Dr. MacPhail,' said the Prince. 'It's Lieutenant Sandes. I was just going to leave but I shall wait to see you two dance it.'[97]

Whether or not the Prince Regent intended to humiliate Lieutenant Sandes and Dr MacPhail, he exposed their awkward position as two foreign women who, despite their enormous sacrifices for his country, occupied its social margins. Flora was, understandably, mortified when forced to waltz with her friend to satisfy the Prince Regent's whim. The episodes in Bizerta and Belgrade demonstrated the fragility of her exceptional position when turned into a public spectacle. As she would later write: 'it's a hard world where half the people say you should not dress as a man and the other half want to punish you for dressing as a woman.'[98] Her painful reflection perhaps explains why so many passing women feared returning to the female sphere.

Flora's ability to straddle these worlds, however problematic this might be, provides insight into the psychological adjustments required to remain in the ranks in disguise. The female combatants who were known to their comrades were accepted once they had 'proven' themselves whether in battle, on campaign or on a ship where the all-consuming struggle for survival superseded relative concerns about social roles. The insights from Sarah Edmonds, Maria Bochkareva and Flora Sandes, among others, might explain why male combatants protected their female counterparts. There is a persistent theme of fellow soldiers and sailors admiring women for sharing the hardships of warfare, for demonstrating admirable courage and for proving their professional competence.

While Flora was befriended by the Serbs, the only other English woman to face combat during the First World War, Dorothy Lawrence, who briefly joined a British Expeditionary Force's tunnelling company, found the men's attitudes varied from respect to horror, anger and confusion. But it was friendships with men that facilitated her access to the battlefield and she depended upon them throughout her brief sojourn at the front. Once her soldier friends had obtained an ID for her as Private Denis Smith of the First Leicestershire Regiment, and with real dog tags and a forged pass, she headed for Albert, the site of a major Anglo-French offensive. Tom Dunn, a Royal Engineer and Lancashire coal miner, found her a place with a mining company within 400 yards of the front line. Once reassured that Dorothy was 'English right enough', and not soliciting business, this 'small soldier' said:

> Now I see thoroughly the sort of girl yer are, I'll help yer. Yer no bad 'un. You're a lady. I followed yer to see what sort of gal yer was. I ain't no better than the rest. All the same it ain't agin to harm any gal. You're straight, that's what yer are. I can see that. So I'll help yer.[99]

Dunn's support was crucial; he moved Dorothy into an abandoned cottage where she could sleep, away from the officers and other men. At daybreak she arrived in the trenches to work as a sapper with an engineering corps, laying mines, and at dusk returned to her hide-out. She avoided the other men, eating only what Dunn brought her and sleeping in her clothes on piles of straw. While in the trenches, however, she remained unwilling to perform 'the duty of setting light to the fuse, preferring that *murder* should not rest on my conscience'.[100] In her mind this disqualified her from being a *bona fide* soldier, an echo of Kati Dadeshkeliani's horror of trench warfare where she felt a sense of 'uselessness, powerlessness, or failing of duty'.[101] Lawrence's reservations, however, failed to arouse her fellow sappers' suspicions.

'Getting away with it': living as a man, among men

Once enlisted within the ranks, the female warrior might quickly familiarize herself with military life and her masculine role; many examples suggest these women revelled in playing their part. Sailor Mary Anne Arnold, who worked, undetected, aboard a British East Indiaman ship in 1838, described her experience as 'performing the character of a man'.[102] Velazquez, the Confederate soldier, revealed that living as Lieutenant Harry T. Buford she 'became accustomed to male attire and to appearing before anybody and everybody in it', and that she 'lost all fear of being found out and learned to act, talk and almost to think as a man'.[103] And as Colonel Barker, Valerie Arkell-Smith was surprised at how easily she convinced people of her military persona. 'As the weeks slipped by I began to experience a sense of exhilaration at the knowledge I was getting away with it', she wrote in 1956. 'As time went on I became more and more daring.'[104] The women often report the benefits of male clothing that allowed them greater physical freedom, unencumbered by restricting items, and the licence to roam freely in previously forbidden places, even at night, where they had access to new pleasures.

Colonel Barker presents the complexities of this phenomenon starkly. While Valerie Arkell-Smith had the courage to escape an abusive husband by adopting a male disguise and to marry Elfrida Haward, the Colonel's brand of masculinity was linked to violent extremism. He became a 'leading light' in the National Fascisti (NF), which he joined in 1927, 'not so much from patriotic motives as from the spice of adventure it introduced into life'.[105] The 'spice' included managing the group's boxing programme – designed to whip members into peak physical condition to combat 'the reds and the pinks' – and joining Sunday afternoon disruptions of Communist Party meetings in Hyde Park.[106]

The NF membership represented a more militant element of the British Fascisti who broke away from the party in 1924 to pursue 'positive fascism'. Small in number and largely confined to London, they adopted a uniform black shirt along with other fascist symbols. Their membership was larger than that of the British Fascisti because of their active and violent pursuit of communists. Their programme was ill-defined but clearly anti-Semitic and anti-communist, and supported the maintenance of the monarch, the preservation of empire and the development of a 'truly national spirit'.[107] The party proposed an authoritarian government of experts with a male executive (of British birth and background) committed to carrying out its agenda. Overall its influence on the public order, policy and opinion was negligible but Colonel Barker became its best-known member.

Arkell-Smith's story is not unusual in its exposure of gendered contradictions. As a woman taking on a male identity she made a mockery of the fascists, military officials, police officers and judges she deceived. The same reactionary social structures that the NF embraced had led her common-law husband to feel entitled to abuse her, forcing her to leave him. Reinvented as Colonel Barker, she felt able to marry her female lover. As Barker's involvement in the NF suggested, Arkell-Smith's implicit critique of gender did not translate into a broader social understanding of oppressive power relations. Rather, the Colonel allied himself with the most hierarchical, authoritarian, racist and hyper-masculine ideology of his era.

There was, of course, more to being accepted amongst men than wearing the correct clothes, or, to use a current neologism, manspreading[108] or proving oneself in a masculine sphere of work. Flora Sandes, who believed 'that men took life much more easily and straightforwardly than women,'[109] may have acquired a fraternal status in Serbia but received a mixed reception outside her adopted country. She describes an incident that took place while she was on a YMCA-sponsored lecture tour about the Serbian cause to British troops stationed in France in 1918. While waiting for a train to Calais she met three Tommies, returning after their leave had been cut short. Sandes, who was a striking figure in her grey Serb uniform and cropped white hair, introduced herself as a fellow soldier, a comment to which they listened politely. But when she went off to find a kiosk and returned armed with several bottles of beer, they exclaimed: '*Now* we know you are a *real* soldier.'[110]

In 1916 Sandes was awarded the order of Karadorde's Star with Swords, Serbia's highest civilian and military decoration. When the 2nd Regiment was fighting to recapture Monastir on 15 November, Sandes was knocked unconscious by a bomb and dragged from the battlefield under fire. A medic poured brandy down her throat and stuck a cigarette between her lips. The alcohol dulled the pain but the wait for transport to a field hospital was agony. Blood dripped through the canvas stretcher from her badly broken arm and more than a dozen wounds that ran down her back and right side. At the hospital, when a doctor probed for bomb fragments, Sandes dug her head into his broad chest and howled.

The doctor made no concessions, telling his patient to 'shut up and remember [that] she was a soldier' which 'did far more good than any amount of petting would have done'.[111] The division commandant Colonel Milić told her that, following her recovery, she would be transferred to the division staff, 'and he would never let me go to the Front again'. She smiled but hoped that Milić would forget this promise because, 'I should lose all caste with the men if I chose a soft billet instead of roughing it with them.'[112] Sandes interpreted Milić's protective impulse as a humiliation since it called attention to her exceptional status. Even in extreme pain she patrolled her behaviour, fearing that any hint of feminine weakness would result in her expulsion from the Serbian Army.

Her memoirs, written in 1916 and 1927, which cover her six months' convalescence in Greece and North Africa, emphasize her sense of how different she was from other women. Even when it came to food, Sandes knew that her comrades, while languishing in hospital, preferred the taste of dark bread and spring onions over the sweetness of pastries. 'Our sergeant knows what we like,' they said. 'The French ladies come and visit us sometimes and bring us cakes. Cakes!' – scornfully – 'food for women and children, not soldiers!'[113] They trusted that Sandes understood their needs and appreciated their tastes. The men expressed their comradeship when the nursing staff placed her, alone, in a tent, rather than with them. The nurses, however, were shocked when she visited the Serbs and 'were rather sarcastic about my supposed wish to be moved into the men's tent'.[114]

Throughout Sandes' memoirs she remains acutely conscious of her contingent status and, like many other female warriors, she could react with anger, irritation or hurt feelings if disrespected. The young Cossack soldier Marina Yurlova observes in her memoir that she reacted differently to violence and aggression from her comrades, a measure of their masculinity. In late 1914 as her regiment crept towards the Armenian front, a Cossack asked an Armenian shepherd to direct them back to their camp and Yurlova, concerned about the elderly man, offered him a lift on her horse. When accused of being soft-hearted, she snapped back, 'A *babba* indeed! I could not have been more grossly insulted. Wasn't I a soldier?'[115] Despite reminding her comrades that she was their equal, later she realized her vulnerability. When an aristocratic officer, whom she found intimidating and who insisted on a royal address, ordered her to tidy his quarters, she complied. Although young recruits often acted as orderlies, Yurlova had to clean his dirty room *and* endure his sexual advances.

> I was astonished to see how stupidly he was smiling; then, as a little saliva crept out of the corner of his lips, I grew frightened. I dared not move.
>
> He pinched my ear, and put one hand around my shoulders; he unbuttoned my jacket with the other hand and his fingers crept inside, stroking me gently. And then – I suppose I was shaking all over – he muttered: 'What is the matter my child?'[116]

Yurlova, who was, in fact, only fourteen, was frightened and insulted at being forced into such a role: 'I did not want to be thought a girl – I was a soldier.'[117] She repelled his advances and was soon riding off to battle with her comrades, hoping 'that they wouldn't think me a soft-hearted *babba*; and I vowed I wouldn't give them a chance.'[118] Although Yurlova glosses over this undercurrent of sexual violence, she considered it significant enough to include in her memoir.

That women soldiers in Russia were expected to remain celibate was a particular form of female sacrifice made explicit by Maria Bochkareva when addressing the 1st Russian Women's Battalion in 1917. At rallies she would remind her troops that they were surrogates for the men who should be, but were not, taking up arms to defend Mother Russia. 'Woman is naturally lighthearted. But if she can purge herself for sacrifice, then through a caressing word, a loving heart and an example of heroism she can save the Motherland,' Bochkareva exhorted her troops gathered in Petrograd in 1917. 'We are physically weak but if we can be strong morally and spiritually we will accomplish more than a large force.'[119] Individual enlistments of female combatants rose rapidly throughout the summer of 1917 even while women's battalions sprang up in Petrograd, Perim, Odessa and Ekaterinodar.[120]

While the Women's Battalion may have appealed to Western readers as a novelty, it did little to further the feminist cause. Rather, it arose from the particular intersection of total war, revolution and a national emergency and, as Bochkareva's address suggests, its spirit was patriotic, public-spirited and directed at all Russian citizens.[121] Her 'harsh and rigid mode of discipline' would prove unpopular with her volunteers, who took a vow of chastity for 'the duration' and were dismissed if they had male friendships.[122] From a peak of 2,000 when recruitment began, so many women deserted that only about 300 saw action on the Russian Western Front a month later.[123] Bochkareva's concern for her soldiers' reputations may have stemmed from her own experience of sexual harassment.

Far removed from public attention, Bochkareva's soldiers found that life on the front was harsh and their male comrades treated them with derision. Even female soldiers who entered regular regiments in disguise held the battalion in contempt. Four days after English nurse Florence Farmborough had cared for the Battalion's wounded soldiers, she spoke with a female combatant whose leg had been badly contused, at a Red Cross station at the front. 'She did not belong to the Women's Battalion of Death', wrote Farmborough. 'She had, however, heard of them and from her curt remarks one could understand that she held them with little respect.'[124] Given that this female soldier served in an all-male regiment, her comments seem hardly surprising. As if recognizing the advantage of being exceptional, Flora Sandes commented on the 1st Russian Women's Battalion: 'I'd very much like to see it but I don't think I'd like to be in it.'[125]

Marina Yurlova, despite her status as a soldier and regimental mascot, endured speculation about her motives for enlisting while recovering from a leg wound in hospital. In 1915 she had travelled with her Cossack regiment from the Armenian plains as they slowly retreated towards Yerevan and the River Arkaxes. Marina was wounded during their first action against the Turkish forces, in which her mentor Kosel was killed, on a dangerous expedition to blow up bridges on the River Arkaxes to block the advancing forces.[126] Marina arrived at the Red Cross hospital in Baku, a Caspian seaside resort, deeply depressed (she described

Kosel's death as losing 'everything that meant gentleness and understanding'[127]), and with a painfully swollen leg. During her long convalescence, rumours spread of a female soldier and Marina became an attraction, 'like a caged animal whom people would poke with umbrellas and walking sticks.' The visitors inquired about her army life, clearly suspicious that she was a 'bad girl'.[128] When she was wounded again in 1916 during the Imperial Russian Army's battle of Erzurum, in eastern Anatolia, Marina met an incredulous nurse who '[found] it hard to forgive me for being of the same sex.'[129] That this girl, a lowly volunteer, was sharing a ward with officers of the Imperial Army was equally galling to the nurses.

Dorothy Lawrence discovered on her return to London in 1915, after serving her brief stint as a sapper in Albert, that her motives for venturing to the Western Front were regarded with scepticism. She endured the accusation that she had been a mere 'camp follower', the term hurled at her by the dismayed British officers who discovered her in their ranks. 'Though I had often heard the term, I supposed it referred to wagons that carried provisions', she wrote. 'Not once had our soldiers removed this idea.' She dismissed any suggestion that the Tommies had behaved inappropriately, explaining that the heavy knife she carried as a sapper had 'no call … for its use'.[130]

During the First World War, English language newspapers often drew on ancient figures such as Jeanne d'Arc to legitimate the female warriors' adventures and assuage anxieties about their sexual purity. Madame Margarita Romanovna Kokovtseva, commander of the 6th Ural Cossack Regiment, was labelled 'the Muscovite militant – a Russian Joan of Arc' by the London *Graphic* in 1915, which made the point, as Frank Mundell had of the French saint in 1898: 'She was above sex and yielded to no one in courage or military virtues.'[131] Flora Sandes was dubbed the 'Serbian Joan of Arc incarnate' by the press following her Australian lecture tour in 1920 – the year that Jeanne d'Arc was canonized. These accounts emphasized the female fighters' pure motives while neutralizing their radical potential.

Another way in which women soldiers might legitimate their presence was through combining combat with nursing duties. While fighting on the Eastern Front with the Tsar's army against the Germans during 1917, Bochkareva was often called upon to provide women with basic medical attention in the villages wherever she was stationed.[132] Sandes, in a letter written home from a trench on 10 November 1916, mentioned that although the Red Cross still supplied first aid to her Serbian regiment, 'when the men near me get wounded they generally get me to do them up.'[133] She also observed that all the Red Cross workers went 'armed to the teeth' in Serbia, suggesting that her position was not much different from theirs.[134]

At several other points in her career with the Serbian Army, Sandes organized medical operations and sourced medical supplies. In 1918 a flu epidemic struck Ćuprija, in central Serbia, and Sandes, after recovering from a bout herself, relieved the lone doctor serving a temporary army hospital. Just as she had during the Valjevo typhus epidemic, she found a hospital 'in a fearful state' with French and Serbian soldiers shivering in filthy clothes, without blankets or sheets and 'dying like flies of flu and pneumonia'. Throwing military discipline to the winds, Sandes assumed control. 'So, as Fate seemed to have landed me there', she wrote, 'I took charge, and the responsibility and hard work soon completed my own cure.'[135] Soon the French soldiers in Ćuprija were seeking out her services and orderlies called upon her to soothe delirious patients.

Unlike her fellow soldiers, on the battlefield Sandes would administer whatever first aid she could to the enemy, often wounded Bulgarians. Her willingness to attend the enemy, often young boys, earned her both her commanding officer's wrath and her comrades' amusement. 'They think quite a lot of my opinion,' wrote Sandes in a letter to her sister Sophia, 'and would even let me keep a pet Bulgar … if I wanted to.'[136] When her responsibilities fell within the female category of nurturing, her comrades gently mocked her motives, revealing yet again the contradictory position the female officer occupied.

Did the female soldiers ever completely overcome their anxieties about being inferior to men, and lesser combatants? For Sandes the lurking fear never seemed to dissipate as she reveals how, recalling the long march of nearly 370 miles from Monastir to Belgrade in 1918, she would whisper Rudyard Kipling's poem 'If' to force herself forward. But the poem's promise of reward for the exertion of body and soul eluded her. 'Often though I have repeated those lines to myself,' she wrote, 'they did not result in making a man of me.'[137]

Over this long sweep of history, women proved their competence, skill and courage; they entered the military and conformed to its masculine hierarchy. As individuals they might occupy the role of mascot or exception that proved the rules. They simultaneously challenged understandings of gender – they were biological women after all – and reinforced them. They were seen as courageous *women* but brave soldiers, their military identity all-encompassing in their temporary passage through the male world during extraordinary historical circumstances. The female warrior's access could be revoked either when her identity was revealed or when her labour or presence was no longer required. Whether the radical potential of her experience and the tantalizing contradictions she embodied really changed historical understandings of sexual difference remains questionable.

Chapter 5

The Denouement

*'Ever since the days of Queen Thalestris, there have been ladies
who aspired to be gentlemen and despised their own position ...
Metaphorically speaking, and in the sense of wishing to rule,
thus it has ever been and is with all her sisterhood, as every
married man is well aware, but the actual inducement of the
garments in question is comparatively rare.'*[1]
CHAMBERS'S JOURNAL, 30 MAY 1863

This jaunty reference to the mythic Thalestris from a popular
nineteenth-century English magazine reveals that, during
Victoria's reign, warrior women still embodied their longing for
masculine power. Frustrated female readers may well have envied
her metaphorical 'gentlemen's garments', but the Scythian queen
Thalestris had, in reality, possessed her own splendid costume.
According to Greek historians, she led 300 mounted women warriors
along the Silk Route in 330 BC to meet Alexander the Great on the
western Caspian shores. These warriors were equals within Scythian
society and it was they, rather than Alexander, who wore the trousers.
Historian Adrienne Mayor describes their exotic dress:

Thalestris's garments shimmered with hundreds of tiny golden
appliques of animals: a long-sleeved silken tunic belted with
an elaborate golden buckle, trousers or a riding skirt over soft

leather boots, and a leopard-skin cape, a dagger at her side, and a quiver and bow at her back. Her horse would have elaborately embroidered saddle blankets and dazzling golden accoutrements.[2]

The female warriors of these ancient nomadic tribes lived and fought amongst men without fear of being cast out to the domestic realm. In later centuries, however, women warriors would prove ingenious in maintaining their disguise, which might involve huge risk, especially when wounded or ill. Some feared punishment, others ostracism, the loss of financial rewards for service, the humiliation of discovery or their comrades' rage at their betrayal. Once they had remade themselves as men, some feared a life back down among the women where, even as veterans, their experience placed them beyond conventional society. They might face an estranged family or lose male friendships forged in extreme circumstances. Instead, these women often longed for a quiet return to Civvy Street along with their comrades when their deception might be forgiven or even prompt a reward. Others had little control over when or how their identities were revealed.

Injury or illness, especially during the long campaigns of the eighteenth century where troops were stationed with civilians and endured wretched battle conditions, posed challenges for the passing woman. By the time that the Duke of Marlborough's famous 'scarlet caterpillar'[3] of 40,000 British, Dutch and German troops crawled across the European continent, dragging the War of the Spanish Succession behind it, Christian Davies was battle-hardened. During this war, disguised as Christopher Welsh, she fought with the 2nd Dragoons, Scots Greys at Nijmegen, Venloo, Bonn and in other minor engagements until the battle of Schellenberg on 2 July 1704. At Donauwörth, as the Scots Greys battled to prevent the French from crossing the Danube and marching on to Vienna, the Habsburg capital, Christian took a pistol shot in the hip. Despite being hospitalized she escaped detection and shared in the victory spoils of Blenheim. Following the extraordinary coincidence of spotting her estranged husband

Richard Welsh after their separation of more than a dozen years, Christian posed as his brother. But a year later, an even more serious head injury, sustained at the battle of Ramillies on 23 May, 1706, finally ended Christopher's existence. The surgeons immediately informed Lord John Hay, commander of the Scots Grey, that his 'pretty dragoon' was, in fact, a woman.[4]

Later, Richard and Christian Welsh were wed again with the Scots Greys as witnesses, and Lord Hay presented the couple with a pouch of gold. The ceremony marked Christian's explicit transition from soldier into woman, as Lord Hay, exercising his paternalistic role, insisted she resume marital relations. Fearing pregnancy, Christian had refused to sleep with Richard until the end of the campaign but now she promised Hay she 'had no objections to … the duty of an honest wife.'[5] She would later claim to have conceived a child that very night and for the next three years devoted herself to foraging for her family. From now on, she would operate as a sutler, supplying food and cooking for the troops, as well as mending and washing clothes.

Even while Christian resumed these domestic duties, she occupied an ambiguous role as both battle veteran and wise woman. She upbraided her fellow soldiers as 'unmanly who treat a woman ill', especially if they falsely promised to marry a lover – 'a practice too customary with our cloth.'[6] Once, following a foraging expedition where she spied enemy soldiers, she chastised the Duke of Marlborough's officers for playing chess while the enemy lurked nearby. When Lord Kerr dismissed her as a 'foolish, drunken woman,' the Duke replied that he would take her advice over that of any army brigadier.[7] However, despite her reputation and experience, without her disguise she was newly vulnerable. Christian fended off an officer's sexual assault by promising him 'the prettiest girl in the camp' and persuaded a younger woman, Dolly Saunders, to visit his tent, hinting that his lordship wanted a dozen shirts made.[8]

Given the conditions for most military wives at the time, it is not hard to appreciate why a passing woman so valued her male disguise. While Christian Davies chose to serve in combat with a pistol ball embedded in her groin rather than admit to her deception, Hannah Snell would endure a similar torment. Snell's contemporary biographer, Robert Walker, describes her receiving wounds in both thighs during the long and unsuccessful British siege of the French fortifications at Pondicherry in August 1748.[9] Throughout her naval career as James Gray, Hannah was often under fire:

> In Case of an Engagement, she was to be stationed upon the *Quarter-Deck*, and, as One of the *After-guard*, her Business was to fight and do what Mischief she could with the Small-Arms which they had on board, so that she was always in readiness in Case of an attack.[10]

Snell was among the crew that arrived at Fort St David, just south of Pondicherry, on 27 July, to seize the town from the French. On 8 August, Hannah shouldered her tent poles, hatchet, camp kettle and musket as her battalion marched from the shore to break camp for the following nine days. By the end of that brutally hot month, they inched towards Pondicherry to dig trenches and set up their cannons. For the next three weeks Hannah hunkered down under a torrent of mortar and gunfire before the monsoon rains arrived, transforming her trench into a muddy gulch. But British stoicism, according to Walker's biography, paid off as the siege collapsed:

> She stood so deep in Water, she fired no less than thirty-seven Rounds of Shot and during the Engagement received six Shot in her Right Leg and five in the Left, and what affected her more than all the Rest, one so dangerous in the Groin ... she remained all that Day and the following Night in the Camp before she was carried to the Hospital, and after that she was brought there and laid in Kit she continued till next Day in the greatest Agony and Pain.[11]

However, Matthew Stephens argues in his 2004 biography of Snell that Walker's account contradicts the Royal Navy ships' musters: on 30 September, James Gray, fit and well, along with a number of fellow marines, was transferred from the *Swallow* to the *Eltham* and set sail for Bombay three weeks later.[12] This casts doubt on Hannah's surviving a shot to her groin and eleven wounds to her legs, and Stephens provides an alternative scenario. He believes that since the marines en route to Bombay were constantly exposed to damp as the ship was leaking badly, Hannah may have been among the crew who contracted scurvy, a disease whose symptoms included bleeding gums and festering wounds. The *Eltham* arrived on 3 January and lay in harbour until the following May. But if Walker had erroneously placed Hannah at Pondicherry, musters record that James Gray's battalion of East India Company soldiers were sent ashore to seize the Fort of Devicotta. While no details survive of his military engagement, the musters reveal that James Gray languished at Cuddalore hospital for two months under the care of the one-legged surgeon Dr William Belchier.[13]

It is possible that Hannah, rather than having to hide injuries that would have exposed her disguise – the leg and groin wounds – was being treated for scurvy. Twenty members of the *Eltham* crew were hospitalized in August and September, while another six marines perished that summer.[14] Illness seems a more plausible explanation for how, despite his confinement at Cuddalore, James Gray was able to board the *Eltham* and sail for England on 19 October, with his secret intact.

Among the powerful incentives for maintaining a disguise were the relatively well-paid trades, skills and crafts a woman might lose if exposed; fear of poverty was a powerful motive and often a tragic outcome. Hannah was among those exceptional cases where a woman could decide when passing had served its purpose and return to womanhood.

After safely returning to Britain, Hannah Snell orchestrated her retirement and exploited her remarkable maritime experiences. On 7 May 1750, the *Eltham* departed Lisbon for Portsmouth, where it weighed anchor two weeks later when Hannah went 'on shore the very Day of her Arrival and took Lodging, together with several of her Comrades and Fellow-travellers at the sign of the "Jolly

Marine and Sailor"'. After enjoying a drunken weekend in port with her crewmates to celebrate their liberty, Hannah collected her five shillings 'conduct money' and, among a company of ten marines, headed for London. Three days later, on 30 May, her sister Susannah greeted her warmly at her home in Wapping and 'almost stifled her with Kisses'.[15]

On 9 June, James Gray crossed the muddy Thames to the regimental agent John Winter's house on Downing Street to collect £15 pay for more than two years' service and to sell two suits for sixteen shillings. Then, at a Westminster pub, accompanied by her sister and brother-in-law, Hannah retired her alias James Gray before witnesses who 'at any time afterwards [would] be ready to testify to the truths of all her merry adventures.'[16] As Hannah suspected her story might be dismissed as 'little better than a romance,'[17] her messmates' eye-witness testimony was vital. Turning to the man who shared her bed, she announced: 'Had you known, Master Moody, who you had between a pair of sheets with you, you would have come to closer quarters. In a word gentlemen, I am as much a woman as my mother ever was and my name is Hannah Snell.'[18] Moody loudly praised her merits, once recovered from his shock, and proposed marriage; she refused, explaining her aversion to matrimony after her first husband's 'hardheartedness and inhumanity'.

Although it's impossible to know whether Hannah had already considered her future employment prospects, her messmates suggested she demand a pension from the Captain-General of the British Army, the Duke of Cumberland. Like other war veterans, the marines championed her financial claim for the battle wounds she sustained at Devicotta. Hannah, dressed once more as James Gray on 16 June, approached the Duke's carriage with her petition which he read and promptly ordered his adjutant-general, Colonel Napier, to authentic her claims.[19]

Half a century later, Deborah Sampson aka Robert Shurtliff, who sustained combat injuries during the Revolutionary War, also needed proof of her war wounds to collect a military pension. According to Sampson's biographer Herman Mann, she was injured while volunteering with a light infantry regiment – 'an elite corps of athletic young men who undertook the hardest duties' – on an ambush in the Hudson Valley in the winter of 1782.[20] Sampson, mounted on an excellent horse, had pursued the enemy into a bog during an early morning raid:

> They rushed on them on the right and left, till as many as could, escaped … The dauntless Fair, at this instant, thought she felt something warmer than sweat run down her neck. Putting her hand to the place, she found the blood gushed from the left side of her head very freely … Coming to a stand, she dismounted, but had not strength to walk, or stand alone.[21]

Looking down, Deborah noticed blood pooling into her right boot from a musket ball in her groin. Despite the agony, her mind raced 'having always thought she would rather die, than disclose her sex to the army!' and in despair, 'she drew a pistol from a holster, and was nearly ready to execute the fatal deed.' But the panic subsided and her fellow soldiers carried her to a hospital at Cron Pond inside a French camp where a surgeon supplied the wounded soldier with 'two bottles of choice wine', and dressed his wounds.[22] The doctor's assistant bathed his patient's head with rum and supplied more 'medicine' and, in private, Deborah extracted the musket ball from her thigh with a penknife.

She would later claim, upon her discharge, that she 'received two wounds, a small shot remaining in her to this day' which prevented her from 'performing the common occupations of life as she otherwise might have done'.[23] But Young, her contemporary biographer, suggests that Mann lifted the whole scene of Sampson's sustaining the musket shots to her groin – and their extraction – from Hannah Snell's 1750 biography.[24] Both were invented to illustrate the lengths to which these passing women went to evade discovery and verify their courage under fire. Since these injuries occurred in intimate and sexually sensitive parts, the women could not be examined for verification. As Young explains, 'In the 1790s, requirements for a soldier trying to establish proof of disability for a pension as an "invalid veteran" were unbelievably stringent, including affidavits from a surgeon or officers about the cause of his disability during the war, and reports from two physicians.' For these exceptional female war veterans, only a midwife could provide evidence of a scar in the groin.[25]

What Sampson most feared about possible discovery was 'the *shame* that would overwhelm me' and that her male friends would desert her, fears which were never realized.[26] But the next time she needed urgent medical attention, she was unable to keep her secret. In the summer of 1783, after a period working as an assistant to Major General John Paterson, at West Point, she 'rode in the company of four gentlemen', following a detachment of 1,500 sent to suppress an uprising in Pennsylvania.[27] By the time Sampson arrived the mutineers had been pacified but an equally deadly threat – an epidemic of smallpox and measles – was raging in the city of brotherly love. Fortunately for Sampson, Dr Barnabas Binney and his assistant Matron Mary Parker rescued her (still disguised as Shurtliff) from 'the loathsome bunks of soldiers' and took her to hospital. As Mann describes the revelation:

> Doctor Bana [Binney] at that instant entered; and putting his hand in her bosom to feel her pulse, was surprised to find an inner waist-coat tightly compressing her breasts. Ripping it in haste, he was still more shocked, not only on finding life, but the breasts and other tokens of a *female*. Immediately she was removed into the Matron's own apartment; and from that time to her recovery, treated with all the care that art and expense could bestow.[28]

Dr Binney and Matron Parker agreed to keep Sampson's secret and made her a 'welcome guest' in their families where she appeared in uniform, was known as Robert Shurtliff, and even introduced to their friends 'as an object worthy [of] their attention, and affection'.[29] While Mann's biography describes a series of unverified adventures that Sampson undertook after her recovery, records reveal that Robert Shurtliff served until 25 October 1783 when he received an honourable discharge.[30] Like other passing woman, upon retirement Sampson would invent another career for herself, trading on her extraordinary adventures.

But more often, the female warrior's return to womanhood was fraught with difficulties. English sailor Margaret Johnson was among those who fell into poverty when she gave up her seaman's career. She shipped out from Liverpool bound for St John, New Brunswick, aboard the *Thetis* in 1843 in search of her husband and successfully avoided detection for five months. Back in Liverpool and without financial support – her husband was never found – she gradually fell 'from the path of rectitude into a vicious course of life' (a euphemism for the sex trade) and appeared in court for assaulting her landlord, who may also have been her pimp. When the magistrate told the court of her exploits as a sailor, 'she cast her eyes on the ground and faintly smiled.'[31] It was an accomplishment of which she knew she could be proud.

Although women returning from sea or military campaigns might be praised for their active service, or held up as exemplars of romantic love for following their lovers, such praise might prove fleeting and provide little hard cash. Like Margaret Johnson, sailor Mary Walker was reduced to begging after her sex was revealed at Southwark Police Court in 1867. Disguised as Thomas, he had spent two years as a ship's steward, and another four working at various jobs as an errand boy, a light porter at a cheesemonger's in London and a barman at a pub in London Road, Hackney. Once deprived of these occupations, Mary, still wearing male attire, was picked up for soliciting money from passers-by in Whitechapel on 30 March 1868. According to an account of her trial, 'she has long been known to the police, not so much as a bad as an eccentric character.'[32]

Even when a passing woman like Walker had proven herself as a highly skilled and reliable worker, once revealed, her female identity was grounds for instant dismissal. After almost four years working as an able-bodied seaman Mary Anne Arnold was found out by her captain aboard an English ship, the *Robert Small*. He became suspicious of his fourteen-year-old sailor during a ritual tarring and shaving of crew members when the ship crossed the equator in 1839. According to Arnold's testimony, she realized that once Captain Scott's questions began 'there was no use denying it ... so his clerk took down all I said in answer to his questions'.[33]

Upon discovery Mary Anne was confined to a cabin where, Captain Scott testified, 'the lady passengers have given her lots of presents; her hair is already getting long and I suppose she will soon think of ringlets.'[34] Locking up such a valuable sailor seemed a waste of her talents since, before joining the *Robert Small*, she had worked below decks and aloft for two years as a cabin boy aboard a Sutherland collier, satisfying the six captains under whom she served. In 1838 after a shipwreck off the Irish coast, she worked as cabin boy in the *Choice* bound for London with stores for the *Robert Small*, Captain Scott's ship. 'I have seen Miss Arnold among the first aloft to reef the mizen-top-gallant sail during a heavy gale in the Bay of Biscayne,' he wrote. 'She has well done her work as a strong active boy in this ship.'[35] According to Mary Anne, along with her last month's wages Captain Scott said she 'was his best man and that he was very sorry to part with me.'[36] Even her brothers – one a boatswain of the *Royal Adelaide* and the other a carpenter aboard the *Britannia* stationed at Portsmouth – approved of her seaman's career. Despite these endorsements, however, once exposed as a woman Mary Anne's seafaring ended. Only when she began to assume a more conventionally feminine appearance – growing out her cropped haircut and wearing dresses – could Captain Scott sing her praises.

Though the fearless Mary Anne was described as 'as good as any man on board',[37] she was forced to find work suited to her sex. The Lord Mayor of London offered her financial support because she was an orphan who 'was herself wholly unacquainted with feminine arts' and appointed a female guardian to provide sewing and childcare instruction.[38] Poignantly, Mary Anne longed for the sea and 'thought she could be of service to ladies who travelled for she was never sea sick in her life and was not afraid of anything.'[39]

A lady's companion would, of course, have neither the status nor the financial or social rewards of being a sailor. Marianne Rebecca Johnson, who had been an apprentice aboard a Sutherland collier in 1807, found that her transition back to womanhood brought fresh anxieties about her vulnerability and insisted on an escort once back in female clothes.[40]

No wonder that the passing woman took such care to evade detection. Another female sailor, and orphan, Ellen Watts disguised herself as Charles Watts in 1838 to escape from her apprenticeship as a farm labourer. 'Before her term expired she determined to leave the plough to plough the deep,' because there 'she could enjoy more freedom than in domestic service.' For more than three years Charles worked aboard ship and enjoyed a reputation for such courage and recklessness that his 'exertions caused a degree of envy among the other lads.' He was discovered only when a tailor attempted to interfere with two lady friends he was entertaining in an orchard while on shore leave. A fight ensued and Charles was forced to leave his trawl ship in Brixham.[41] But like Mary Anne Arnold, Watts swore that exposure was the only thing that stopped her returning to sea.

For some women this loss appeared to leave permanent psychological scars. George Wilson, an unfortunate sailor imprisoned for several years in Baltimore for horse-stealing, was severely punished for refusing to accept the transition without a fight. George (who never divulged a female name) had enlisted as a sailor in England while still a teenager and made the Atlantic crossing several times. George claimed to have been arrested in New York 'for creating a disturbance in the street' and sentenced to serve two years but when sent to Bridewell prison, 'not liking her companions, she disclosed her sex'.[42] She remained at Bridewell, however, and upon her release moved to Baltimore where, in 1838, she was arrested for stealing horses. While serving a second sentence, she was flogged for resisting her prison duties since 'she, of course, knows nothing of women's work; she can handle a needle with no further dexterity than will enable her to sew a button on her pantaloons.'[43] The newspaper reports implied that Wilson, 'a singular and hardened creature', was punished for refusing to perform these feminine tasks. Dressed in trousers, answering only to a male name, the story of the tall woman, 'as muscular as a pugilist' is a stark reminder of the social pressure exerted on those who dared to pass. For Wilson and others, trading men's for women's work was a demotion and a source of deep resentment.

Although Wilson's violent behaviour led to her exposure, many passing women found that, within the military ranks, their disguise was unproblematic until those in authority discovered their identity, or a mate threatened their exposure. If a woman enlisted as an ordinary soldier the men who shared her class and ethnic background might willingly keep her secret. As an exception and one of their own, she could occupy the position of mascot, a flattering imitation of masculine values, but to those in power she might represent an inconvenient or even disturbing breach of authority.

In 1805, the young Orkney woman Isabel Gunn defied the titanic authority of the Hudson's Bay Company when she signed an 'x' against her labourer's contract as John Fubister. In an institution organized along quasi-military lines in colonial North America, she survived with her fellow Orcadians' support. Before the dramatic revelation of her identity, she canoed more than 1,800 miles along an inland waterway, was given a pay rise, and wintered at the Pembina fur trading post on the Red River (now in North Dakota). While celebrating Hogmanay, Fubister was among the HBC men who had joined their rivals, the Northwest Company, at the home of their officer, Alexander Henry. Fubister, feeling unwell, asked Henry's permission to lie down, an incident he recorded in his journal of 29 December 1808:

> I was surprised at the fellow's demand; however, I told him to sit down and warm himself. I returned to my own room, where I had not been long before he sent one of my people, requesting the favour of speaking with me. Accordingly I stepped down to him and was much surprised to find him extended on the hearth, uttering dreadful lamentations; he stretched out his hands toward me, and in piteous tones begged me to be kind to

a poor, helpless abandoned wretch, who was not of the sex I had supposed but an unfortunate Orkney girl, pregnant and actually in childbirth. ... In about an hour she was safely delivered of a fine boy.[44]

Once the spring thaw had broken up the ice on the rivers, Isabel Gunn had canoed with James, her fine boy, along the inland waterways to Albany Factory on James Bay. There the baby was regarded as a novelty, the first white offspring in the North-west since the HBC fur traders were barred from bringing their families to the West. Isabel named as the father John Scarth, an experienced HBC man who had gone out from Orkney with her in 1805, a claim which he would deny.

Trapper Peter Fidler heard rumours of the Orcadian woman travelling along the Red River that spring. In a diary crammed with topographical notes, weather reports and navigational degrees, Fidler scribbled as an aside on 1 May 1809 that three days earlier Isabel Gunn, who 'worked at anything and well like the rest of the men,' had passed through.[45] Back at Albany Isabel was made a laundress for her former mates and asked to mind the eleven HBC officers' Metis children at the fort. William Harper, the local school teacher, records in a letter home that Isabel was pleased neither with laundering nor with minding the bairns. His compatriot was living 'with her child and her chief employment is washing for all hands which indeed she is no witch at as far as I think she has been washing for me,' he wrote, adding that 'she seems not inclined to go home.'[46] Although she was never again employed to transport heavy loads of furs and supplies by canoe, Isabel Gunn stayed at Albany that summer before sailing back to Orkney on 20 September 1809.

Perhaps John Hodgson, the chief factor at Albany Factory, considered the implications of this white woman who, contrary to the HBC fears about how European wives might fare in the harsh climate and rough conditions of the North-west, had survived the brutal winters and succeeded at the work. Perhaps the Orcadians might question why their wives and families were kept at home if

Isabel Gunn thrived in the North-west. Hodgson had subverted company policy by marrying a Metis woman, Mistigoose, whose father was the previous chief factor, Robert Godwin, and whose mother was Puckethwanisk, a Cree. William Harper, the teacher who later became master of the HBC sloop that ran between Moose Factory and Albany, also married a Cree woman with whom he had three children.[47] Isabel Gunn no doubt feared the shaming from Orkney's deeply Presbyterian community when she returned with an illegitimate child. Harper's comment on Isabel Gunn's frustration at being demoted from labouring to the menial, domestic chores (most likely without pay) epitomized the fears of other passing women. No longer an equal among the men with a well-paid job, she might be abused, mocked or humiliated for her transgression. If Gunn had been allowed to remain as Scarth's wife, her position would have changed dramatically.

A few passing women in the early nineteenth century received better support than Isabel Gunn whose presence posed a particular threat in the all-male HBC. A contemporary of hers did appear to enjoy the protection of her fellow sailors, even after her status was made public when she appeared as a witness in a sodomy case. When Elizabeth Bowden, a female tar, testified in a court martial held aboard the *Salvador del Mundo* moored at Plymouth, on 2 October 1807, no comment was made about her eight months serving at sea. Bowden, a fourteen-year-old orphan from Truro, Cornwall, claimed that she was motivated 'through want, to disguise herself, and volunteer into his majesty's service' on the *Hazard*, taking the name John. The *Annual Register* suggests that Bowden alerted Captain Charles Dilkes and the ship's officer to her disguise but once her sex was known, they 'paid every attention to her'. Rather than dismissing their cabin boy, she remained on board ship as 'an attendant', and was praised for climbing the masthead in the middle of the night and reefing the sails in bad weather, tasks performed only by the most dexterous sailors.[48] Bowden's testimony also provides insight into the intimate conditions in which the crew lived and reveals the loyalty of her shipmates who kept her secret while she kept theirs.

Bowden testified in the case of First Lieutenant William Berry, a twenty-two-year-old naval officer, who was charged with a 'horrid and abominable crime which delicacy forbids us to name' with Thomas Gibbs, a boy who worked aboard the *Hazard*.[49] She appeared in court 'dressed in a long jacket and blue trowsers' and said she had witnessed the crime on a Sunday afternoon in August as the vessel was returning to Portsmouth and the crew were off duty.[50] According to the Admiralty records:

Elizabeth, alias John Bowden (a girl) borne on the *Hazard's* books as a boy of the third class, was sworn and examined:

Prosecutor: Did you ever, during the time you have been on board the *Hazard*, look through the keyhole of Mr. Berry's cabin door and see the boy Thomas Gibbs in any way in an indecent manner employed with his hands with the prisoner?

Bowden: Yes, a little before we came in [to Portsmouth] I looked through the keyhole and I saw Thomas Gibbs playing with the prisoner's [Berry's] privates. I went up and called the gunroom steward and told him to come down and look through the keyhole and see what they were about. He did come down, but did not look in and called me aloft and told me to sit down.

Prosecutor: Have you frequently observed Thomas Gibbs go into the prisoner's cabin, and the door shut, and the prisoner at the same time in the cabin?

Bowden: Yes.

Prosecutor: Did Thomas Gibbs ever relate to you or in your hearing what passed between him and the prisoner? And what induced you to look through the keyhole?

Bowden: Gibbs had never told me anything that has happened – he was called in several times, and I thought I would see what he was about.

Prosecutor: Are you sure that it was the prisoner's private parts that you saw Thomas Gibbs have hold of?

Bowden: Yes.

Court: What light was there in the cabin at the time?

Bowden: One candle.[51]

The court found Berry guilty and he was sentenced to be hanged from the yard-arm of the *Hazard,* an act carried out on 19 October 1807. Bowden's testimony suggests that she understood that what she witnessed between Gibbs and Berry constituted a crime and by alerting the gunroom steward, she involved herself in the episode. It reveals a certain courage and confidence in her shipmates since as a lowly 'third boy', she became the key witness in deciding the fate of an officer.

If Bowden's presence aboard ship was unremarkable in 1807, two decades later, seventeen-year-old Ann Jane Thornton's service aboard several American merchant vessels and on the *Sarah* of Belfast earned her praise from a London court. Captain McIntire had hired this Anglo-Irish girl-disguised-as-boy to work as a cook and steward aboard the *Sarah,* where he 'participated in the most severe toils of the crews'.[52] Ann dressed as a sailor to enlist in St Andrews, South Carolina, at $9 per month. Although Captain McIntire never questioned the lad's presence, the crew became curious when he refused to drink grog, and later confirmed their suspicions when Ann was 'seen washing in her berth'.[53] Although Captain McIntire had been kind, Ann recalled that on the journey across the Atlantic to Liverpool, she had been 'struck by some of the sailors because she could not work as hard as they did – a thing she found difficult to do in a gale of wind.'[54] Thornton was fearless in her duties. Captain McIntire described how she would 'run up to hand the topgallant-sail in any sort of weather, and when we had a severe passage. Poor girl, she had a hard time of it, she suffered greatly from the wet, but she bore it all excellently and was a capital seaman.'[55] When the ship pulled into port, McIntire pleaded her case at the Mansion House before a judge who funded her journey back to her family in Donegal.

Femmes soldats

While nineteenth-century British newspapers regularly published accounts of women disguising themselves to become combatants, the French briefly experimented with female soldiers during the Revolution and the Napoleonic campaigns. Whereas these conflicts produced several hundred cases of French women in arms, they served in an official capacity, in disguise, or as wives who were present as sutlers (*vivandières*) who, like their British counterparts, picked up arms on the battlefield. While only a few of the officially recognized *femmes soldats* who served with French military units between 1775 and 1820 were rewarded with pensions or medals, these sisters in arms had an enormous impact on women of the Revolution who believed that military participation would advance their civil rights.

The French woman warrior during this tumultuous period is very different to her counterparts elsewhere in Europe. Their short-lived access to the military, with its implications for women's rights, demonstrates how passing female soldiers negotiated their combat role as an expression of nationalist commitment. Once their identity was exposed, they could argue that they transgressed only to serve their country's cause. Their story begins as the Old Regime of Louis XVI crumbled, and gender roles were hotly debated. Although these ultimately became more rigorously defined, women did enjoy a brief moment of access to male occupations and privileges. Women activists such as Pauline Léon in 1791 marched through Paris to the National Assembly with a petition, signed by 319 female citizens, demanding their right to form militias, to train and to engage in combat should war be declared.[56] Under the First French Republic in 1792, women enlisted in both military supply and combat roles for which they were later recognized in the *Annales du civisme*.[57] At least seventy-eight women soldiers served in international conflicts after France declared war against Austria. Even in foreign campaigns women were ubiquitous, passing frequently from suppliers of goods to active combatants in the French and Indian Wars in North America.

But this relaxing of gender boundaries proved short-lived and when the Jacobins came to dominate French politics, they regarded the female volunteers as a contagion; rumours circulated that they made poor soldiers and exploited the state by absconding or selling their uniforms. Opponents regarded women in arms, the 'Amazon battalions', as insulting to men and undermining of male physical superiority. In October 1793, the National Assembly prohibited women's political clubs with deputy Fabrice d'Églantine arguing that if women 'ask for the red cap [of liberty], [t]hey will not rest there; they will soon demand a belt with pistols ... These societies [of women] are not at all composed of mothers, daughters, and sisters of families ... but rather of adventuresses, female knights-errant, emancipated girls, and amazons.'[58] The Committee of Public Safety hardened its stance on women 'who wanted to be men' and ruled that the female fighters of the Revolutionary Army be paid off to return home; 80 per cent were discharged that year.[59] A number of *femmes soldats* flouted the rules, many with the collusion of their commanders and comrades, and stayed put; a few even rose to fame.[60]

Thérèse Figueur was among those who survived the Jacobin purges of 1793, taking active combat roles during the Revolution and Napoleonic Wars for which she was later recognized. She fought throughout twenty campaigns, was wounded twice, had horses shot from underneath her and was twice taken captive. Figueur, a dragoon with the 15th Regiment, was nicknamed '*le petit Sans-Gêne*' when she enlisted with the Republican Legion of Allobroges aged nineteen. It was a nickname she shared with the former laundress and wife of the Napoleonic general François-Joseph Lefebvre, who was famously outspoken and which was suggestive of Figueur's character. Popular with her comrades, she proved so courageous during the siege of Toulon (serving under a young Napoleon) that she escaped the Committee of Public Safety's ban on female soldiers.

Perhaps the Jacobins found Sans-Gêne's story more palatable than others because, in a reversal of the army wife-turned-soldier trope, she married a fellow soldier, a hussar, Henri Commarmot, on 21 December 1797. When her husband was transferred to the 1st Carabiniers six months later, Sans-Gêne remained with his hussar regiment, the 8th, and three months later transferred to the 15th Dragoons. During the Italian campaign, she was badly wounded at Savigliano, in Piedmont after her horse was shot out from under her. She was taken prisoner but French royalists arranged her escape by dressing her in a frock to return across French lines.[61]

The harsh conditions of the campaign and her injuries forced Figueur into temporary retirement to Paris in 1804, when Napoleon authorized a twenty-four franc per month pension in recognition of her services.[62] But Figueur quickly grew bored with civilian life and so volunteered the following year for a brief period with the Grande Armée before returning to Paris. In 1809 she campaigned in Spain where, in 1812, she was made a prisoner of war by the guerrilla chief Merino, imprisoned by the English and sent to Alba in 1814; she was finally freed after Napoleon's abdication in 1815.[63]

The daughters of an Alsatian philosopher and military officer were among the era's *femmes soldats* whose deeds were considered patriotic enough to enter public consciousness. Félicité and Théophile de Fernig 'felt their warlike ardour stirring' when their father Louis Joseph de Fernig was appointed commandant of a National Guard detachment in the district of Mortagne in 1789.[64] A contemporaneous letter documents how they offered their services to the Republic: Fernig's daughters, who describe themselves as 'two brave Amazons' whose 'patriotism equals their courage', submitted an official request from their village on the Franco-Belgian border, on 7 June 1792:

Gentlemen, though our sex is accused of weakness and timidity, although we are excluded from the honour of the oath, as well as civic inscription, we nevertheless dare to offer our country our arms and our lives; therefore, we beg you gentlemen, my younger sister and I, not only to register us on the volunteer list of the National Guard of our city, but also to take the civic oath to be faithful to the nation, to the law, and to the king, to hold with all our strength the constitution of the kingdom. We are happy to pay homage to the Homeland and to share the victory with the brave volunteers and our brothers in arms.[65]

The Fernig sisters regarded their military participation as an entrée into the political sphere, as they challenged assumptions about women's inferiority. Most versions of their story suggest that before they volunteered for their father's detachment, they were dressing in their brother's clothes and carrying arms.[66] In disguise, they surreptitiously joined the troops – aided by their male comrades – exchanging fire with the Austrian forces in Maulde, before returning home so their father 'did not suspect that his own daughters had fought in the front rank of his skirmishes and sometimes preserved his own life.'[67]

After several nights in the field, the sisters' disguise was revealed when the commander of a neighbouring detachment (also their father's friend) noticed that two young soldiers refused to meet his gaze. Puzzled, General de Beurnonville asked Fernig to call the shy volunteers forward. The women parted the ranks, unrecognizable in their uniforms, their faces sooty and their lips black from the bullet cartridges they tore open with their teeth:

M. de Fernig could not understand how it was he did not know these two members of his little army.

'Who are you?' he sternly demanded.

At these words the whole company began to exchange smiles and whispers.

Théophile and Félicité realising their secret was out, fell on their knees, blushed and burst into tears, acknowledging their misdeeds, and flinging their arms around their father's knees, implored him to forgive the deceit they had practiced upon him.[68]

Accepting his daughters' apologies, Fernig was so moved by their 'marvellous display of love and self-sacrifice' that he wept.[69] The

Fernig sisters accompanied their father, 'as models of patriotism and an augury of a glorious victory', in General Charles Francois Dumouriez's march towards Paris through the Argonne Forest.[70]

In a nineteenth-century telling of the Fernig sisters' exploits, on 6 November 1792, at the battle of Jemappes, near Hainaut in Belgium, when Dumouriez's forces faced the Imperial Army of Field Marshal Albert Casimir, Duke of Teschen, Théophile shot two Hungarian grenadiers, before disarming and 'with her own hand', taking prisoner its commanding officer. Meanwhile, sixteen-year-old Félicité, in the 'thickest of the melée', amidst the wrecks of Dumouriez's retreating battalions, charged her horse across the battlefield, 'holding her bridle with her teeth, and with a pistol in each hand' to shame the fleeing soldiers into rallying behind their commander, the young general, the Duke of Chartres.[71]

A week later, as the French Revolutionary Army advanced on Brussels, then in Austrian possession, Félicité demonstrated again her grace under fire. Caught in an exchange between the French advance guard and the Austrian rear, she and her horse wove their way through a circle of swords to rejoin her column. En route she rushed to rescue a Belgian officer, thrown from his horse, and engaged in a sword fight with the Polish cavalry, the Uhlans. She shot two of them, before escorting the wounded Belgian to a field hospital and returning to Dumouriez.

This chance encounter between Félicité and the Belgian, Vanderwallen, may have ended in romance. The wounded officer could never forget the 'apparition he beheld on the field of blood', and after leaving the army he travelled through Germany 'in search of his fair liberator'. Apparently, he even eventually tracked down and married Félicité 'who had resumed the habits, the graces and the modesty of her sex.' Théophile, the younger sister, followed the Vanderwallens to Brussels, where she 'died young without having been married'.[72] The *soeurs soldates* of the Revolution were tamed through the agencies of marriage, spinsterhood and jam making. In the Belgian author O. P. Gilbert's telling, the sisters 'threw themselves into the part with zest, [and] displayed no small talent for coquetry, took great interest in the upbringing of children as well as in the making of preserves.'[73] Their foray into the violent, masculine world of war left no mark upon them.

What the romantic version of the Fernigs obscures, however, was the sisters' political influence among their generation of French women. Their heroic actions when they served under General Dumouriez in Belgium became known to the National Convention and the public. In 1793, a petition entitled 'Departure of 900 Female Citizens from Paris Who Enlisted, Disguised as Men, to Leave for the Front to Combat the Tyrants of the Nations' demanded that women be permitted to form the 'Fernig Corps', named in honour of the sisters. Up to 10,000 female citizens aged between eighteen and forty, it proposed, would be organized in 100 companies of combatants in twenty battalions and five legions. The women would be armed with pikes, muskets, pistols, hatchets and sabres with mottoes inscribed on the flag of each legion bearing such ferocious slogans as 'Free Women', 'Live Free or Die', 'The Republic or Death'. The women would have their hair cut short, for convenience, their heads would be covered with a bronze helmet that featured 'a brim and visor of chamois, plume, and panache tricoloured at its end'. A song followed the petition that identified the wearing of trousers with female liberation:

> Long live the sansculottes,
> And you will wear them;
> Abandon your hearths
> Dressed as lads. Let us march …
> We wear pants
> That's the way that women are now[74]

While the petition was ignored, it indicates the Fernigs' influence on women's struggle to establish a new form of equal citizenship.

The sisters' decision to follow Dumouriez in swapping the French for the Austrian Army, however, would later be regarded as treasonous. Although they soon realized that their loyalty to Dumouriez was a mistake, and deserted the Austrian Army for the republicans, the National Convention considered them turncoats.

They fled to Belgium where they petitioned the government to return home; the right was granted only in 1801 and when they did return, they felt so unwelcome that they soon moved back to Brussels.[75]

Despite such disappointments in advancing women's cause during the Revolution, more women than ever before served during the Napoleonic Wars and rose to celebrity status.[76] Among them was Angélique Marie-Josèphe Brûlon, who survived several campaigns to receive the Legion of Honour in 1851. She was born into a Breton military family in 1771; her father and two brothers were killed on active service in the Italian campaign. She married a soldier, aged seventeen, and in 1792, while stationed in Corsica her husband was killed during a battle at Ajaccio. Soon after, she dressed in his uniform and demanded that she replace him within the 42nd Regiment of Foot. Long after she gained international fame as an 'extraordinary female military character' she told an American journalist in Paris in 1856: 'My heart, head and hand burned to send destruction to the English and the rebel Corsicans.'[77] Brûlon joined her husband's regiment in defending the artillery fort of Calvi from a combined British and Corsican military operation in 1794. After several weeks of close fighting, when the French positions were sufficiently damaged, General Charles Stuart launched a major assault, driving their enemy out of the forts and into the town. When the siege ended, Corsica had become a British colony.

Brûlon actively defended the fort and, using the *nom de guerre* Liberté, served in three different regiments, working her way up from fusilier to corporal, lance-corporal and sergeant-major.[78] Despite being wounded in the siege and with her regiment losing ground, she still managed to organize a female resistance.

> I did not mind my wounds in each arm, nor did I fear the dark, but set out alone, at midnight, evaded the guards, roused sixty starved women and led them to the fort, which we reached at two o'clock in the morning. We gave the women each half a pound of rice, which we all considered an excellent bargain.[79]

Despite recruiting this ad hoc group and even as Brûlon joined the defence, the artillery men were falling under enemy fire at Calvi, and when she aimed a sixteen-pound cannon at the enemy, a bomb burst, wounding her left leg, which would leave her permanently disabled.[80]

Brûlon's military family and her role as a war widow and patriot provided acceptably feminine motives for entering the front line and by the mid-nineteenth century she was an exotic figure, sought out by wealthy travellers as a curiosity. Lady Charlotte Guest, a literary editor and wife of Welsh ironmaster Sir Josiah John Guest, who visited Paris from Wales in April 1851, was disappointed not to meet the famous Madame Brûlon. In Lady Charlotte's telling, Liberté's military career conformed more to the activities of a bit player or female mascot. She had heard that Brûlon was best known for snatching the regimental flag from her husband's corpse to carry it through the action at Marengo in 1800 where the French defeated the Austrians.[81] Though Brûlon's military skills and courage were officially recognized when she received the Legion of Honour, the popular conception of the *femme soldat* had become a mere extension of military wife or daughter. As Napoleon's Grande Armée expanded to include conscripts from foreign territories, it incorporated foreign women on an unprecedented scale. As *femme soldats* became mythic creatures, more *vivandières* fought with musket and sabre alongside their men who could be honoured by the Empire for participating in combat but only if they fought in self-defence.[82]

The First World War

In the early twentieth century, women disguising themselves to enter the ranks found their secret became more difficult to hide from recruiters or commanding officers. This may explain why the most celebrated cases were those of Maria Bochkareva, Marina Yurlova, Princess Kati Dadeshkeliani, and Flora Sandes, all of whom either signed on without subterfuge or with an officer's complicity. Aside from the steady trickle of stories about the other Russian women soldiers, scattered reports surfaced in the European and North American press about passing women whose military service was either fleeting or failed completely. Although such references remained exceptional during the First World War, the women's presence still carried symbolic weight for their readers.

Dorothy Lawrence, the aspiring journalist, suggests that despite her brief time at the front, British military authorities acted swiftly to suppress reports of her adventure, and were perplexed by her motives. Her stint as Private Denis Smith lasted a mere ten days during which she was plagued by rheumatism, chills and chafing from her tight swaddling. Eventually, Dorothy requested to speak with her immediate superior, hoping that once the sergeant in charge knew her true identity, he might offer her proper accommodation. He smiled and patted her on the back, raising her hopes, and she returned to the mine fuses she was preparing with her pal Tommy Dunn. A few minutes later, however, two meaty hands grabbed her arms as the military policemen hauled her from the trench.

Lawrence was furious at the sergeant's betrayal and scowled as she passed him. 'You are the biggest blackguard I have ever met,' she shouted, 'If I *were* really a man I'd knock you down here and now.'[83] Lawrence believed naively that the sergeant could have kept her secret and, instead, she was marched to British Third Army headquarters. There an astonished colonel, thinking she might be a spy, made her a prisoner of war.

Despite the grave charge, Dorothy found her situation both amusing and ironic as she faced a panel of intelligence officers. 'So utterly ludicrous appeared this betrousered little female, marshalled solemnly by three soldiers and deposited before 20 embarrassed men,' she wrote years later. 'On arrival I heard, "Oh-o-o! (groan) it is a woman. Certainly we shall never get even with a woman if she wishes to deceive us."'[84] Rumours of her arrest spread quickly through St Omer, the British Expeditionary Force headquarters, prompting visits from several young officers. One exclaimed angrily that the 'episode' would soon pass like rapid-fire along the front line and Lawrence heard murmurs of 'what would they say back home?' The army's reputation, they seemed to suggest, might be sullied by her presence.

The Secret Intelligence Corps' officers scrutinized her private letters, fetched from the cottage in which Dunn had housed her, for intelligence violations. With her adventure over, and seated at a wooden table watching the men, Lawrence 'lapsed into feminine attitudes despite [her] little khaki uniform,' since concealment was no longer necessary.[85] The 'lapse' into innocence and passivity were the only weapons in her arsenal. Finally, the commanding colonel dismissed his prisoner for the night and told the guards: 'Whatever you do take her away from here! I don't know what to do with her.'[86]

Her military escorts shuttled Lawrence, on horseback, across the countryside as they searched for 'suitable accommodation'. When they reached Calais, Major-General Sir Henry Seymour Rawlinson instructed her escorts, 'to find some decent clothes for her and get her out of here.' Then they stopped at Senlis before returning to St Omer for another examination. Then Lawrence was thrown into a guard room which was policed by eight soldiers with strict instructions to refuse visitors. She remained there for three nights while her guards, she claimed, grew increasingly ashamed of her treatment.[87]

During her final interrogation Lawrence was seated before three British generals, including Sir Charles Munro, twenty staff officers and other military officials. Throughout the questioning she swung between amused irony and anger at the officers' unwillingness to believe her story. One admitted: 'They simply don't know what to make of you … One thinks that you are a spy and another says you must be a camp follower and everyone has his own views on the subject.'[88] If Lawrence were a spy or a prostitute, her transgression would have been clear. But since she denied the charges and any patriotic claims, she could not be pigeon-holed as an Amazonian heroine. 'Our higher command surely lacked imagination and proper perspective otherwise this trivial escapade never could have assumed such proportions,' she wrote, although she understood their legitimate concern.[89]

Uncomfortable under cross-examination, Lawrence blustered: 'If masculinity, as nature's endowment, had fallen to [my] lot, probably [I] would have tried to be in the navy, if not a member of the law.'[90] Her breach of military security occurred as Britons grew anxious on the home front about the consequences of women entering a wide range of occupations to release men for the front. The officers failed to appreciate that for Dorothy enlisting was a way for all women to expand their political rights and, in her case, to get a journalistic scoop. Unwilling to accept 'the consequences of nature' she suggested that her improvization at the front might inspire other women. When Lawrence challenged her interrogators '*you* rest in *my* hands not I in yours' she attempt to usurp their masculine authority.[91] When she was housed, under guard, for two weeks at the nearby Convent de Bon Pasteur, a cloistered order, she believed it was a deliberate attempt to break her adventurous spirit. In isolation, Lawrence was unable to file reports about the front whose content, in any case, would have been out of date by the time she reached London.

But if the British officers assigned to her case puzzled over her motives and regarded her as a nuisance, other women and many serving men found her fascinating. The nuns of de Bon Pasteur affectionately labelled her the 'female desperado', as they were 'utterly enthralled at the adventures of a woman who had got out to the big world ...'. Lawrence wrote, 'I eventually became quite a popular heroine.'[92] Out of respect and curiosity all the off-duty soldiers in St Omer shook Lawrence's hand before she left for England. Among the small crowd who gathered to see her off, an English Tommy confessed, 'Most of us would have come, only the authorities have kept rather quiet about it; not all the men know.' She might inspire other women to rebel, or to resist a passive female role, but once elevated as a heroic figure possessed of superlative or supernatural qualities it was less likely others would follow in her wake.

In fact, two years after Dorothy Lawrence returned to London, a passing woman was caught attempting to stow away aboard a US army transport ship bound for France. Hazel Carter was held at a New Jersey police station awaiting charges which took the sting out of her success at outwitting the military authorities. While contemporary press reports praised her ingenuity, they simultaneously trivialized her motives. Carter had deceived the army authorities and her husband, Corporal John Carter, had no idea his wife was sitting in the last carriage when his troop train left Douglas, Arizona. She had stolen a uniform, cropped her black hair short and pulled a service cap low over her eyes, and for two days avoided detection. A suspicious officer put her off at a remote station where the train was switching tracks. But the indefatigable Carter simply hopped back on among a crush of soldiers when the 'all aboard' sounded.

When the regiment reached Hoboken, New Jersey the following day, Hazel was easily lost amidst the soldiers crowded on the dock. She found her husband's ship and slipped into the baggage hold where she stayed for several days. She was eventually discovered when her squad was paraded onto the after-deck for a medical examination after a rumour circulated about a woman on board. According to Hazel, she had enlisted after the Red Cross rejected her application and 'because I was born on a ranch and was used to riding and looking after myself since I was a child ... I decided to disguise myself as a soldier and go [to France] anyway.'[93] She identified independence and courage as essential qualities for her mission.

While Carter waited for the federal authorities to decide her fate, charges of impersonating a soldier and stowing away on an army transport were dropped, and the townspeople of Hoboken took up her case. Although Mayor Patrick Griffin refused Carter's offer to remain as a war worker, he used the city's 'poor fund' to outfit her return journey to Douglas. The police officers told reporters that 'she was the handsomest and smartest-looking soldier they had seen in Hoboken since the war started, which cheered the corporal's wife considerably.'[94] In the police officers' eyes, the new clothes transformed Carter from an androgynous figure with 'somewhat masculine features' that made it difficult to detect her true sex into a 'corporal's wife'. Though the police revealed a lingering admiration for the 'pseudo US infantryman' whatever threat she posed, the new outfit easily resolved it.

Reports of the female combatants from the Eastern theatre carried a similar theme that soldiering for women, and its attendant masculine identity, was an aberration. An English journalist recorded Zoya Smirnova's decision to quit the Tsar's army after she was wounded in 1915. Smirnova and a group of her twelve female friends left their homes to volunteer, concealed on a train bound for the Austrian front where they borrowed uniforms from sympathetic officers. Although they were soon discovered, they persuaded the commanders to let them participate in numerous battles.[95] After being wounded a second time, Smirnova spent a month recovering at a military hospital, following which she was unable to rejoin her regiment. 'The girl lost her presence of mind and for the first time during the entire campaign began to weep, thus betraying her sex and age,' wrote a *Times* correspondent. 'Her unfamiliar country-men gazed with amazement upon the strange young NCO with the Cross of St. George medal on her breast who resembled a stripling and finally proved to be a girl.'[96]

A similar case is recorded in 1915 of seven German women volunteers, in military uniform, who were captured in Russian Poland. A report in the *New York Times* of the 'German Amazons Dressed as Men' described most of the volunteers as recovering from battle wounds in a special hospital ward in Galicia where one had already died.

They are fine specimens of Teutonic womanhood, and the Russian nurses greatly admire their finely developed muscles, which seem to indicate that they have belonged for years to German gymnastic societies. In captivity they behave with the same haughty and contemptuous indifference which characterises the Prussian officers. One of the nursing sisters brought to them a Russian newspaper, the Petrograd Herald, which is printed in German, but they indignantly rejected her offer and said they did not believe anything which appeared in a Russian paper, even when printed in German. They refused to talk of their homes and families but, judging from their demeanour, they seem to belong to the upper or upper middle class.[97]

A later report claimed that Russian soldiers on the Dvinsk front, in southern Latvia, had been capturing up to 200 women per week: 'These women were all in German uniform and apparently serving as soldiers.'[98] However, these reports – often translations of translations – may have confused the thousands of women serving in the Prussian War Ministry as auxiliaries with the more rarefied cases of the 'German Amazons'.[99] A year earlier, a Don Cossack in Petrograd reported that during a raid on the German-held town of Częstochowa, they had captured 300 enemy cavalrymen and, '[w]hen these came to be examined, forty were found to be women dressed in soldiers' uniforms.'[100]

Georgian princess Kati Dadeshkeliani's memoir describes her preference for practising medicine rather than front-line combat. Dadeshkeliani, as Djamal, endured the front line's brutality for a week before joining a regimental ambulance. Humiliated by her inadequacy in battle, a medical role offered her 'abundant scope for my womanly faculties, for my energy and my will-power.'[101] Away from the intimate contact of the dug-out, she was free to bathe, once again comfortable with her female body (and in more civilized accommodation) and was no longer concerned about accidental discovery. As Dadeshkeliani feared sexual harassment, ridicule and dismissal rather than imprisonment if her sex were discovered, she was keenly aware of the need to maintain a masculine appearance.

The female warrior preferred to choose her own moment of disclosure, return to her true sex and embark on a new career or occupation. Some had used their male disguise to accomplish a goal that once realized, rendered their masquerade unnecessary. Others looked forward to resuming or beginning motherhood, to renewing female friendships and their place among other women. No one who witnessed the carnage of war yearned for its return and some openly expressed their battle fatigue and a growing revulsion of violence. But the female soldier uniquely experienced the tension of withholding emotions from her comrades who, however sympathetic, could not completely understand the strain she had endured, the horrors she had witnessed.

It was sometimes in another woman's presence that these emotions arose most poignantly. Following the Vardar offensive of September 1918 on the Bulgarian border Flora Sandes was introduced to the women in a Turkish harem. The 'hideous, old hags', 'screeched' and covered their faces when Sandes entered the room and 'it took a long time before I could persuade them that I was a woman.'[102] A few days later Sandes' regiment broke camp at Nish in northern Serbia where the women grew curious about the English lady in the uniform of a Serbian officer. The wide-eyed group 'carried [her] off' to a cottage, seated her on a three-legged stool and bombarded her with questions'.[103] Her discomfort is evident in her description of this meeting, written in 1927:

> Though I could understand the men perfectly I could not understand half the women said. They talked too fast, and their voices were very shrill, unlike the men who have rather soft voices. I was beginning to feel rather dazed, so was relieved when a couple of the men came in, laughing and saying they had been hunting for me everywhere and had come to 'take care of me'.[104]

Sandes experienced Serbia through male eyes and from her privileged perspective as a middle-class foreigner. It is unsurprising that she felt so little affinity for these women who appeared rough, uneducated and somehow menacing. Perhaps Sandes was made uneasy when reminded that she would inevitably re-enter the female ranks, cut off from her male friends. She would never lose her Britishness, a social status that placed her above the village women, but upon demobilization in 1922, the circumstances that allowed her equality with her Serbian friends, would change.

Peace did not end the female fighter's predicament and she shared her loss of status and sense of purpose with her former comrades in arms. Sandes noted that during the Serbian Army's 1916 campaign, she experienced 'incessant fighting weariness indescribable but hand-in-hand with romance, adventure and comradeship which more than made up for everything.'[105] She found a unique sense of belonging during the war; as she wrote to her sister on 14 October 1916, 'for anyone to say they are proud of anything I do is such a novel experience – it's generally so much the other way – that it had quite bucked me up.'[106] But she added in a postscript written a week later, after a close friend was killed, that she had renounced her earlier descriptions of war as a form of sport and said, 'I've changed my mind … and loathe war and everything to do with it with all my heart, but if I wrote particulars the Censor would not pass it.'[107] The exhilaration, pain and brutal hardships of war formed her attachment to the Serbian cause for which she remained forever grateful.

If Flora Sandes suffered long-term trauma, she never expressed it. But other former female combatants of the First World War were more open about their relief when their military service ended. Wounded a second time in 1916, Marina Yurlova regained consciousness during a battle, a sensation like 'a waking nightmare' that 'bruised' her mind and for months afterwards jolted her awake with visions of dead men, 'lying with their eyes staring up at God.'[108] After three years in combat she began a slow process of recovery; her fantasy, in 1914, of an adventure that would enable her 'to find my place … to do things', had vanished.[109] And what price had she paid for her search? She had lost her home, her family and, finally, her identity. Women combatants did not uniquely experience the terror of war but once retired from active service many could not even acknowledge their part in an armed struggle. Back in skirts and dresses, married and perhaps raising children, they were shunned by fellow veterans. Along with their uniform they shed their male status.

Inevitably there were women who were able to parlay their military service into celebrity status, or to exploit its political and financial possibilities. But how, and in what circumstances did they transform their adventures into a script for the stage, publish their memoirs, campaign for pensions or gain public recognition for their war efforts? Some returned home to find that their reputations preceded them and they were already immortalized in ballads or published stories. Whatever future they made for themselves from their celebrity or notoriety, as we shall see, they found audiences fascinated by their extraordinary lives and adventures. Others were unable to make the transition back to womanhood, foundering alone, penniless, confused, and broken. These women inhabited neither a male nor or female space, to live as outcasts, permanently transformed by their experience. But for some, the return to an acceptable social identity with its profoundly different meaning marked the beginning rather than the end of a life split in two.

Chapter 6

Back to Civvy Street

The Amazons of Greek mythology always die a beautiful death, leaving a corpse on a barren battlefield after a violent end that guarantees their eternal fame. These 'admirable, athletic, beautiful, sexually desirable valiant women' are neither objects of contempt for usurping masculine powers, nor victims of ancient misogyny but heroes. Unlike mortal women, the various mythic biographies of Amazons, from Queen Melanippe to Queen Penthesilea, are worthy opponents for Greek heroes.[1] Yet the tales of these strong foreign women, whom their male adversaries always vanquish, contrast sharply with their more realistic appearance in Greco-Roman histories. Here they forge alliances with former enemies, have male lovers, become mothers, and even sometimes win their battles.[2]

The history of women's participation in armed conflict is, of course, scored with myths of the female warrior's after-life which is as ritualized as her wartime exploits.[3] Just as the Scythian women's histories were erased or rewritten to conform to the contemporary mores of their storytellers down the centuries, so the biographies of the female warriors from the eighteenth century onwards were refashioned for their readers. Among those who survived the war, or were exposed and returned home to rebuild their lives, a few narrated their experiences on stage, through newspaper interviews, or in memoirs. Those who managed to control their own mythmaking, or to produce more realistic depictions of their experience, would be remembered for their exceptional endeavours.

The eighteenth century

The publications, ballads and stage performances from the long eighteenth century in Europe reached back to the ancient Greek myths as their reference point for the female warriors. Readers were familiar with tales of the warrior heroines from their appearance in ballads and stage performances, in newspaper accounts, chapbooks, portraits and illustrations, and even the naming of pubs. In England these stories became so commonplace that they established their own literary and performance genres. A few retired soldiers and sailors were able to parlay their experiences into these forms of popular culture which might supply them with the income they had lost. While most passing women's military experiences were never recorded beyond a fleeting mention in official accounts, in newspapers or as military anecdotes, a few rose to fame and even managed to work at 'male' trades.

Relying on her reputation as a former soldier with the Duke of Marlborough's army, Christian Davies ran a pub in Paddington, London, while she waited for her soldier husband's discharge. The pub, however, was a short-lived venture and, to escape an impoverished old age, Christian was accepted into the Royal Chelsea Hospital where her husband was a guard. She may have sold her story, which appeared soon after her death in 1739, and was reprinted in 1741 with a lengthy appendix; in 1742 it was published as the work of J. Wilson, a former army surgeon. Perhaps playing on this popularity, in 1740 actress Peg Woffington, famed for her male roles, made her breeches debut in *The Female Officer* in Dublin, Christian's former home. Woffington twice performed as 'The Female Volunteer', mocked up as a militiaman wearing a sheathed sword, at London's Covent Garden.[4] The woman warrior was enjoying a surge of popularity.

When Hannah Snell's adventures appeared in the *Whitehall Evening Post* in the summer of 1750, Robert Walker, a canny London publisher, approached her with a proposition. Snell signed over the contemporary equivalent of 'life rights', swearing an affidavit before the Lord Mayor of London on 27 June that summarized her 'surprising adventures'.[5] A short, forty-six-page soft-bound edition followed less than a week later and another edition appeared within a fortnight. Walker mounted an impressive publicity campaign, which included Hannah appearing on stage, in uniform, at New Wells Theatre in Goodman's Fields, Aldgate, as 'the British Amazon' on 29 June.[6] Throughout that summer her theatrical appearances were billed almost daily in London newspapers.[7]

The *General Advertiser* described Hannah's impressive performance as she sang and demonstrated 'all the manual exercises of a soldier in her regimentals' at New Wells Theatre:

> Here she and her Attendants fill up the Stage in a very agreeable Manner. The Tabor and Drum give a Life to her March, and she traverses the Stage two or three Times over, Step by Step, in the same Manner as our soldiers march on the Parade in St. James's Park. After the Spectators have been sufficiently amused with this formal Procession, she begins her Military Exercises, and goes thro' the whole Catechism (If I may be allowed the Expression) with so much Dexterity and Address, and with so little Hesitation or Default, that great Numbers even of Veteran Soldiers, who have resorted to the Wells out of mere Curiosity only, have frankly acknowledged that she executes what she undertakes to Admiration.[8]

In just over two months Hannah made sixty appearances, confidently demonstrating her martial skills, to the approval of 'Veteran soldiers', and belting out ballads, copies of which were 'sold at the Bar of the Wells'.[9] But this venture was, like Christian Davies' pub, short-lived and after her final appearance at the New Wells on 15 September she retired from the stage except for brief stints in Bath and Bristol.[10] Two months later, without the promised thirty pounds per annum pension from the Duke of Cumberland, Hannah was forced to follow Christian Davies into the Royal Chelsea Hospital. Hannah

Snell's military experience is summarized as belonging to the '2nd Mar. [Marines] ffrazer's [regiment] ... aged 27. Time of service 4 ½ months in his & Guise's Regt ... Wounded at Pondicherry in the thigh of both legs, born at Worcester, her father a Dyer.'[11] Despite the massaging of the truth (Hannah was wounded at Devicotta rather than in the better-known siege of Pondicherry), the Royal Chelsea Hospital provided sanctuary.

Walker claimed that Hannah aspired to open a sailor's tavern in Wapping called the 'Woman in Masquerade' and a few years later a Mrs Coles, upon her retirement from sea, happened upon the same idea. The *Annual Register* for 1782 records that Mrs Coles, described as 'a very polite and elegant woman', who had served aboard several men of war, aspired to become a publican in Poplar, in East London. She had seen actions during the American Revolutionary War and had inherited 'a small fortune' which, along with her naval contacts, would ensure the pub's success.[12]

Mary Lacy, the female sailor, was eventually able to exploit the secret of her naval career in her memoir *The Female Shipwright*, published in 1773. By then Lacy had retired from her seafaring adventures after serving eleven years at sea and in the Portsmouth Dockyard as a shipwright. Lacy, as Bill Chandler, was forced to end her career, finally receiving her shipwright's certificate after a long apprenticeship. Her memoir chronicles how, after an absence of eight years, she had visited her family in Kent where a chance meeting with a family friend led to her discovery. In the summer of 1767 Lacy was granted leave and travelled back to Ash where her mother, unfazed that Mary was now living as Bill Chandler, welcomed her daughter warmly.[13]

A year after the fateful reunion, Lacy was lodging in Portsmouth with Mrs Reading when rumours began to circulate at the dockyard: 'it was whispered about that I was a woman; which threw me into a most terrible fight, believing that some of the boys were going to search me.' One morning, two dockers confronted the shipwright: 'What think you, Chandler, the people will have it that you are a woman! which struck me with such a panic that I knew not what to say. However, I had the presence of mind to laugh it off, as if it was not worth notice.'[14] After an older man, Mr Penny, chased off the accusers, Bill broke down, 'and gave full vent to my tears, which were not few.'[15]

Then Bill's trusted mentor, Mr Corbin, and his mate demanded that he either prove his identity by allowing a body-search, or they leave him to the boys' mercy. 'They put the question to me very seriously, which I was ingenuously answered, though it made me cry so that I could scarce speak; at which declaration of mine, in plainly telling them I was a woman, they seemed greatly surprised; and offered to take their oaths of secrecy.'[16] Corbin and his friend agreed to keep Bill's secret, swearing to the dockyard bullies that their mate was a man, and pointing to his success with women as the ultimate proof. 'As one said, "I thought Chandler could not be so great with his mistress if he was not a man ... I'm sure he's no girl"'. Even Bill's girlfriend, Sarah Chase, brushed aside the rumours and a few days later, 'the matter quite dropt'. Reassured, the shipwrights wondered 'how it should come into the heads of people to think that Chandler was a girl [telling each other]: I am sure there is not the least appearance of it in the make or shape of him'.[17]

But while Bill won the trust of his workmates, the reprieve was fleeting. Keeping her secret was a constant stress so Lacy was pleased when a family friend from Ash, the aptly named Mrs Low, moved into the seaside town. Bill moved into Mrs Low's lodgings in Tree Rope-Walk on Portsmouth Common where, 'I could freely unbosom myself ... being perfectly satisfied of her fidelity'.[18] The trust, however, was misplaced as Mrs Low lit aflame the recently dampened rumours so that Lacy again feared discovery:

> I fretted myself quite sick, and thought I should have broke my heart; but could not tell who [Mrs Low] had told: and the apprehensions I felt from persons meddling with me, greatly affected me. So that by fretting and hard working, I was reduced very low, and thrown into a fit of illness.[19]

Although Lacy remained at Gosport for several more months, she was 'very uneasy, less something disastrous should happen to me', and felt 'continually apprehensive of being surprised unawares'. Meanwhile, the physically demanding work and poor living conditions (she was again bunking onboard ship and sleeping on 'the softest plank [I] could find'), caused her arthritis to flare up.[20] She left Portsmouth, and a heart-broken Sarah, on 2 December 1771 for London. Lacy outlined in a petition to the Lords of the Admiralty how she 'disguised herself in Men's Cloaths and enter'd on board His Maj[esty's] Fleet', serving aboard the Royal William and as a shipwright in Portsmouth Yard, and was granted £20 for life.[21]

Lacy's memoir *The Female Shipwright* sold well with its three editions, never rivalling those of Christian Davies or Hannah Snell, but adding to the growing history of the female warriors. Two decades later, Deborah Sampson, the Continental soldier who seemed acutely aware of Snell's adventures, published, with Herman Mann, her memoir entitled *The Female Review* (1797). By then, this veteran of the American Revolution had had three children with Benjamin Gannett, a hardscrabble farmer whom she married in Sharon, Massachusetts in 1785. The collaboration with Mann was a godsend, leading to a book tour of New England in 1802 where, dressed in her Continental Army uniform, Sampson reflected on her wartime experiences and, like Snell, performed military exercises with her musket. The theatrics, which took place in venues across Massachusetts, Rhode Island, and New York, supported Sampson's petition to Congress for an invalid-veteran pension. The Gannetts needed the income, as Paul Revere the American Revolution's famous patriot and family friend wrote of her claim after visiting them in Sharon in 1804: 'They have a few acres of poor land which they cultivate, but they are really poor.'[22] Whatever money Sampson made by lecturing was sorely needed to clear debts or pay medical bills.

In these instances, the female warriors might appear on stage as novelties, mythic creatures made flesh. Their adventures were endlessly reworked in street songs and ballad operas, in musicals and plays, and, in England, as live performances at 'pleasure gardens'.[23] One bold Hannah Snell tribute act appeared in 1803 when the New Wells Theatre debuted 'the British Amazons or Army without Reserve' featuring 'female volunteers in scarlet doing military exercises accompanied by patriotic songs praising the loyalty of all British countries and a vision of Bonaparte in the temple of British victories.'[24] The 'Invincible Brigade or Female Cavalry' offered 'ladies of the establishment' in uniform, manipulating lance and sabre, a performance which appeared at the Royal Amphitheatre near Westminster Bridge, in August 1828.[25] These acts reflected nationalist sentiments while providing male audiences with the titillating spectacle of women in military costume and handling weapons; as a charming amusement and devoid of social critique, their gender-crossing was tamed.

Since the woman warrior also endured as a newspaper staple throughout the nineteenth century, a female combatant might arrive back from a rough campaign or long ship's voyage to discover that she was already immortalized. The female tar Mary Anne Arnold read with interest Captain Scott's letter about her discovery aboard the *Robert Small* in 1839 when it was reprinted from the *Times* in an Indian newspaper. Reaching London a few months later, she capitalized on her fame by asking Sir Chapman Marshall, the Lord Mayor, for financial assistance while she awaited her return to Asia.[26] Her story added to the growing popularity of ballads about seafaring women, making their experiences more believable and familiar to contemporary audiences.

Four years earlier, London's Lord Mayor William Taylor Copeland had sent City Police Inspector McLean to offer 'assistance ... if required' after reading about sailor Anne Jane Thornton in the local press. Under the heading, 'a romantic adventure' it was reported that a female tar had arrived at Fresh Wharf aboard the *Sarah* just returned from St John, New Brunswick, in February 1835. After Thornton's appearance at Mansion House a book chronicling her years at sea was quickly published. It cast aside any lingering doubts from the Fresh Wharf dockers who had 'exposed [Anne Jane Thornton] to much annoyance from the jeers and obscene language'.[27] If the written word wasn't enough, the *Sarah*'s captain allegedly invited 'some gentlemen to see his phenomenon fly up the shrouds'.[28] Thornton's adventures even appeared in a second edition, published in Providence, Rhode Island and accompanied by a ballad entitled 'The Female Sailor', reassuring readers that 'the following song is founded on fact, however romantick [sic] it may appear.' [29] Whether in London, Boston or Amsterdam, readers needed little convincing of the female sailor's existence and ability to perform her duties aboard ship.

By the end of the American Civil War, warrior women had gained a new popularity with memoirs by Sarah Edmonds and Loreta Velazquez, alongside news stories, and many other fictional or fictionalized accounts. Edmonds claimed that she donated the proceeds of her first book *Nurse and Spy*, which sold more than 175,000 copies in 1865, to the Sanitary Commission, the Civil War's equivalent of the Red Cross.[30] *Pauline of the Potomac*, an account of Pauline Cushman, an actor turned spy for the Grand Army of the Republic (GAR), which Edmonds pronounced 'a low quality of fiction', was published in 1862. Written by her friend Ferdinand L. Sarmiento, it dramatized Cushman's operations as an intelligence agent for the Union Army, gathering information about enemy fortifications and operations, under cover of her reputation as 'a die-hard secessionist'.[31] Edmonds' may have regarded Cushman as something of a literary rival since she also served as a federal courier whose work took her through Kentucky, Tennesse, northern Georgia, Alabama and Mississippi.[32]

In the same year Madeline Moore's 'perilous adventures and hair-breadth escapes' as a GAR soldier were featured in *The Lady Lieutenant* and widely read, while Velazquez waited until 1876 to publish her account of fighting with the Confederates, *The Woman in Battle*. These stories found a ready market for female readers who appreciated heroines who had trespassed into forbidden spheres of action. Cushman's biographer regarded her military experience as proof that 'it is neither unladylike nor inelegant to serve one's country, or to overstep the ordinary rules of conventionalism in behalf of our glorious Union and its brave supporters'.[33] Female readers awaiting their husbands' return, enduring the privations of

war, or restless with their own desires to enter the fray, could live
out a particular fantasy.

Although the Civil War heroines might be passing as men,
their authors often downplayed their masquerade. Edmonds self-
consciously concealed her disguise until halfway through the book,
presumably to lend credibility to the Union cause. Describing
the battle of Bull Run where the Army of the Potomac met the
Confederate forces for the first time on 21 July 1861, Edmonds
wrote, 'Col. R's wife … Mrs. B. and myself were, I think, the
only three females.'[34] This was one of several instances where she
obscures her identity as Frank Thompson. To reinforce this sleight
of hand, Edmonds describes Mrs B. as her constant companion
when, in fact, she would admit to missing female friends while in
the army.[35] But however carefully she explained or obscured her
male identity, Edmonds' behaviour proved controversial.

Edmonds opened *Nurse and Spy* exclaiming that 'patriotism was
the grand secret' of her success and that:

> it makes little difference what costume [a woman] assumes
> while in the discharge of her duties – perhaps she should have
> the privilege of choosing for herself whatever may be the surest
> protection from insult and inconvenience in her blessed, self-
> sacrificing work.[36]

Costume, however, made an enormous difference to a woman's
'blessed' work. Years later Edmonds, no longer concerned with
claiming patriotism as her motive for passing, acknowledged the
'freedom and glorious independence of masculinity' that trousers
afforded her.[37] Yet her memoir advocates that women send their
lovers skirts and crinolines until they enlist, accompanied by a note
as follows:

> We send you the buttonless garments of women!
> Cover your face lest it freckle or tan!
> Muster the apron-string guards on the common
> That is the corps of the sweet little man.[38]

The irony escaped Edmonds that her poem equates female clothing and behaviour with weakness in a classic shaming strategy. While many of her female readers could not enlist themselves, they could surely insist their men honour this masculine calling. Edmonds herself argued that a woman's nature made her inherently more suitable for nursing – an extension of the domestic sphere – but celebrated her own masculine adventures.

Contemporary accounts of passing warrior women simultaneously recorded their experiences while revealing women's hidden desires. For some readers these figures were, no doubt, erotic fantasies and reflected the ways in which women of the labouring classes found spaces to enact their fantasies. As the English writer A. J. Munby observed, women embodied male roles as a form of street theatre or in private venues for their own entertainment.

On a frozen evening walk through London to Walworth along Blackfriars road in January 1861, Munby passed the Surrey Gardens where he recorded that among 150 shopmen, milliners and 'loose-women' gathered there, he deemed the best dressed woman wore a jacket, trousers and a cap.[39] In Camberwell, London in 1862, Munby encountered a military volunteer he mistook for a man until someone called her Jenny.[40] At a Derby Day ball that summer, Munby observed that more than half the women 'were in male clothing – as sailors, highlanders or swells'. Dressed as men they swore freely and were 'slapped around and pulled about in unfeminine ways'. Munby spoke to a woman drinking at the tavern bar alongside the men, sporting a sailor's outfit of white shirt, trousers, and (naval) hat and smoking a cigar. She told Munby that she was a bonnet maker but, 'I often come to these balls masques and always in men's clothes because it's a greater spree. I come in a different character every time. I like smoking very well, but don't smoke when I'm in women's clothes – oh no!'[41] Here young women and artisans could rent a costume at the door for three half-crowns, drink alcohol, smoke, dance and escape life's drudgeries while enacting an invented persona. Munby, who himself followed news of the American Civil War closely, still regarded the women in military uniform as harmless and even innocent amusement.

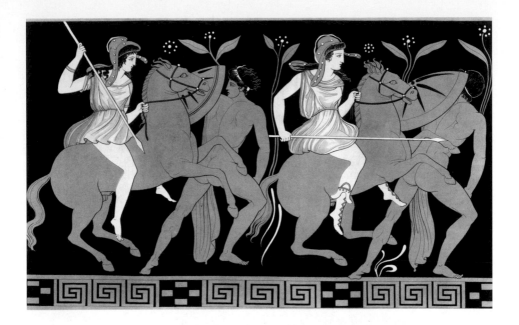

A Greek vase depicting Scythian women in battle, imagined as the Amazons. (Photo © Historical Picture Archive/CORBIS/Corbis via Getty Images)

Mary Read and Anne Bonny, pirates who joined the infamous Captain Jack Rackham's crew. (Hulton Archive/Getty Images)

Seen here as Christopher Welsh, Christian Davies was an Irish publican who became the eighteenth century's most famous female warrior. (Granger Historical Picture Archive / Alamy Stock Photo)

A portrait of Hannah Snell, who served as James Gray, in her Royal Marine uniform. (Image courtesy of the National Army Museum, London)

Mary Anne Talbot, whose adventures as a cabin boy in the British Navy and on French and American merchant ships were the subject of a popular but wholly fictional biography. (Photo by The Print Collector/Heritage Images via Getty Images)

Angélique Brûlon, a French veteran who served through seven campaigns from 1792 to 1799, including the defence of Corsica. She became the first woman to receive her nation's Legion of Honour, awarded in 1851. (UtCon Collection / Alamy Stock Photo)

Nadezhda Durova, a Russian officer in the Napoleonic Wars, later published her memoirs and was fictionalized as a heroine in girls' adventure stories, inspiring later generations of feminists and soldiers. (Historic Images / Alamy Stock Photo)

DEBORAH SAMPSON.
Published by H. Mann. 1797.

A portrait of Deborah Sampson, a Continental soldier during the American Revolutionary War, painted by Joseph Stone in 1797. (Photo by Hulton Archive/Stringer/Getty Images)

An eroticized image of the 'Maid of Saragossa', who defended her city from the French forces in 1808 and demonstrated bravery under artillery bombardment. (iStock)

Sarah Emma Edmonds, seen here as Franklin Thompson, soldier, nurse, postal carrier and spy with the 2nd Michigan Regiment. (Photo by Fotosearch/Stringer/Getty Images).

American Civil War soldier Loreta Janeta Velazquez as Confederate scout Harry T. Buford. (Bettmann/Getty Images)

Loreta Janeta Velazquez in her post-war 'female' attire. (Granger Historical Picture Archive / Alamy Stock Photo)

The Amazons of Greek mythology continued to inspire artists into the fin-de-siècle, with Austrian artist Gustav Klimt reimagining the female warrior as a femme fatale. (Photo by Imagno/Hulton Archive/Getty Images)

How the girls of England would like to treat the Scarborough baby killers if they could catch them.

An illustration from the popular English magazine *Ally Soper's Half Holiday*, 2 January 1915, depicting female soldiers with stereotypically exaggerated bottoms and breasts and tiny feet.

SAPPER DOROTHY LAWRENCE

The English journalist Dorothy Lawrence, who served as Private Denis Smith of the First Leicestershire Regiment on the Western Front in 1915. (© British Library Board. All Rights Reserved / Bridgeman Images)

The Georgian princess Kati Dadeshkeliani, in uniform as Prince Djamal, served under Colonel Khogandokov in Galicia, 1915. (Author's collection)

Emmeline Pankurst (right), founder of the Women's Social and Political Union and supporter of Maria Bochkareva (left), leader of the 1st Russian Women's Battalion of Death in 1917, believed that women's military participation was a route to their equality in public life. (Chronicle / Alamy Stock Photo)

While in her teens, Marina Yurlova served for two years in a Cossack regiment during the First World War. (Author's collection)

Marina Yurlova as she appeared in her 1934 memoir, *Cossack Girl*. (Author's collection)

The internationally famous Maria Bochkareva with the 1st Russian Women's Battalion of Death, 1917. (Photo by Fine Art Images/Heritage Images/Getty Images)

Sergeant Major Flora Sandes, an English nurse who joined the Serbian Army, sits at an outdoor café with her comrades, *circa* 1917. (Flora Sandes Collection)

Right. During her public speaking tours, Flora Sandes handed out postcards of herself dressed in Serbian uniform and attracted huge crowds. (Flora Sandes Collection)

A 1917 US Navy recruitment poster which alludes to the history of female sailors and of women in uniform being used to shame men into enlisting. (Photo by Swim Ink 2, LLC/CORBIS/Corbis via Getty Images)

Valerie Arkell-Smith as Colonel Victor Barker, who trained young men to box while a member of the National Fascisti. (Photo by Daily Mirror/Mirrorpix/Mirrorpix via Getty Images)

The Colonel Barker sideshow at the Blackpool marquee, 1937. (Philip Trevelyan/From the Collection of Bolton Library and Museum Services)

SOVIET RUSSIA *Today*

15

OCTOBER, 1942

LIUDMILA PAVLICHENKO — HER OWN STORY
CABLED ARTICLES by SOVIET WRITERS
RELIGION IN THE USSR by ALBERT RHYS WILLIAMS

Lieutenant Lyudmila Pavlichenko on the front cover of *Soviet Russia Today* during her 1942 US tour. The magazine features an article by this 'heroic Soviet markswoman'. (Author's collection)

Diana Barnato Walker, an English pilot with the Air Transport Auxiliary during the Second World War who flew 80 types of aircraft, delivering 260 Spitfires, and later became the first British woman to break the sound barrier. (Photo by Keystone/Stringer/Hulton Archive/Getty Images)

Barnato Walker's American counterparts, members of the Women Airforce Service Pilots, look over flight plans around the cockpit of a Curtiss A-25A at Camp Davis Army Air Field, North Carolina, *circa* 1944. (Photo by PhotoQuest/Getty Images)

The 'Ack-Ack girls', members of Britain's Auxiliary Territorial Service during the Second World War, broke new ground for women in the services by operating anti-aircraft guns alongside men. (Photo © Hulton-Deutsch Collection/CORBIS/Corbis via Getty Images)

More than 5,000 American women served in the US military during the Vietnam War, the majority of whom were nurses. (Photo courtesy Janis Nark/Vietnam Women's Memorial)

In the more recent conflicts in the Persian Gulf, Iraq and Afghanistan, US and British servicewomen have served in a range of front-line occupations, many newly opened to women. (Photo by Matt Cardy/Stringer/Getty Images)

During Eritrea's thirty-year-long war for independence from Ethiopia, women made up more than a third of the guerilla fighters, but after the conflict ended, many were ostracized and regarded as unfeminine and unmarriagable. (Photo by Alex Bowie/Getty Images)

'Natalia', DAMTOYS' Russian Airborne Troops doll. Some action figure fans have seen a connection between 'Natalia' and real-life VDV fighter Yulia Kharlamova. (Reproduced with kind permission of DAMTOYS)

Munby's observations from Victorian England shed light on the confusion around gender exemplified by the anomalies he encountered on his city walks. On a November evening in 1861, at a South London music hall he watched a Miss Stuart, 'dancing a Highland fling in full male costume, kilt and bare legs'.[42] A year later he observed the performance on Oxford Street of Madeline Sinclair, another Highland dancer, accompanied by an Italian organ-grinder. She appeared as 'a tall, young man in full Highland costume; wearing a Glengarry bonnet, a scarlet jacket, a sporran and tartan kilt and stockings, his legs bare from the knee to the calf.' The crowd debated the dancer's sex:

> For no one could make out whether she was a man or woman. Her hair and the set of her hips indeed were feminine; but her hard weather-stained face, her large bony hands, and her tall strong figure became her male dress so well that opinions were equally divided as to her sex. 'It's a man!' said one, confidently: 'I believe it's a woman', another doubtfully replied. One man boldly exclaimed, 'Of course it's a man; anybody can see that!'[43]

As the debate sallied back and forth, Munby offered Madeline a sixpence for her story: she had been living in Paris for the past five months and was currently at Saffron Hill, dancing every day in a male costume. Whether it confused the punters or not, it earned her a living.

Munby, who kept extensive diary notes about the lives of cross-dressing women, frequently attended their court hearings when they ran into trouble, often for engaging in petty crime. He attended Mary Walker's trial in 1867, before a magistrate 'pompous and petulant and grandiose', who appeared as confused as the Oxford Street crowd by a woman in male guise. Munby's diary entry of Wednesday, 20 February empathizes with Walker's pain at being discovered – 'poor Thomas' – a confession given to avoid a prison bath:

There she stood in the dock, conspicuous and central: and to the outward eye she looked a bluff and brawny young man, of four or five & twenty. A broad bronzed face, full cheeked & highboned; well cut straight nose, sharp eyes, determined mouth: rough dark hair, short as a man's, and evidently worn in man's fashion for a long time past. Her head was bare, and so was her strong bull neck: about the waist she wore nothing but a blue sailor's shirt, with the sleeves partly rolled up. Standing there, with broad shoulders squared and stout arms folded on the dock rail, she seemed just such a fellow as one many see drawing beer at an alehouse, or lounging about a seaport town; and it was almost impossible to believe that she was not a man.[44]

Munby's concern for Walker was not misplaced. When she appeared at Thames court a year later for begging at Cable Street, the prosecutor Mr Benson 'condemned the conduct of the prisoner in degrading herself as she had done; she had not the vigour or the strength of a man'. While Walker explained that after leaving her native village in Bedfordshire, 'the desire to act the part of a man and to adopt the garb and condition of the sterner sex grew into a passion', Benson showed her no mercy.[45] Despite her destitution, she was immortalized as the 'She-He Barman of Southwark', in a comic ballad that nodded toward Mary's motives for becoming Thomas.

The ladies like the trousers,
Of that there is no doubt.
Many would be a barman,
But fear they'd be found out.[46]

Throughout the nineteenth century cross dressing remained integral to pantomime and was regarded as family entertainment, featuring, from the 1870s, female actors in military uniform such as Vesta Tilley, Hetty King and Ella Shields performing jingoistic songs for largely working-class audiences.[47] A variation on the classic warrior heroine ballad featured in 'The Belle of Cairo', performed at the Royal Theatre in 1903 where a young woman escapes from a Greek sex trafficker by disguising herself as a butler and travelling to Sudan (a reference to the 1885 battle of Khartoum); there she meets an English officer, who falls in love with her.[48]

Lower down the theatrical rankings, the female warrior featured in parodies of the earlier romantic ballads such as 'William Taylor', now sung with a Cockney accent as 'Billy Taylor'.[49] Dramatizations of those who 'put on the Guernsey and chucked away her shift' became so popular that by 1863 a magazine article entitled 'modern Amazons' would claim that women more commonly enlisted as soldiers despite 'the rapid naval promotion of the female sailor with which we are all familiar through ballad.'[50] The on-stage performers enacted the known experiences of military women alongside their sisters who belonged to more fantastic realms.

Despite such rich traditions, the female warrior was about to face a challenge. While she would appear on theatrical billings as a bit of fun for the family, military historians and writers, concerned about her suitability for middle-class young women, began to regard her more critically. News or magazine reports began to suggest the passing female warriors were archaic creatures rather than romantic models of patriotism or citizenship. Popular accounts often hid traits that, as the century progressed, seemed to clash with new codes of feminine behaviour to which women of all classes were expected to aspire.

A contemporary example of such shaming is reflected in the fate of Isabel Gunn, the Orcadian who had successfully worked for the HBC and sailed back home with James, her infant son. 'Discharged' on 14 September 1809, the Company records note: 'We cannot think of keeping this Woman any longer, as she is of a bad Character, and has not answered the intentions for which she was detained.' A week later, Isabel and James (who had been baptized by William Harper, the local school teacher) boarded the *Prince of Wales* at Albany Fort on James Bay, and sailed across the Atlantic for Stromness.[51] The following year, the ballad 'Canada-I-O' was published, featuring the story of a woman whose lover threatens to drown her when he discovers her aboard a ship sailing for the North West. But the captain intervenes, falls in love with the stowaway and 'she's now a captain's lady in Canada, heigh-o', giving Isabel the happy ending denied her in reality.[52]

While John Scarth, the putative father of Isabel's child, remained with the company without sanction, his lover was shamed as 'a bad Character' for bearing his illegitimate child. The 1821 census records that despite Isabel's large family of four siblings who lived locally, she, James, and eight-year-old Nelly Craig lived together in Stromness. By 1851, Isabel had moved to Hellyhole Street and is listed in the census as a 'stocking knitter', a euphemism for a sex worker. Ten years later she appears at Main Street south end, where her death was recorded on 7 November 1861.[53]

At the Selkirk settlement on Red River, Manitoba, the settlers knew of this Orcadian woman who had birthed the first white child in the West. John Scarth's friend Donald Murray claimed that back in Orkney, Isabel 'became, with her daughter [perhaps a reference to Nelly Craig], public characters and were known as vagrants under the name of the "Nor-westers"'.[54] Later versions suggest that Isabel was a witch who sold 'love-philters [potions] and charms to the young men and maidens of the country-side' or was the daughter of Bessie Millie, the witch of Walter Scott's novel *The Pirate*, who sold good winds to sailors.[55] These retellings of Isabel's story cite her power in the supernatural while diminishing her achievements of canoeing, while pregnant, on six trips inland covering 1,800 miles and working, as trapper Peter Fidler, recorded in 1808, 'at anything and well like the rest of the men.'[56]

The process by which Isabel Gunn was mythologized suggests how, increasingly, passing women's success in masculine occupations clashed with emerging concepts of femininity. The warrior heroine's exploits also became an uncomfortable reminder that women, whether supplying services or active in combat, were often present in wars. As military services were increasingly professionalized in British forces from the mid-century, the old tales of passing soldiers and sailors were held up as counter-examples. Writer Menie Muriel Dowie, whose travelogue, *A Girl in the Karpathians* (1891), featured an illustration of her wearing trousers, a vest and man's jacket, also introduced a volume on adventurous women in which she argues that female cross-dressing was passé. Despite Dowie's masculine 'Karpathian costume', Victorian women, she claimed, could now adventure in 'the cold seriousness of skirts' and that equality between the sexes rendered male disguise redundant. She was, she wrote, 'not a woman's rights woman in the aggressive sense ... I do not rejoice in ugly clothes ... and I am not desirous of reforming the world or doing anything subversive.'[57] Such ambiguity is evident in other published collections which feature female warriors from this period.

An early example is James Caulfield's two-volume set of 'remarkable persons' that included, along with famous murderers, conjurers and thieves, potted biographies of the famous female warriors. Christian Davies, Hannah Snell, (the possibly fictional) sailor Anne Mills and pirates Mary Read and Anne Bonny, all featured as women who 'pleaded the tender passion as an apology for assuming masculine pursuits and habits.'[58] Even Mills, whom Caulfield claims was famous for decapitating a French sailor and keeping his head as a trophy, enlisted to 'follow the fortune of a favourite lover who had gone to sea.'[59] While these writers strained to ascribe their heroines with acceptable motives such as romance, their readers were invited to celebrate their unfeminine achievements – their 'female masculinity'.[60]

By 1824, *The Soldier's Companion; or, Martial Recorder* recast the female warrior in a softer light. Christian Davies' story appeared under the heading 'Female Courage', emphasizing her role as service-provider rather than soldier.[61] Published in the aftermath of the Napoleonic Wars, Davies' masculine authority and boisterous self-confidence are muted as the spotlight turns on exemplary wives and mothers who perform a national sacrifice under hazardous conditions. The stories simultaneously acknowledged women warriors' presence in the British Army and Royal Navy while narrowing their reasons for enlisting to love of a man and love of country.

Among other military wives that *The Soldier's Companion* singled out for honour was 'Frederica of Waterloo' who accompanied her husband, McMullen, on to the battlefield and 'whilst employed in the offices of mercy to a wounded comrade received a wound in the leg.'[62] McMullen lost both of his arms but survived and the couple returned to London where they recovered from their wounds and where Frederica gave birth to a daughter. The Duke of York, touched by the story, 'gave to the infant his own name', but his tiny namesake did not survive.[63] These stories grew in popularity, reflecting the reality of military wives caught up in conflicts who, like so many others who had gone before, slipped from serving their men to bearing arms.

English travel writer Sir John Carr varied the theme of the woman caught up in the thick of battle by happenstance with his description of Augustina Saragossa who fought against the French. When Napoleon sent troops into Spain in 1808, only the city of Saragossa stood against them and 'the Maid of Zaragossa' became an emblem of its resistance; from June to August the city was besieged and its irregulars engaged in street fighting to defeat the French. Brigadier-General Doyle, an Irish officer in the Spanish Army, introduced Carr to Augustina, the heroine, in a local café where the writer recorded their exchange. Carr's description emphasizes the physical beauty of this 'lower class' twenty-three-year-old Spaniard, noting her 'light olive complex' and 'her countenance soft and pleasing', and that 'her manners, which were perfectly feminine, were easy and engaging'. Her medals testified to her 'brilliant exploits' about which she was modest, preferring to describe her comrades' bravery.[64] During the worst fighting, she had snatched a burning match from a dying soldier's hand and fired off a twenty-six-pound cannon. Augustina had been seen fighting in the streets, 'with a knife or sabre in her hand, and her mantilla wrapt around her body, cheering and animating the soldiers by her example'.[65] Like the British female soldiers during the American Revolution, Augustina's trespass could be accommodated since her masculine action in combat was both transient and patriotic.

After the war, Augustina's comrades 'were uncommonly pleased with her', so supported her reward of 'prize money', a pension and an artilleryman's pay.[66] Although she was now a veteran, Carr suggested that Augustina retained a warrior's habits, leaping up from her chair when the evening gun was fired and when inspecting one, treating it with 'the satisfaction with which other women would speak of a cap'.[67] However, the English travel writer noted that in nearby Cadiz, residents feared that Augustina might set a dangerous example. 'There were many ... who coldly called this young heroine "the artillery woman",' wrote Carr. '[They] observed that they should soon have nothing but battalions of women in the field instead of attending to their domestic concerns if every romantic female was rewarded and commissioned as Augustina had been.'[68] Despite generations of earlier warrior heroines, according to Carr, Augustina's war record renewed contemporary Spanish anxieties about women's military role.

Thomas Carter's 1860 volume *Curiosities of War* was published four years after the Crimean War, which saw Florence Nightingale professionalize nursing services at Scutari and the Russians create a new women's nursing hospital. His military history also reflected a renewed interest in the female warrior and campaign wives, including biographies of Christian Davies and Phoebe Hessel alongside less well-known examples of 'Women in Battle'. Such popular representations of the British Amazons coincided with a period when organizational changes within the military directly affected the lives of its women. Their once-vital presence became redundant as camp life and 'official duties' were increasingly segregated and as soldiers' sexual and marital relations were brought under direct military control for the first time.[69] In 1869, the American biographer James Parton acknowledged that Nightingale's organization of medical services coincided with 'the loss of the history of army women [and] made the rise of military nursing and the opening of restricted careers for uniformed women's auxiliaries, appear to be something new.'[70] The roles that women had once performed in a variety of services for the army and navy were reduced, domesticated or excluded altogether.[71]

Mrs Retson, a sergeant's wife, who appears in Carter's military history, illustrates how war heroines, now receding into the past, assumed a feminine hue. An account by Sir William Napier, a former soldier, describes 'an astonishing display of female heroism' from the battle of Bussaco, in September 1810, when the French were laying siege to Cadiz. During the attack, when a drummer boy is frozen with terror and cannot fetch water for the regimental surgeon, a cool-headed Mrs Retson takes over. She tells the doctor, 'The poor thing's frightened, an nae wonder; gie me the bucket my man, an I'll gang myself.'[72] However, these exemplary wives and mothers remain at the margins of history, prompting Carter to suggest that, 'It was left to the nineteenth century to exemplify woman's true sphere of duty on the battlefield – this was shown by Florence Nightingale and her devoted sisterhood.'[73]

Yet in 1847, only a few years before the conflict in Crimea, claims for the general service medal for the navy revealed women's presence and vital role with the British fleet during the Napoleonic Wars. An Admiralty Order on 1 June stated that all 'officers and men present' at any of the 18 naval actions for which flag officers or captains had already received gold medals would also be rewarded. Initially, the directive was issued for anyone, regardless of their sex[74] and Sir T. Byam Martin, who sat on the Admiralty committee that considered the applications (23,000 were submitted), argued that Jane Townshend who was aboard the *Defiance* at the battle of Trafalgar in 1805 was deserving. He noted that 'The Queen in the *Gazette* of 1st June [1847], directs that all who were *present* in this action [the battle of Trafalgar] shall have a medal, without any reservation to sex, and as this woman produces from the Captain of the *Defiance* strong and highly satisfactory certificates of her useful services during the action, she is fully entitled to a medal'.[75]

However, the committee later reconsidered such applications, which were closed by 1851, because, 'There were too many women in the fleet equally useful and it will leave the Army exposed to *innumerable* applications of the same nature.' Claims from Ann Hopping and Mary Ann Riley who had served at the Royal Navy battle of the Nile in 1798, were promptly refused.[76] The comment, buried in the wealth of detail on naval awards, suggests the military authorities realized the potential cost of acknowledging and rewarding women's contribution to the war effort.

As the 'useful' army and navy wives faded into obscurity, women's suffrage campaigners would rediscover the women warriors as exemplars of female courage and physical strength. Ellen Clayton, a writer best known for a dictionary of women painters, published the two-volume *Female Warriors* connecting women's historic participation in war with their capacity to govern:

> Popular prejudice, having decided that woman is a poor weak creature, credulous, easily influenced, holds that she is of necessity timid; that if she were allowed as much as a voice in government in her native country, she would stand appalled if war were even hinted at.[77]

Clayton criticized those who dismissed these rebellious women as 'masculine' and unnatural. Instead, she argued that the female warriors went undetected partly because they were not subject to a physical examination, but 'more especially because the female soldiers behaved themselves quite as *manly* as their comrades.'[78] She acknowledged that their hard, muscular bodies and weathered faces, much like the passing women Munby encountered, contradicted Victorian ideals of feminine beauty. Clayton was determined to introduce these historic heroines to a new generation of readers.

Dowie's influential collection followed but opposed Clayton's openly feminist interpretation. Although identified as a New Woman writer,[79] her edited collection acknowledged the significance of characters like Christian Davies and Hannah Snell but warned her female readers against emulating them. 'It is difficult to take them seriously, these ladies of the sabre,' she wrote. 'They are to me something of a classic jest: their day is done, their histories forgotten, their devotion dead, and they have left us no genuine descendants.'[80] Modern 'ladies' should follow Florence Nightingale's lead in identifying appropriate roles for women in war.

Dowie's claim that the ancient viragos left 'no genuine descendants' was contradicted by accounts of passing women and female warriors who would remain a British newspaper staple for many more decades. Munby's article in *Notes and Queries* from 1881 suggests their prevalence, providing sixteen contemporary examples of modern equivalents and 'scores' of women who worked in male clothing as bricklayers, grooms, navvies and at other occupations.[81] Munby had impeccable sources, culled from newspaper reports collected by the Romeike and Curtice Press Cutting and Info Agency on the subject throughout the 1880s and 1890s.[82] While Munby celebrated labouring women, often photographing and questioning them about their work, Dowie advised her readers that women 'do well to keep to their own clothes. An air of masculinity, however slight, goes against the woman who would be successful in the public eye.'[83] Presumably Dowie's readers understood the class implications of the passing woman's displays of 'masculinity', especially in a military context.

Leslie Stephen, editor of the Dictionary of National Biography, shared Dowie's disregard for the ancient viragos, writing in 1888 of Christian Davies' 1741 biography: 'the book is uniformly disfigured by the revolting details of many unseemly and brutal acts, related in a tone of self-glorification which is suggestive of nothing so much as an unsexed woman.'[84] The historian George Trevelyan pencilled this comment in his copy of Davies' biography: 'There are many next to incredible things in the narrative and the Dictionary of National Biography holds it as untrue – in everything except that she *was* a female soldier and died in 1739 of which there is external evidence.'[85]

Despite such scepticism, British antiquarian booksellers swapped details of chapbook heroines and the faded news cuttings which inspired them. William J. Thomas, an expert on centenarians, replied to a reader's inquiry of 1873 to *Notes and Queries* about Phoebe Hessel, that he had 'often been addressed privately' about her life with much discussion about whether, or not, she died aged 108.[86] Mr Thomas confirmed that Hessel's claim to surviving 108 years was 'unproved'.[87] An 1892 *Daily Telegraph* article about Hannah Snell sparked a debate about her military career, with one reader claiming she was 'an impostor [who] never was in either the army or the navy.'[88] Stories of female combatants that filtered back from the American Civil War were also regarded with scepticism, with Munby commenting on his indifference to the subject: 'Politeness forbids me to answer.'[89] That the female warrior heroines still generated debate within the pages of widely circulated magazines throughout the nineteenth century suggests their enduring public fascination.

In a period of rapid European imperial expansion, readers were also offered travellers' accounts of female warriors from exotic lands. These writers viewed 'masculine' women through an imperial lens as they struggled to interpret radically different cultural practices. A traveller who observed female combatants in Africa wrote in an 1872 magazine article entitled 'What Can Women Do?' that 'Some of the African potentates have Amazonian armies and Mrs. [Anna] Leonowens, in her recent interesting account of her governess-experience at the Court of Siam makes frequent mention of the body-guard of Amazons at the Palace.'[90] Leonowens' memoir *The English Governess at the Siamese Court* (1870) regarded the women who cross-dressed in the Maha Phrasat, where all court ceremonies were performed, as refugees from 'the most disgusting, the most appalling, and the most unnatural [crimes] that the heart of man has conceived.'[91] The English traveller Richard Francis Burton described the 'Amazonian' guards of the West African King of Dahomey in *A Mission to Gelele, King of Dahome* (1864) while John Duncan's *Travels in Western Africa* (1847) included 'pictures' and Frederick Edwyn Forbes noted how they wore 'the dress of a soldier ... a dress, short trousers, and skull-cap'.[92] Munby himself wrote about a Crystal Palace exhibition in 1893 of thirty-seven female soldiers that the French had taken prisoner in Dahomey.[93] Reports of these extraordinary women, who were in reality not royal wives but the army's *corps d'elite* and often independent traders, were all written by foreign men at a time when European armies were employed to establish new empires.[94] Powerful women were still framed through classical Amazonian mythology as writers puzzled over the African warriors they had observed.

By the early twentieth century, while most British middle-class readers would regard the woman warrior as little more than an ancient myth, a music hall trope or an exotic species, she was about to reclaim her place in the public consciousness. Author A. R. Hope Moncrieff, writing in 1913 about women's place in the military, summed up this attitude: 'In our day a certain ridicule attaches itself to the character of a woman in arms, made admirable only by such religious enthusiasms as inspired Joan of Arc.'[95] Ironically, it was through the engines of both the nationalist military glory of the Great War and the women's suffrage movement that such 'characters' found a new place of honour.

The First World War and the New Women

The female combatants who featured in Western press reports during, and after the war, remained a crucible for a public conversation about women's role in combat. They became inspirational figures for other women as examples of heroism, and even roused a few to attempt to enlist. British and North American news reports of women participating in foreign conflicts raised public awareness, showing that while these female warriors remained exceptional, they proved women's capability in combat.

Despite the eventual defeat of the 1st Russian Women's Battalion's at the final Russian offensive – six were killed and thirty wounded – women confined to traditional non-combatant services appreciated that it proved women's ability to fight. An American woman working at a Red Cross night canteen in Beauvois on the Western Front in 1918 fantasized about forming her own women's battalion. 'Oh [war's] a wretched business,' she wrote, 'but my fighting blood is up and I'd give anything if I could be a man.'[96] The women in her camp ran an efficient lorry depot for six months until the Red Cross administration sent a series of inexperienced and incompetent male supervisors. 'I wish I could form a "Legion of Death",' she wrote in a letter home, reflecting on her frustration.[97] Fascinated onlookers assumed that the Russian female soldiers had been granted the equality that seemed to elude women working in auxiliary services elsewhere.

However, Florence Farmborough, the English Red Cross nurse stationed at the Galician front in 1917, was disappointed by the Women's Battalion's mixed success on the battlefield. The 'deep impression' it had originally made on Farmborough melted away with reports of women's terror. Farmborough had noted in her diary that when someone read aloud a Moscow newspaper report about Bochkareva around a campfire near a Romanian village, 'we sisters, of course, were thrilled to the core'. When she nursed wounded female soldiers two weeks later, however, Farmborough was disheartened when she learned that a few had cowered in the trenches, 'fainting and hysterical' or crawled back into the rear. 'Bochkareva retreated with her decimated battalion,' she wrote. 'She was wrathful, broken-hearted but she had learnt a great truth. Women were quite unfit to be soldiers.'[98]

If the 1st Russian Women's Battalion would suffer a blow after its engagement on the Russian Western Front, Flora Sandes' combined roles of nurse and soldier continued to inspire the British nurses she met in Serbia. Ishobel Ross, working with the Scottish Women's Hospitals, wrote of her first meeting with Sandes at Ostrovo, Serbia in September 1916: 'We [nurses] felt so proud of her and her bravery.'[99] The *Nursing Times* commented on Sandes' enlistment, 'we have always thought women would do invaluable work in the Army Service Corps. This proves it.'[100] When Red Cross nurse Elsie Corbett was having a difficult time setting up a hospital in Leskovatz in October 1918, she 'kept on wondering what Florence Nightingale or Flora Sandes would have done.'[101]

Perhaps it was this same admiration that brought women to hear Sandes while on her Australian tour to raise funds for Serbia in 1920 where she was often feted by charitable women's groups such as the Soldiers' and Sailors' Mothers' and Wives' Association, the Red Cross and local sewing circles. In Coffs Harbour, New South Wales, Sandes inspected a local hospital where admiring nurses took her photo and where 'lady war workers' held a dinner in her honour.[102] A largely female audience gathered to hear the 'lady sergeant' when she spoke in Sydney and in Brisbane while newspapers advertised her talk in the 'Women's Realm' and 'Women's World' sections.[103] Fundraising was an acceptable role for a middle-class lady despite the incongruity of her secondary function as military attaché to the Serbian Army. Her female audience surely admired how she escaped her suburban spinster's life to become an international celebrity: despite the uniform, they embraced her as one of their own.

The influence of the women warriors' stories was also reflected in British reports of passing women at the close of the Great War. After an outbreak of female stowaways aboard ships in 1919 a Liverpool newspaper warned 'romantic maidens' against taking such risks. Potential 'jolly Jack Tars' and their mothers were reminded of the horrors that awaited those foolhardy females:

> The war has bred a new spirit amongst the rising generation. It is full of glorious adventure. … Women were imitators ever and the history of all nations knows how women have emulated men not alone in deeds of valour but in personal habits and ideals. … But there is one direction in which woman's desire has been checkmated. She would have fought on the battlefield and was not allowed to, although she managed to get to the fringe. … She has imbibed the spirit of our own gallant masculine youth and she is clamouring for an outlet for the newly-inherited spirit of adventure.[104]

Aside from the reality that sexual molestation was a hazard for all working women, this journalist cautioned them against invading the male territory of merchant vessels even if tempted by the well-paid 'masculine' occupations.

Among Liverpool's female stowaways was a young war widow who had served four years as a transport driver and found post-war life dull. Since the former driver 'could not settle again to domesticity, she pined for adventure [and] she too rigged herself in trousers' and boarded an American merchant ship. She pleaded at her arrest, 'I did not mean any harm. It was just bravado and a bit of fun.'[105] This war widow had weighed up the risks of illegally boarding a ship to find work that would replace her previous well-paid, high status job as a driver. A magistrate interviewed about this phenomenon was sympathetic to women's motives for becoming stowaways. 'The trouble is, these girls want an outlet for their enthusiasm,' he said. 'They want freedom from restraint, the opportunity to enjoy life and not to be compelled to spend their days in a band-box tied up with pink ribbons. They want to come out and be in touch with realities.'[106] Since alternatives to 'pink ribbons' were still scarce, such inventive and risky means to a better wage and to adventure appealed to young women.

The following chapter looks at the legacy of the female warriors' experiences of war, how they fared as veterans, and the lasting impact on their lives. Even where women served for relatively short periods, their battlefield exploits would continue to reverberate. Many passing female warriors were often forced to document their accomplishments to gain a pension. That fight might bring them to public attention and garner patronage via funding or book sales or performances but rarely did it lead to financial security. Often these women, like their male counterparts, suffered from disabling war wounds and developed mental illnesses. Some found ingenious ways to employ skills learned during their military services to their advantage while others became public advocates for women's rights. All were involved in shaping the collective memory of the woman warrior.

Chapter 7

The Legacy

'And dost thou ask what fairy had inspired
A NYMPH to be with martial glory fired?
Or what from art, or yet from nature's laws,
Has join'd a FEMALE to her country's cause?
Why on great Mars's theatre she drew
Her FEMALE pourtrait [sic] though in soldier's hue?'[1]
DEBORAH GANNETT, 1802

At the age of forty-two, the highly respected Mrs Benjamin Gannett, née Deborah Sampson, was proud to pass for a youthful soldier in her Continental Army uniform. Leaving her husband and three children, she lectured and toured through New England and New York from March 1802 to April 1803, thrilling audiences with her daring stories of fighting the British forces. In female attire, she addressed her audience, apologizing for her 'uncouth' actions as a soldier that were, nonetheless, justified by her 'good intentions of a bad deed'. Warming to her subject, this living symbol of 'Liberty and Peace' described how she 'burst the tyrant bonds which held my sex in awe and clandestinely or by stealth, grasped an opportunity which custom and the world seemed to deny, as a natural privilege'.[2]

With the address completed, and after a chorus of military songs, Mrs Gannett would leave the stage for a brief costume change. In Providence, Rhode Island, on 5 May 1802, as she mingled among the audience dressed in her breeches and uniform, she heard the audience swear 'that I was a lad of not more than 18 years of age'. When the uniformed soldier mounted the podium, her public were 'full of unbelief – I mean that in regard to my being the person that served in the Revolutionary Army.'[3] Then Gannett would perform with her musket while a company of officers barked their commands, and rounded out the evening with a patriotic anthem.[4]

Mrs Gannett was motivated to climb back into uniform for the same reason she first took to wearing breeches. As she admitted in *The Female Review*, she had enlisted, 'to have a little frolic and to see how it would seem to put on a man's clothing but chiefly for the purpose of procuring a more ample supply of money.'[5] Once her bounty was secured, 'A new world now opened to my view, the objects of which seemed as important as the transition before seemed unnatural.'[6] In her uniform she could exercise not only her musket but her intellect. As the Honourable Peter Force of Washington, DC wrote of her, 'she conversed with such ease on the subject of theology, on political subjects and military tactics that her manner would seem masculine.'[7] Gannett, 'a master of self-promotion', may have used her humble address to deflect criticism of her 'demonstrative, illustrative style' and arouse audiences' sympathy.[8] Addressing the women, Gannett expressed her 'most sincere declaration of friendship for that sex ... which neither in adversity or prosperity could I ever learn to forget or degrade.'[9] As Robert Shurtliff, she had neither exploited other women nor sacrificed her own sexual integrity with her comrades. Despite her adventures, Gannett reassured her audience that while 'our Masters' and our Lords' proper spheres are the field and cabinet', the 'Mistress and Lady' belongs in the kitchen and the parlour.[10]

Mrs Gannett observed women's enthusiasm for her speech, and reflected on whether she represented a challenge to conventional femininity, noting in 1802: 'I think I may with much candour applaud the people for their serious attention and peculiar respect, especially the ladies.'[11] She believed, 'it is [only] one of my sex who are exposed to the storm, who can conceive of my situation'[12] since only they could understand that she apologized, not for harbouring such a desire, but for acting upon it.

The retired soldier's claims to embrace hearth and home, however, were contradicted by Gannett's own circumstances since she abandoned both to undertake her highly profitable speaking tour. The lectures also raised her public profile which, in turn, supported her request for an increased military pension. Her travels enabled her to visit former officers including Captain George Webb in Holden, Massachusetts, and in Lisle, New York, General John Paterson, then a judge, who would later serve as a Congress member. No doubt these social occasions enabled Gannett to discuss her pension request, which was eventually granted in 1805 (but backdated to 1803), after Paterson had entered Congress.[13] Despite her protestations to the contrary, this mistress and lady had pragmatically ventured from the kitchen and parlour with roaring success.

The struggle for financial recognition of her military service had begun several years earlier when Deborah petitioned the Massachusetts Legislature. In January 1792 she asked to 'receive pay for her service in the army but being female and not knowing the proper steps to be taken ... has hitherto not received one farthing.'[14] Her claim was passed to the House of Representatives who granted her $34, stating that:

> Deborah Sampson exhibited an extraordinary instance of female heroism by discharging the duties of a faithful, gallant soldier and at the same time preserving the virtue and chastity of her sex unsuspected and unblemished and was discharged from the service with a fair and honourable character.[15]

On 11 March 1805 she received an additional $4 per month from the Washington, DC pension office which was increased to $6.40 per month in 1816.

Gannett, however, swore another oath in Washington two years later, relinquishing her invalid pension to receive benefit of a Congressional Act passed on 18 March 1818. Increasing her monthly payment from the following year to $8, it provided 'for certain persons engaged in the land and naval service of the U.S. in the Revolutionary War.'[16] In 1820 she applied for but was denied further aid giving her a retroactive pension covering the period between the war's end and January 1803. After her death in 1831 the pension office again struggled with Gannett's case when considering her estate. A special act of Congress directed the Treasury to pay $466.66 to her surviving relatives because 'as there cannot be a parallel case in all time to come the committee do not hesitate to grant relief.'[17] It was easier for the US government to reward an anomaly than risk setting a precedent, a realization that female combatants often exploited.

There were, of course, other female soldiers who fought in the Revolutionary War, including Sally St Clair, who died at the battle of Savannah; Margaret Corbin, killed at the battle of Fort Washington in November 1776; and a woman known only as Samuel Gay who served as a corporal in the 1st Massachusetts Regiment and was discharged in August 1777, 'being a woman dressed in men's clothes.'[18] That none of these women received pensions suggests that Gannett understood the value of publicizing her story in persuading the state to acknowledge her service. Her humble address as a member of the 'softer sphere', reassurances of her chastity and advice against women following her lead proved effective. Despite her breeches and manual exercises, Gannett had repented of her sins while privately savouring her adventures.

Gannett never attacked the oppressive social structures that motivated her passing but cultivated friendships with powerful men and female admirers. A generation later, Civil War soldier Sarah Edmonds, married and a mother, also relied on her public profile and former comrades to support her claims for a military pension. As she complained rather bitterly to her friend Albert E. Cowles:

I have thought, of late, since my health has failed me that perhaps it would be no more than right if Uncle Sam should pension one female soldier who has actually served two years, or nearly so – faithful, hard service when he has pensioned so many male effeminates who never smelt powder on a battlefield.[19]

Like Gannett, Edmonds realized the importance of emphasizing her long service record, which went without the same financial reward as those 'male effeminates' who took fewer risks.

Edmonds had already begun gathering testimonials in 1882 and by February 1884, a private member's bill proposed that Franklin Thompson alias S. E. E. Seelye's charge of desertion be removed and that she be awarded outstanding back-pay, allowance and bounty. An act granting her pension was passed in the House of Representatives on 28 March, and referred to the Committee on Pensions on 1 April.[20]

Central to Edmonds' campaign was the testimony of her former officer, Byron M. Cutcheon, a Michigan congressman who corroborated her explanation for Frank Thompson's desertion. Edmonds' memoir described how, wracked with malarial fevers, she left the army after obtaining a medical discharge which, she later confessed, the regimental doctor had actually denied her. Rather than risk detection she fled.[21] Her comrades supported her claim of serving in the 2nd Michigan Infantry regiment for two years without discovery, which was only partially true given Jerome Robbins' diary confession.

But other soldiers and officers came forward with testimony of her courage and skill under fire. In 1884 Captain William R. Morse described how, 'She followed through hard-fought battles, never flinched from duty, and was never suspected of being else than what she seemed ... The beardless boy was a universal favourite.'[22] General Orlando M. Poe wrote that, 'her sex was not suspected by me or anyone else in the regiment' even though he resigned along with her alleged lover, Assistant Adjutant James Reid, in April 1863.[23] The officials who weighed the evidence of her case, Edmonds realized, would be more sympathetic if they believed she had always been in disguise.

As her health began to fail, the pension increase became so crucial to her survival that she pleaded with veteran Richard Halsted to alter his testimony. 'Just after the statement [of evidence], "She was my bunk mate considerable of the time" please just add – But I *never knew* she was a woman [emphasis in original],' Edmonds wrote in January 1897. 'Our lamented General Poe put those words in his testimony and they turned the scale for my pension,' she reported and, on 15 November 1897, Halsted received her thanks for the vital 'correction'.[24]

After Edmonds' appearance at the 2nd Michigan Regiment's reunion in Flint in autumn 1884, she became aware that, although now respectably married to carpenter Linus Seelye and a mother of two adopted children (she had given birth to three but all had died in childhood), moral censure was never far away. Colonel Frederick Schneider noted that even though 'the slender and wiry Frank Thompson of 1863 now appeared as a woman of above medium height and had grown rather stout and fleshy,' rumours circulated about her possible sexual misconduct.[25] She wrote to Halsted from Fort Scott, Kansas on 27 January 1885:

I was properly punished for going to the reunion – God forgive me for going. It has always been the pride of my life that I had ever been a member of the beloved 2nd Michigan but I discovered while at Flint that the honour of membership has cost me more than I am willing to pay – that of slurs against my character.[26]

However, her comrades' 'unanimously and highly eulogistic' testimony ensured that the Committee on Pensions recommended her application and placed her on the pension roll, an act approved by the Senate on July 1884. Edmonds was awarded $12 per month and, two years later, the senate and house removed the charge of desertion against Franklin Thompson.[27]

Upon retirement from the 2nd Michigan, she had planned to work abroad for a foreign mission, perhaps fearful of how her wartime experiences might be misinterpreted. As she wrote to

Jerome Robbins on 10 May 1863: 'My intention is to go at once into the missionary work, notwithstanding the protestations of my friends to the contrary ... Miss Lizzie H. wants to go with me on a foreign mission but I must not encourage her for she is not strong enough.'[28] Instead, Edmonds found philanthropic work closer to home. Following the death of her children, Homer in 1871 and Linus in 1872, she and her husband worked for the Freeman's Aid Society, running 'a coloured orphanage' for the next three years.[29] After the death of their six-year-old daughter Alice in 1880, Edmonds became gravely ill and the couple moved to Fort Scott, Kansas. Her charitable endeavours, while bold and unconventional, seemed motivated by a genuine desire for public service and as a means to regain social approval. She spent her final months rewriting her memoir but died before its completion.

The publicity that came from a memoir, theatrical performance or charitable venture served to enhance the female veteran's social reputation and provide vital income, especially for those suffering from war-related injuries and illness. Loreta Velazquez, who served as Confederate Lieutenant Harry T. Buford during the Civil War, supported herself and her son (whose father was absent) with revenue from her 1876 memoir.[30] However, her story, entitled *The Woman in Battle*, proved to be controversial. Jubal Early, a sceptical Southern general, provided compelling evidence for his claims that Velazquez's account was full of 'inconsistencies, absurdities and impossibilities'. He challenged, for example, the impossibility that in June 1861 she took 'the train bound north' from Columbia, South Carolina to Richmond, Virginia, since there was then a gap in the line 'from Gainsboro, North Carolina to Lynchburg, Virginia.'[31]

However, some forty Southern members of Congress believed Velazquez and cheered her as a Confederate heroine. Early wrote to Southern Congress member W. F. Slemons with his doubts. Early, who never swore his allegiance to the United States of America, objected to both the tone of Velazquez's account and its falsehoods. If it were written as fiction, he argued '[it] ought not to be patronized by Southern men or women for it is a libel on both.'[32] He found descriptions of Confederate officers as 'drunken marauding brutes whose mouths are filled with obscene language', and Velazquez's assertion that women threw themselves into Harry T. Buford's arms 'without waiting to be asked', deeply offensive.[33] Early felt duty-bound to criticize Velazquez publicly since she was 'no true type of Southern woman'. Fearing that Early was 'endeavouring to injure me and my book', Velazquez fought back, defending it as an honest account, although she admitted to writing it from memory 'having lost many of my notes'.[34] Moreover, she argued that despite Early's indignation about his fellow officers' behaviour, it was painfully realistic.

Velazquez's livelihood, reputation and social standing rose or fell on her memoir which she defended with vigour. Early first heard about it in the winter of 1878, on a visit to New Orleans, from a 'gentleman from Virginia' who had recently travelled with Velazquez. Early skimmed the volume and pronounced it a fake. A few months later, when Early was visiting Richmond, he learned from a Confederate veteran who had once met Harry T. Buford that Velazquez was in town. Early arranged to meet the author and after 'a brief interview with Madame Velazquez,' he wrote, 'I thus became satisfied that she had not written the book of which she purported to be the author or that it had been very much changed and influenced in style by her editor.'[35] But Civil War historians Elizabeth Leonard, DeAnne Blanton and Lauren M. Cook corroborate much of her narrative from contemporary newspaper accounts, the testimony of fellow Confederates and government documents.[36] Early's pronouncements against this Confederate veteran's achievements were simply wrong.

Ironically, Early's criticism only served to boost sales of the memoir. The Southern politicians who endorsed it and Velazquez's correspondence with the press were vital to her survival. Her service in the Confederate Army was substantiated by officers such as James Longstreet, a former lieutenant-general, who verified 'that there was a woman in the ranks with us who became Lieutenant and called her name Buford.'[37] Early's criticism missed the point since its readers approached it not so much as an accurate history of the Civil War but as the adventures of an independent woman. As a result, his accusations did little to curb her popularity or to discredit her claims. Dowie reprinted it in her 1893 collection of female adventure stories praising its 'air of truthfulness which comes ... with very great refreshment to a connoisseur of the elaborated adventure of the average adventurer.'[38] Whatever the official pronouncement of her authenticity, the warrior heroine appealed to an audience willing to believe in her.

Public opinion of the Civil War female soldiers only became an issue for those whose identity was disclosed and a few pensions were even quietly awarded to women under male names. Despite claims to Sarah Edmonds' exclusivity in serving with the GAR, Jennie Hodgers alias Pvt. Albert D. J. Cashier of the 95th Illinois Infantry also received a soldier's pension. Jennie, Irish-born, was nineteen years old when she enlisted as Cashier at Belvedere, Illinois, on 6 August 1862; he served for a full three years, and was among the Union troops that laid siege to Vicksburg under General Ulysses S. Grant in 1863. In Louisiana, Cashier fought with his regiment through the Red River campaign, taking part in more than a dozen battles and skirmishes then marching hundreds of miles before the campaign ended in May 1864.[39]

Private Albert Cashier mustered out on 17 August 1865 having kept his identity so closely guarded that Jennie would later claim that no one had ever seen her naked.[40] After leaving the army, Jennie lived as Albert, moving around Illinois, taking jobs as a farmhand, handyman, day labourer and property caretaker, and even as a town lighter. In Chesbro, Albert's employer grew so fond of their handyman that they bought him a house, welcomed him at their dinner table and reserved him a plot in the family cemetery.[41] In 1890, Private Cashier applied for, and was granted, a veteran's pension of $70 per month, with an increased allotment granted nine years later due to his deteriorating health.[42] Cashier's female identity was only discovered in 1911 when the former soldier was hit by a car and broke a hip; the attending surgeon realized Albert's biological sex but agreed to keep it secret. Although the fracture mended, it disabled the now-elderly veteran who was admitted into the Illinois Soldiers' and Sailors' home in Quincy. Three years later, with his physical and mental health declining, Cashier was transferred to the women's wing of the nearby Watertown State Hospital. For the first time in more than forty years Albert Cashier was, despite his opposition, forced to wear a dress.

In long and unaccustomed skirts, Cashier tripped, fracturing a hip, after which he never regained his mobility and died on 10 October 1915, six months after admission.[43] Although Jennie Hodgers' origins remained obscure, Albert's former comrades, who attested to his bravery in battle, and former employers provided their support; none seemed betrayed or perplexed by Jennie's choice to live as a man. The GAR buried Albert D. J. Cashier with full military honours at a funeral with no family members in attendance.[44]

Jennie Hodgers created her own mythology – telling whoever asked that she had been born in Ireland and stowed away to the United States aboard a ship, then found casual work around the east coast before enlisting. There were other versions where she had a twin brother and their mother dressed them both as boys. Or, as she told her Chesbro employers, that she had enlisted with her lover but that he had been mortally wounded. So Jennie, like so many heroines of contemporary ballads, vowed to avenge his death and refused to wear female dress again. In another telling, it was her stepfather, whom her mother married in New York, who insisted that she wear trousers to secure a job in a shoe factory. When her mother died, Jennie-as-Albert left the city for the West.[45]

Epilogues for Europe's warrior heroines

If the American female warriors struggled for public recognition and financial reward for their military service, those across the Atlantic had no easier time. While the pension records of Christian Davies, Mary Lacy and Hannah Snell attest to the military authorities' willingness to reward female warriors who could prove their service records, these funds were often limited. The women relied on persuading royal personages or their former commanding officers or on finding other champions to speak on their behalf with the relevant army or naval authorities. By many accounts the women survived their retirement, often with chronically painful injuries, dependents and ruined reputations, through sheer force of personality.

Christian Davies used a variety of means to press her former officers for money when she returned to London at the end of Marlborough's campaigns in 1712. She persuaded the Duke of Argyll to compensate her as a campaign veteran and a widow (her second husband Hugh Jones, a grenadier, was killed at the siege of Saint-Venant in 1710). Despite the Duke's original reluctance, when informed that Davies was living in a 'house of civil conversation' – a brothel – he invited her to dinner. After an evening where the old soldiers 'ripped up old stories and were as merry as so many new-paid-off sailors', Davies departed, clutching a petition drawn up for Queen Anne which swore to her twelve years' service in Orkney's regiment.[46]

In her best clothes, Davies presented her petition to the queen on bended knee; it was received 'with a smile and helping me up [she] said it should be up to her to provide for me and perceiving me with child added, "if you are delivered of a boy I will give him a commission as soon as he is born."'[47] Christian gave birth to a daughter and was granted £50 and a shilling a day for life. She further supplemented her income by chiding other English nobles with reminders of her soldiering in Marlborough's campaigns. While guarding the King's tent at a Hyde Park encampment, she collected several guineas from officers without which she 'must have either perished or gone upon the parish [become a charity case].'[48] Later, Christian Davies relied on the patronage of well-placed friends to established her ill-fated pub in Paddington. Rather than being granted a financial reward for service, like so many other female soldiers, she fought for it. Typical was an incident when two veterans whom Christian met at the Chelsea College Board became furious at hearing of her increased pension. One shouted that she had 'never done anything for the government', an accusation to which she responded by cracking a wooden plank over his head.[49]

In Davies' old age, like that of many widows of the eighteenth century, she faced illness and poverty. A stranger had appropriated her Dublin pub when Christian left in 1692 to search for Richard Welsh and she could not afford a lawyer to reclaim it. When she returned to Dublin in 1712, her eldest child had died and the youngest was in a workhouse. She set up a pub and pie house there and married her third husband, a soldier named Davies, who re-enlisted in the army after a drinking binge, forcing her to return to England. When Davies' service brought him back to London, through Christian's contacts the couple were admitted to the Royal Chelsea Hospital. Suffering from dropsy (oedema), rheumatism and various other ailments, she caught a fever and died on 7 July 1739.[50] Her wish to be buried at the Royal Chelsea Hospital was granted and three grand volleys were fired over her grave as her casket was lowered into the ground.

When family or wealthy patrons proved scarce, the veterans fell back on whatever charity was available. Phoebe Hessel, who served as a private soldier, received a pension only after she attracted the attention of the Prince Regent, later George IV. On a royal visit to Brighton in 1817 the Prince noticed Hessel selling fruit and gingerbread from a house near the main road. When he learned that she had fought in the War of the Austrian Succession (1740–48), the Prince awarded her a weekly half-guinea and more if she needed it.[51] Thereafter, Hessel received small sums from the parish in 1792, 1797 and 1806 and was 'admitted into the workhouse but her spirit was uneasy in such a situation.'[52] When she became bed-ridden at her home on Woburn Place her case 'awakened the deep sympathy of the good people of Brighton' and attracted many visitors. Remembering the Duke of Cumberland's regiment, and the battle of Fontenoy, she explained away her soldiering as 'the error of her former ways'.[53] Soon after her death, a local jeweller, Hyam Lewis, paid for her tombstone in a Brighthelmstone parish churchyard, along with an inscription encapsulating her details as an infantryman. The epitaph skipped over her marriage and celebrated 'poor Phoebe' who 'strove to act the soldier's part, A female form that held a manly heart'.[54]

The discrepancy between the romantic fantasy and the often mean reality of the female warriors' later life persisted. Their moment in the limelight was often brief and masked their more difficult task of finding financial and emotional support for themselves, and their families, once they could no longer engage in professions reserved for men. But in many cases they discovered ingenious ways to forge other careers, often finding unexpected success and a surprising degree of support from friends, family and even strangers.

Hannah Snell, only a few days after her retirement from the British Navy, was granted a pension of £30 per year for life.[55] The first publication of her story in 1750 informed readers that after her unhappy marriage she was 'resolutely bent to be lord and master of herself and never more to entertain the least thoughts of having a husband to rule and govern her and make her truckle to his wayward humour.'[56] However, in November 1759 Hannah, heavily pregnant (or with a newborn son in arms, George Spence), married carpenter Samuel Eyles at St Nicholas Church at Newbury, Berkshire. The couple would have another son, Thomas, in 1763 although Samuel died sometime during that decade, along with Hannah's supportive sister Susannah and her brother-in-law James Gray (from whom she may have borrowed her male name), who contracted consumption in a workhouse.[57]

Hannah avoided the workhouse and, with a third marriage to Richard Habgood at Wickham Chapel in Welford, Berkshire in 1772, was prosperous enough to fund George's education as an attorney.[58] Their comfort and security, however, was brief and by 1778 the Reverend James Woodforde describes her reduced state when they met at Weston Longville, Norfolk. Hannah was working as a pedlar and the Reverend was accompanied by his cousin who claimed to have served with her abroad:

May 21 ... I walked up to the White Hart with Mr. Lewis and Bill to see a famous Woman in Men's Cloaths, by name of Hannah Snell, who was 21 years as a common soldier in the

Army, and not discovered by any as a woman ... She went in
the Army by the name of John [sic] Gray. She has a Pension
from the Crown now of 18.5.0 per annum and the liberty of
wearing Men's Cloaths and also a Cockade in her Hat, which
she still wears. She has laid in a room with 70 Soldiers and not
discovered by any of them ... She is now about 60 years of age
and talks very sensible and well, and travels the country with a
Basket at her back, selling Buttons, Garters, laces, etc.[59]

Although the Reverend's details are wrong (she used the name
James Gray and served for four years not 20), she is earning her
living, still in men's clothes which she has the right to wear, and
proud of her achievements. But her seventies were less kind and a
decade on from her encounter with the Reverend she petitioned
the Royal Chelsea Hospital for an increase to her pension, because
'she is now quite infirm'. Snell's contemporary biographer Matthew
Stephens noticed that the 1785 petition coincided with George
facing a bill of £100 for his Articles of Clerkship. Hannah's
daughter-in-law was also pregnant with the couple's third child.[60]
Despite George's professional standing, by December 1789 he was
in debt so concocted a money-making scheme to publish and sell
on subscription a portrait of his mother.[61] Two years later, perhaps
broken down by poverty or the inevitable exhaustion of a long
life, she was admitted to the hellish conditions of Bethlem Royal
Hospital, otherwise known as Bedlam.

Ironically, the former warrior-heroine, who had graced the
London stage with her musket and her Amazons, now occupied
a venue that only a generation before had exploited its patients
in 'London Spy' shows where visitors paid a penny to observe
their cells. The women were kept in galleries, about ten to a room,
with an arm or leg chained to the wall, barefoot and dressed in a
'blanket-gown' without a front fastening.[62] Poor Hannah, to reach
such an ignominious end. She died on 8 February 1792, having
survived in these appalling conditions for less than six months,
and was buried, like Christian Davies, in the grounds of the Royal
Chelsea Hospital.[63]

Perhaps Mary Lacy, the Portsmouth shipwright, prospered because her apprenticeship had given her the skills for a very masculine trade: construction. In a variation of the female warrior's apologia, Lacy's memoir claimed that when she collected her superannuated pension of £20 (the equivalent to six months' wages for a carpenter) from the Royal Admiralty in London, she met her future husband. Although Lacy writes that Mr Slade had 'not seen me before in womens' [sic] apparel', he was unconcerned about her former identity and they married in 1762.[64] She suggests that she modestly returned to womanhood, and through Mr Slade, found 'the important truths of Christianity'.[65] With her frocks and piety came appropriate heterosexual behaviour.

Mr Slade, however, was a chimera. There is no marriage registration for the couple but Mary did use Slade as a surname in her 1773 memoir which listed a publisher on King Street, Deptford. Mary moved into a property with an Elizabeth Slade in 1777 where the women may have passed as sisters.[66] For a decade, Mary was a speculative house builder; she grew prosperous and spent her dotage in a substantial, mid-terrace double-fronted house built with her own labour and named, perhaps in honour of her partner, 'Slade's Place'.[67] Her memoir, along with her success as a woman in a male artisanal trade, is rare, as the next generation of female warriors found themselves repeating the cycle of brief celebrity before falling into obscurity or penury.

In France, a few women were afforded the public recognition of Christian Davies or Hannah Snell with pensions and lodgings at the French equivalent of London's Royal Chelsea Hospital. Among them was Thérèse Figueur, who used her prize money after retirement to open a public house. With Jeanne Geneviève Garnerin, a well-known balloonist, she opened a *table d'hôte*, near the barracks on Rue de Babylone in Paris. Madame Garnerin, a celebrity in her own right, had in August 1802 risen in a giant balloon from the Vauxhall Pleasure Gardens in London. A crowd of several thousand spectators held their collective breath and cheered as Madame Garnerin and her husband, André Jacques, 'let drop from the car, a small parachute to which was suspended a cat'. The crew landed without incident at Hampstead Hill later that day and the cat, safe in 'its little vehicle', followed.[68] Whatever the success of the *table d'hôte*, conveniently located near the barracks to attract a regular clientele of her former comrades, by 1818 Sans-Gêne had taken her third soldier-husband, Clément-Joseph-Melchoir Sutter.

But Figueur was widowed again by 1823. With her health already compromised by her war injuries, she petitioned for a place at Les Invalides, the national veterans' hospital in Paris. However, the administrators refused her admission because she was female, even though they had another female veteran, Angelique Duchemin.[69] The city's Hospice des ménages, however, came to the rescue, recognizing Figueur's right to medical treatment and from there she wrote her memoirs, which were published in 1842.[70] Her book included episodes from her life as 'a celebrity in military circles' where she dined with generals (five attested to her distinguished service), and was once the guest of Joséphine Bonaparte at Saint Cloud. She died at the Hospice des ménages in 1861, where she had 'astonished everyone by her unremitting charity' and would later be credited as the inspiration for Victor Sardou and Émile Moreau's 1893 play, *Madame Sans-Gêne*.[71]

During Napoleon's reign, more women served in the French military than ever before, the vast majority as sutlers, or *vivandières*, with many from occupied foreign territories. The *vivandières*, who were responsible for procuring supplies and providing services such as laundry, mending and cooking, often crossed the line to fight with a musket or sword alongside their men.[72] Figueur as a *femme soldat* was exceptional and even more so as a memoirist of her experiences. In the post-war period the genre of life-writing flourished, imbued with Romantic notions of the individual and a turn towards reflection.[73] This outpouring, however, was dominated by male publishers and writers who considered women's opinions on history or politics an act of 'appropriating male experience', so female accounts were relatively rare.[74]

Regula Engle was among those who managed to publish their accounts of the Napoleonic Wars. Her memoir *L'amazone de*

Napoléon (1821) found eager readers, perhaps because she defied the Napoleonic code's insistence on a 'private sphere' for women, in which transgressions from their 'natural' role were forbidden. She revealed the hardship she had endured accompanying her common-law husband, Colonel Florian Engle, on campaign over two decades of conflict. During that time she bore twenty-one children, ten of whom died, and was widowed after the battle of Waterloo. As a combatant, she participated in the Egyptian campaign, in the battle of Marengo, in Italy, and at Waterloo, following Napoleon to Elba during his first exile.[75]

Another wife-turned-soldier who gained notoriety was the Prussian Madame de Xaintrailles, née Marie Henriette Heineken, who, in 1791, became the common-law spouse of Charles-Dominique de Lauthier de Xaintrailles, a French officer stationed in Germany. The following year she accompanied him to the 6th Battalion of Light Infantry in the Army of the Rhine and was later appointed as his unofficial aide-de-camp. Two years after Madame Xaintrailles was forced to leave the military in the 1793 purge of female soldiers, she re-enlisted, possibly with the support of Lazare Carnot, the former Minister of War and member of the Directory government. After she separated from Charles-Dominique in 1798, she remained with the armies, serving as aide-de-camp to General Menou during the Egyptian campaign.[76]

Madame Xaintrailles was seriously wounded in 1779 and retired from the military in 1801. An account of a masonic lodge, *Les Frères Artistes*, where she was given a *fête d'Adoption* [initiation ceremony], lent veracity to her account, and demonstrated her comrades' respect for her:

> Among the visitors who were waiting in the ante-chamber [to the lodge] was a young officer in the uniform of a major of cavalry. He was asked for his certificate. After hesitating for a moment, he handed a folded paper to the senior Deacon, who, without opening it, proceeded to take it to the Orator. This paper was an aide-de-camp's commission issued to Madame de [sic] Xaintrailles, wife of the general of that name, who, like

the Desmoiselles de Fernig and other Republican heroines, had distinguished herself in the wars of the sword. When the Orator read to the lodge contents of the commission the astonishment was general. They grew excited and it was decided unanimously that the bearer should be admitted at once to the order. Madame Xaintrailles was acquainted with the decision of the lodge and asked if she would accept the hitherto unprecedented favour. Her reply was in the affirmative. 'I am a man for my country,' she said, 'I will be a man for my Brethren.' The initiation took place, and from that time Madame de [sic] Xaintrailles often assisted in the work of the lodge.[77]

The lodge provided access to a powerful network of generals who were potential allies in her fight for a military pension. In 1804 Madame Xaintrailles wrote to Napoleon I, pleading for either financial support (she had been badly injured after falling from her horse during the Egyptian campaign), or a job. 'Sire, it was not, in any manner of speaking, as a woman that I went to war,' she wrote to the Emperor, 'I made war as a soldier.' Without an official dossier, the French military clerks questioned her service record and assumed 'she was just another [general's] wife'. Her struggle with the civil service eventually resulted in a 2,400 livres settlement from the Grand Marshal of the palace and Ministry of the General Police.[78]

As Madame Xaintrailles railed against her designation as wife rather than combatant, she shared the frustration of many female veterans that their military achievements were ignored or trivialized. Jeanne Merkus, the Dutch social reformer who supported the Herzegovinian revolt against the Turks in 1875 before joining the Serbian Army, was equally frustrated that the press chose to ignore her political motives to 'liberate Christian people'[79] while highlighting the novelty of a woman in trousers. As the Serbian writer Geza Kon described her appearance in Belgrade:

She was a young, rich, but far from beautiful Dutch woman ... As she dressed like a man and rode horseback, she was known as the Amazon of the Herzegovina uprising. All Belgrade seemed to go mad about this female revolutionary. The poet Jura Jaksic sang, 'Our Joan, not the one from Orleans, yet her equal, as pure as an angel.'[80]

On Palm Sunday an evening torchlight procession was held in her honour. According to one observer, when Merkus appeared on a hotel balcony, a Montenegrin cap covering her large mop of blond hair, she 'caused more excitement than if Peko Pavlović [leader of the revolt] had turned up in person'.[81] Even though Merkus supported the revolutionary cause, according to Kon, it was her exotic blondeness that held the crowd's attention.

The female veterans of the nineteenth century who have left accounts describe feeling diminished, and estranged from male fellowship. Nadezhda Durova, four decades after retiring from the Russian light cavalry, would remember her shock in 1816 when, stripped of her officers' identity, she dressed again in civilian clothes. '[T]he first sentry I passed did not come to attention … as he was supposed to at the sight of an officer … I could not bear this complete estrangement from the main element of my life.'[82] Fiercely independent, Durova claimed her privileges where she could. Acquaintances in the 1830s described her as a 'middle-aged, rather ugly woman with cropped hair who usually wore a frockcoat, sat with her legs crossed, smoked a pipe, chose to join the men for discussions of military matters, and escorted the ladies to dinner'.[83] Wealthy patrons often invited her to dine, not as an honoured former officer, but as a novelty.

However, while Durova retired quietly to her family's estate in Tartasan, she would profoundly influence generations of Russian women, including those of the Red Army, through her published journals and short stories. Her memoir, *The Cavalry Maiden* (1836), recounted her military service action against Napoleon's forces in East Prussia in 1807, in the 1812 invasion and in the European campaign of 1813–14. Durova provided exquisite reflections on the dilemmas of the female warrior. By the 1860s, women campaigning to participate in reforms to the 'Woman

Question' during Tsar Alexander II's reign sought out the Calvary Maiden in Tartasan.[84] After her death in 1866, Durova's exploits were resurrected as the adventurous heroine of Lidiia Charskaia's 1908 novel *A Daring Girl*.

The life of Nadezhda Durova – the prototype for Charskaia's tomboy heroine Princess Nina – fed the growing appetite of privileged girls in Europe and America who yearned to travel and enjoy forbidden experiences.[85] Rather than the 'rather ugly woman with cropped hair who usually wore a frockcoat', Princess Nina was an appealing paragon of beauty, intelligence, bravery, talent, pride, determination and passion.[86] No wonder then that Elena Iost was among several young recruits who cited Durova as the motive to petition the Tsar to enlist with the Imperial Army in 1917:

> I pray to your Imperial Majesty to allow me to join the ranks of the troops with the same kind of noble and radiant outburst for the MOTHERLAND, with which the heart of Durova was filled and with which my own soul, filled with courage and fearlessness and unwomanly boldness, burns ...[87]

Despite Durova's dread of irrelevance, her legacy endured even into the twentieth century when the Soviet authorities, hoping to recruit more women soldiers, republished her journal during the Second World War.[88]

The First World War

Female veterans of the global conflicts a century after Durova's retirement recognized her despair at the 'complete estrangement from the main element of my life'.[89] Returning home where the public regarded female warriors with curiosity rather than gratitude, and where they no longer had the comfort of companionship or shared experiences, could be brutal. Flora Sandes captures these complex emotions and difficult negotiations in her 1927 memoir. The isolation and the loss of 'my old pals' that followed her demobilization from the Serbian Army in 1922 was vivid:

> Though still quite friendly they were now quite different. Never again could it be quite the same. As long as I had occasion to notice, men are never quite so naturally themselves where there are women present, as when among themselves. Formerly they had been so used to me that I did not count.[90]

Without her uniform, that physical and symbolic marker of regimental unity, Sandes was newly and awkwardly exposed as female to her Serbian comrades.

According to her friend Dr Katherine MacPhail, after the war, and before being demobbed, Flora strode through Belgrade, 'marching with her soldiers through the streets in the early morning and drilling them at the barracks in the fortress.'[91] Despite Flora's status as a decorated war hero – visitors frequently paid homage at her home – her comrades struggled with appropriate social cues when she appeared in women's clothes. Her former commanding officer, who lived in southern Serbia, was horrified when Flora arrived for a visit in a newly purchased hat and frock. He ordered his wife to find an old uniform and insisted Flora wear it before they could talk. 'He didn't know where he was with me,' wrote Sandes, 'nor how to talk to me.'[92]

While Flora faced a particular dilemma as a veteran in her adopted country, many other women shared her search for meaning in the post-war years. Female veterans who had served either as auxiliaries or as combatants might readily bury their memories of war and settle into maternal and domestic roles. Others, like Flora Sandes, yearned for an active life and realized that their military experience left them with 'a permanent incapacity to settle down to anything.'[93] Although Flora, in 1927, published her second memoir of war experiences and married a fellow officer, Yurie Yudenitch, a Russian and former White Army general, she continued to seek out new adventures. Before even this modest settling down began, however, she had acquired a speed boat licence, and with

Yurie, moved to Paris for two years. For a period she chaperoned a dancing troupe, the John Tiller girls, but without steady work, they returned to Serbia in a new car that they hoped would become Belgrade's first taxi. Instead, Flora worked as a typist and English teacher to supplement her military pension.[94]

Despite her wartime fundraising for the Serbs, and role as an unofficial ambassador after 1918, there was no prospect of her entering government. The Serbs may have been grateful for her military, medical and diplomatic service, but, like so many other female veterans, recognition was hard won. In April 1919 Flora was left off the army's promotions' list despite all sergeant-majors (her rank) automatically being raised to second lieutenants. Although the military authorities justified their oversight by claiming that no woman or foreigner had ever occupied a Serbian army post, she complained to her commanding officer. Eventually a special Act of Parliament approved her promotion to the higher rank.[95] As a newly commissioned officer in the 2nd Company of the 3rd Battalion, she rode with her men through Belgrade where citizens shouted, 'Bravo Sandes' while a windowful of girls – an ironic gesture Flora thought – sprinkled the second lieutenant with rose petals.[96] On 11 September 1926 she was promoted to reserve captain.

Flora lamented her return to 'becoming a woman' after her demobilization in 1922. Wandering through the streets, she clenched her fist to stop herself saluting, and restrained herself from removing her hat in restaurants or friends' homes. She grated at the passive 'femininity' she was expected to resume. Like Durova, she was comfortable with giving orders and having men respect her authority rather than making decisions on her behalf. 'It was impossible at first,' she wrote, '… to wait till I was asked instead of saying, "Come along, where shall we go to-night?"'[97] In the Serbian Army's hierarchy, she had authority and power which, when lost, would never be regained.

Sandes' deep loyalty to the Serbian Army would draw her back into the fray during the Second World War. Despite her age and being classed 'war disabled' from injuries suffered in 1917, she offered her services at the War Office in Belgrade, ahead of

Operation *Punishment* when the German Air Force bombed the city days after the Yugoslav military's *coup d'état* of March 1941. Undeterred, Flora, aged sixty-five, pulled on her old uniform, picked up a blanket and kit bag, and, after a tender goodbye with Yurie, walked six miles through a blizzard to army headquarters. As she would later explain, 'You can't stay out of the fighting – can't let other people do it for you – not if you hold the Kara George Star.'[98] After the valiant attempt by Flora's battalion to resist the German march towards Belgrade, she was taken prisoner but escaped after a few days and returned home to Yurie. On 24 June, the Gestapo arrested Flora and Yurie but released the couple eleven days later, due to Yurie's declining health. Flora's liberty came with particular conditions that, 'I would not speak to anyone but Serbs, nor receive letters (must show them to the Gestapo) nor say anything to offend Germany.'[99] Yurie died at home, two months later, from tuberculosis. As Flora wrote that day: 'At 1:30 heard a little gasp and then a sound – the death rattle – rushed to Yurie but it was all over. Yurie had died in his sleep. Could not believe it and spoke to him frantically but no heartbeat and no pulse.'[100]

With help from the British Adriatic Mission, Flora returned to her family in England via Italy, Palestine and South Africa in August 1946 and retired to a cottage in Suffolk, a few miles from her childhood home at Marlsford Rectory.[101] Her mobility was restricted so Flora travelled round the country lanes of her childhood in an electric car and settled into a life that was 'very safe but not very exciting!'[102] In a more direct moment she revealed: 'I hate old age and retirement. I'm bored to tears. I missed soldiering – I loved it.'[103]

Flora had been flung onto the world's stage, honoured for her courage and skill, and her immense sacrifice for her adopted country. As the war's intensity faded, she grew nostalgic:

Sometimes now, when playing family bridge for three pence a hundred in an English drawing-room, the memory of those wild, jolly nights comes over me and I am lost in another world. So far away it all seems now that I wonder whether it was really myself, or only something I dreamed. Instead of the powdered nose of my partner I seem to be looking at the grizzled head and unshaven chin of the Commandant, and the scented drawing-room suddenly fades away into the stone walls of a tiny hut lighted by a couple of candles stuck into bottles and thick with tobacco smoke, where five or six officers and I sit crowded on bunks or camp stools ... I return to the prosaic drawing-room with a start, and the realization that I am a 'lady' now and not a 'soldier and a man'.[104]

According to her niece Betty Russell, Flora was happiest adopting the pose of her army days: a cigarette in one hand, a drink in the other and, though wearing a sensible skirt, her knees planted firmly apart.

The conundrums of being a female veteran, however, would continue to plague Flora. At the Salonika Reunion Association's annual parade in 1950, she grew anxious about her place among the veterans. 'I'm wondering where I'll stand as I can't, of course, go with the men and I don't belong to the nursing sisters and I don't know anyone,' she wrote, convinced that she would be unrecognizable to her former comrades as 'a very old lady not a bit like the Sergeant you knew.'[105] Flora, as ever, found a compromise: she wore a skirt and walked with the nurses but displayed her medals on her chest and afterwards 'had a jolly good chinwag' with the men.

Was it the 'soldiering' she missed or the social privileges and sense of purpose that the military granted her? Perhaps it was both and, while she missed her male friends and the intensity of soldiering, she never criticized the social structures that left no post-war role for a female veteran. Amongst her possessions Flora kept an article by J. G. Lucas entitled, 'Nostalgia for War,' with relevant passages underlined in black ink. 'You don't forget learning in war that a man could love the other more than himself,' wrote Lucas. 'I didn't know that kind of living before I went to war. I haven't known it since. I miss it. The absence of it, the brutal contradiction of it in peace makes it harder to forget.'[106] These were intimate considerations and according to a close family friend, ones Flora rarely shared.[107]

But the consequences of nursing typhus patients, of living in trenches and barracks, of fighting through bloody campaigns and enduring serious bodily injury reverberated. She received a comfortable disability pension of 300 dinars per month from the Yugoslav government, which circumscribed her old age.[108] Perhaps post-war English society might have offered her more but Flora Sandes remained committed to her adopted country, the place where she had redefined herself and found meaning. Jeanne Merkus only returned to the Netherlands in old age where, like Flora Sandes, she grew reticent about her past. A young cousin recalled that, 'She was thin, of medium height with short grey hair, a sort of raincoat and a cigar! … I do not believe she ever told anything about her experiences.'[109] Perhaps anecdotes and their days with the Serbian Army would raise uncomfortable questions or memories too traumatic to express in polite company.

Old age and obscurity seem almost a luxury for the female veterans of the First World War who faced tragedy, disability and loneliness. Florence Farmborough met Maria Bochkareva, the former leader of the 1st Russian Women's Battalion, aboard an American ship destined for San Francisco in 1918. 'She has eluded the spy-net of the Red Guards and is making good her escape to the US,' wrote Farmborough.[110] According to the journalist Rheta Childe Dorr, Bochkareva published her memoirs in 1919, 'dazzled by the lure of money she was to receive from her story dictated to a well-known magazine writer' before she faded into obscurity.[111] Or so they thought.

The truth about Bochkareva's life following the collapse of the Women's Battalion was much stranger and much sadder. The Bolsheviks arrested her in Petrograd in 1917 and took her to the Smolny Institute, then the seat of Soviet power, where Lenin and Trotsky failed to persuade her to enlist with their cause. She was released, and after convalescing with her family in Siberia, undertook a spy mission for Major-General N. S. Anosov, a former Tsarist war minister, to contact the White Army general

Kornilov. Wearing a nun's habit and under a false passport, she travelled to the general's headquarters in the Caucasus where the Bolsheviks again arrested her. She escaped execution only because a soldier-friend, who had served with her in the Tsar's army, intervened with his superiors. After a military tribunal in Moscow, she was released and travelled abroad, with her fifteen year-old sister, Naja, to raise support for the anti-Bolshevik cause.[112]

The international press now opened doors for Bochkareva in Washington, DC where Florence Harriman, the philanthropist and women's rights activist, feted the Russian officer. On Sunday 23 June 1918, Mrs Harriman described the deep impression Colonel 'Batchkarova' and her interpreter made at their first meeting. 'I can't understand her Russian, of course, but I hung on her words just the same, drawn by her magnetism and the vociferousness of her gestures. Everyone thinks she rings true.'[113] The following day, Mrs Harriman escorted Bochkareva, dressed in her Russian army uniform which the American thought was 'not at all a feminine sight', to inspect a motor corps. Although Bochkareva was, of course, dressed in military fatigues, she announced: 'I don't approve of women's wearing breeches. I don't approve of women's being soldiers. They aren't physically intended for such a hard life.'[114] Flustered, Mrs Harriman persevered in supporting Bochkareva's cause and on 10 July accompanied her to the White House where they discussed Russian affairs with President Woodrow Wilson. As Mrs Harriman recalled:

The Batchkarova [sic] interview was intensely dramatic. Beside her own interpreter, there was another one from the State Department to check up. Batchkarova started off her story in a fairly matter-of-fact way; then suddenly she began to tell the tale of the suffering of her people and her tongue went like a runaway horse. She would hardly wait for her interpreter to put what she was saying into English. Her face worked. Suddenly she threw herself onto the floor and clasped her arms around the President's knees, begging him for help, for food, for troops to intervene against the Bolshevik. The President sat with tears streaming down his cheeks, and assured her of his sympathy. The little party finally got away from the White House, all very much shaken.[115]

After this extraordinary encounter Mrs Harriman 'raised a small purse' for Bochkareva's return trip to Russia. Naja was left in the care of Mrs Harriman, who organized a summer stay at a girls' boarding school and camp. While her American benefactor grew fond of Naja, her mother in Tomsk wrote her letters about 'all the fine things the Soviets had brought to the peasants' and a year later Naja returned home, escorted by a Red Cross agent. As Mrs Harriman concluded of Colonel 'Batchkarova': 'She was a wonderful woman and I was glad to do anything for her.'[116] Mrs Harriman's greatest contribution on behalf of Bochkareva's cause, however, was probably the introduction to Isaac Don Levin who would write the 'Russian Joan of Arc's' biography. Meanwhile, Bochkareva returned home via Manchester, meeting with Emmeline Pankhurst, and then London for an audience with King George, and a meeting at the War Office.

Despite such high-profile support, Bochkareva, even with British government funding, was unable to muster enough volunteers for a second women's battalion. At Allied headquarters in Shenkursk, Archangel, she descended into pathos, with one American officer describing her as a lonely figure by late 1918, who spent her days smoking and drinking heavily, her weight having ballooned to 250lbs. General V. V. Marushevskii, leader of the regional anti-Bolshevik unit, even forbade her to wear her uniform and on 27 December 1918 declared that women in the ranks were damaging. White Army authorities scorned an attempt to raise a women's medical detachment in support of Admiral A. V. Kolchak's Russian Army. A few months later the Bolshevik secret police tracked Bochkareva to Tomsk and transported her 370 miles east to a prison in Krasnoyarsk, where, after four months of interrogation, the head of the 5th Red Army ordered her execution and she died on 16 May 1920.[117]

While Bochkareva and the Russian female soldiers won international fame during the Great War, ironically, they left few traces in Soviet history. According to historian Melissa K. Stockdale, when the Soviet leadership began preparing its citizens, including women, to confront the fascist enemy in the late 1930s, it was without reference to the earlier female soldiers.[118] Dorothy Lawrence's short-lived career with a BEF tunnelling company also suffered the fate of silencing. On the ship going home after her two-week stint at the Western Front in 1915, Lawrence claimed to have met Maria Bochkareva's friend, Emmeline Pankhurst, who invited her to speak in Manchester. Lawrence was, however, forced to decline since the Defence of the Realm Act prevented her for speaking or writing about her experience until after the peace.[119] The delayed publication of *The Only English Woman Solider* also killed public interest in the subject and despite modest sales in America, Australia and the United Kingdom, it was remaindered within a year.[120]

Lawrence's brief front-line experience and her subsequent disappointment that her memoir failed to boost her career or provide her with an income would prove deeply psychologically damaging. By 1925 she was renting rooms in Cannonbury, North London, when her neighbours became concerned about her mental health, describing her as 'strange and mysterious in her manner'.[121] On 2 March she was admitted to the London Mental Hospital after she recalled a childhood trauma to the attending psychiatrist: following her mother's death when Dorothy was thirteen years old, a clergyman was appointed as her guardian and, three years later, 'improper conduct took place and continued from time to time'. The medical notes record that she 'served in the trenches for three months in France – passing as a man' and 'there is a sex trauma at the back of her mental state ... a sexual past which she dwells on with great interest.' Later that year she was diagnosed with 'systematized delusional persecution', followed by medical notes months later declaring that the 'patient is evidently blessed with a superabundance of ovarian hormone.'[122] Since the sappers who hid Dorothy Lawrence suggest that their friendship was purely platonic, it seems that it may have been the 'sexual trauma' of her young adulthood, the stress of her wartime experiences, lack of income and social isolation that shattered her mental health. Diagnosed with 'chronic mania' and later 'chronic schizophrenia', she was housed in a series of London institutions, enduring periods of 'seclusion', and died on a psychiatric ward in 1964.[123]

Although the details of Dorothy Lawrence's fate would not be revealed for decades, her incarceration coincided with a change in public perceptions of the passing women warriors. The post-war era in Britain saw the end of their gender ambiguity as a playful and even gentle critique of women's desire for masculine privilege fit for family entertainment. On stage, the cross-dressing female was regarded as sexually provocative, and off-stage she was subjected to new psychological readings of her behaviour. Women who expressed a desire for the same 'masculine' jobs they had undertaken during the war, or wore 'mannish' clothes and desired same-sex partners were suddenly problematic, pathologized and needing psychiatric support. By the 1920s the English novelist Radclyffe Hall became the emblem of this disturbing new trend; her male dress symbolized assertiveness, modernity and sexual freedom. In her hats, scarves and suits, Hall epitomized post-war concerns about the actual source of women's desire for emancipation.[124]

Although psychologists had been encountering female transvestites (defined as biological women who either identified or dressed as males) since 1910, the post-war period saw an expansion of their interest. Cross-gender identification acquired new meaning and by 1934 the German psychologist Magnus Hirschfeld, president of the World League for Sexual Reform, and others identified a woman's desire to enter the military as a sign of transvestism, homosexuality or sadism. Moreover, Hirschfeld argued that women whose 'psychic attitude' was masculine found the soldier's life particularly appealing.[125] The sexologist Richard von Krafft-Ebing also linked a woman's desire for a 'male' occupation with lesbianism, although acknowledging that 'the consciousness of being a woman and deprived of the gay college life, or to be barred from a military career produces painful reflections.'[126] Yet this pursuit of masculine inclinations, he argued, might suggest a congenital form of psychic disorder.

Richard von Krafft-Ebing, an Austro-German psychiatrist, had begun his research into women's 'congenital antipathic sexual instinct' before the war, publishing his groundbreaking book, *Psychopathia Sexualis,* in 1886.[127] He cited cases of women who preferred playing soldiers to dressing dolls, neglected their appearance and dropped art for science lessons. Krafft-Ebing described such women as possessing a 'masculine soul heaving in the female bosom'.[128] He observed that his patient, Miss N., even in early childhood preferred games with boys rather than with girls. Longing to roam the world, Miss O., aged twenty-three, ran away from home dressed in male disguise. C.R., a maid servant, had an inclination for boys' sports, loved to hear shooting and would gladly have enlisted as a soldier. 'She knew,' wrote Krafft-Ebing, 'very well that all of this inclination was unwomanly but she could not help it.'[129] W., a cleaner who preferred cigars to sweets, 'bewailed the fact that she was not born a man, as she hated feminine things and dress and would much rather have been a soldier.'[130] His patients all expressed sexual desires for other women which, he believed, were manifested in masculine pursuits and male clothes. While Krafft-Ebing labelled women's conflicts about their identity examples of sexual inversion he also believed they were persons of unusual development and labelled them as 'stepchildren of nature'.[131]

But Hirschfeld, whose work on female cross-dressing would prove vital to Britain's sex reform movement, appreciated that the war had sexually freed both heterosexual and lesbian women. As part of the erotic enlightenment movement and as the World League's president, he argued against social forces and conservative attitudes that perpetuated sexual repression. He saw the connection between economic independence through 'masculine' roles and the jobs women had enjoyed during the war, and their social, political and sexual emancipation.

However, Hirschfeld's analysis had its limits for feminism. While he understood the practical rewards for women in male jobs and masculine dress, he still regarded such behaviours as symptoms of sexual confusion. Female combatants were a prime example, as he wrote in 1934:

> Women who feel an uncontrollable urge and compulsion to put on masculine clothes and to practice a masculine calling and all other members of the weaker sex whose whole psychic attitude is masculine obviously will have a particular predilection for the soldier's life which has always been regarded as the masculine occupation par excellence. It is understandable then that such women, when the opportunity is offered will seize it gladly and largely devote themselves to active warfare. We must not ... overlook the suspicion that in certain cases, the predominant motive was a sadistic one.[132]

Hirschfeld's introduction to his research on female soldiers added that, 'we shall certainly not be wrong in assuming that in a great number of these cases we are dealing with transvestical [sic] and homosexual impulses.' Cited in his study, among others, are Maria Bochkareva, Flora Sandes, Zoya Smirnova and Clara B. of Insterburg who enlisted with the army after the military campaign of East Prussia put her out of work. Hirschfeld concluded that all women who longed for 'the glorious independence of masculinity' were female transvestites. The psychologists' redefinition of cross-dressing irrevocably influenced popular understandings and representations of these female warriors. Newspapers still reported on cases of adventurous women escaping from home in men's trousers while former combatants published memoirs, and the female warrior might draw crowds to music halls, but elsewhere there was now a subtext of deviancy attached to the woman in trousers.[133]

In the inter-war period, while women passing as men might be regarded as symptomatic of psychological disturbance or lesbianism, the female warriors remained ever popular. In 1931, novelist Percival Christopher Wren won critical acclaim for his edited diary of the pseudonymous Mary Ambree's five years' service in the French Foreign Legion, bolstering the book's authenticity with news that the Legion had introduced a bathing parade to filter women from the ranks.[134] Travel writer Rosita Forbes championed the female warrior as 'inspiration for the women of those post-war years, now emancipated in large measure, [who] were still but gingerly feeling their way along the paths trodden heretofore only by men'.[135] Forbes' weekly magazine, *Women Of All Lands*, featured portraits from conflicts and revolutions, including China. 'From Lily Foot to Army Boot' identified the Chinese Army as a great liberating force, freeing women from the torture of foot binding.[136] Spain's Republican militia featured happy female soldiers while members of the Japanese Patriotic Association demonstrated their skills, firing guns at aeroplanes. A Somaliland woman shouldered a rifle across her naked chest and modern Turkish women at the University of Ankara were reported to 'have taken quickly and with eagerness to the modern idea of uniforms.'[137]

Forbes covered extensively the career of Halide Edib whose name she heard whispered at a women's raki party (risqué behaviour for devout Muslims) in Turkey. 'Hard and purposeful they told me the story of the woman who played Joan of Arc to Kemal's version of the Dauphin.'[138] Halide had left her husband's harem to work for Mustafa Kemal Ataturk's cause, addressing crowds in Istanbul, and attending revolutionary meetings in attics and alleys. She was arrested but escaped by throwing herself into the Bosphorus and was rescued by a fishing crew and transported to Ataturk's headquarters. After Halide served as an officer in a Turkish battalion, Ataturk promised that the nation's women, 'having done a man's job', should have their freedom.[139] Forbes claimed that Halide became her country's first female education minister, but when she argued for liberating women from the veil, the opposition was so violent that she fled to America.

Forbes' portrait of the Turkish Joan, however, now appears woefully inaccurate and obscures a disturbing reality. Although raised in a harem, Halide was the daughter of an upper-class Istanbul intellectual, had a degree from an American college, was a published novelist and translator, ran a salon for Turkish nationalists, and was as much a journalist as Forbes. When her journalist-husband demanded a second wife, Halide divorced him. According to Aghavnie Yeghenian, a college friend, the media's superficial portrait ignored Halide's deeply conservative politics and participation in the Armenian genocide.

Rather than championing freedom from the veil, Yeghenian described her friend as 'in utter contradiction of the new type of Turkish woman whose leader she was to be'. After two years in Damascus where Halide joined the harem of Jemal Pasha, the Syrian dictator who oversaw the Armenian deportations, she became a school superintendent. This included enforcing the 'Turkification' of Armenian children seized from their parents, at the College Saint Joseph orphanage in Antoura where her charges were cruelly treated, according to Yeghenian. 'So this little woman who so often boasts of her American ideals of womanhood ... after calmly planning with her associate forms of human tortures for Armenian mothers and young women, undertook the task of making Turks of their orphaned children.'[140] Far from seeking exile in America because of her liberal, feminist views, as Forbes claimed, Halide was sent to Malta for her war crimes and, after several years in Britain, returned to Turkey in 1939.

Forbes conceded that revolutionary armies might represent only a shallow and transient liberation for women, but British women may have found these superficial glimpses of female warriors just as exciting as Dowie's collections or Charskaia's fictionalized portrait of Durova. While girls' adventure stories remained popular throughout the decade, the public mood was shifting. A stark revelation of the increased intolerance for masculine women and those who chose to love other women is revealed in the fate of Valerie Arkell-Smith, aka Colonel Barker, who remained a notorious figure.

On a dark December day in 1929, Arkell-Smith was released from Holloway Prison. 'Determined to become a man again',[141] over the next few years Arkell-Smith moved from menial job to menial job, always in fear of employers and landlords discovering his female identity. Despite a litany of careers as a car salesman, a film extra, a salesman, and an assistant to a fortune-teller on the Isle of Wight,[142] he was often in debt and at least twice was picked up for petty crimes. In 1934, as John Hill, he appeared in West Sussex Quarter Sessions dressed 'in a brown tweed sports jacket and flannel jacket and ... horned-rimmed glasses' on a charge of stealing a purse, but was found not guilty.[143] On 22 March 1937, then working as a 'domestic servant', he appeared in a London court, charged with stealing from his employer in Hanover Square. *The Gloucester Citizen's* coverage was typical, devoting the court report to the front page with the headline, 'Woman who posed as "Colonel Barker" pleads guilty to theft'.[144] It may have been this relentless exploitation of Arkell-Smith's notoriety that finally led him to appear in a Blackpool show as himself. Under the banner 'Colonel Barker and His Bride', sightseers could 'feast their eyes' on the spectacle of Arkell-Smith in male drag, living with a woman named 'Eva' playing the part of his bride.[145]

A Mass Observer, whose comments would be filed under 'freak shows', provides a remarkably detailed account of punters who loitered outside the Colonel's Blackpool marquee on a chill autumn night. Two middle-aged women teased each other under a sign that read, 'On a Strange Honeymoon? Love calling, Colonel Barker, admission two pence.' A large woman giggled behind her hand and chided her friend, ''Ere's Colonel Barker, your old friend. You'd better go and see how she's getting along.' Her friend laughed uproariously. A girl broke away from a nearby clutch to look up at the sign and commented, 'Ay, I'm not going in there – make me blush it would.' An older woman, in her sixties, said to herself, 'Ee, isn't it a sensation!'[146]

During the season, thousands of people paid to encircle a pit and glimpse down at Colonel Barker in red pyjamas and his 'bride' in a nightgown – lying in single beds. A Belisha beacon and a taped-on cross-walk divided the floor while a description of the act was splashed across the marquee: the couple were pledged to refrain from touching each other, or leaving their cage, until the season had ended.

Billed as 'the most famous intersexual character of our time,' Colonel Barker's' popular seaside show provoked complex reactions. The details of Barker's relationship with Elfrida Haward, revealed at the sensational 1929 trial, lent the Colonel an aura of illicit eroticism. It was rumoured that the Colonel's new 'bride', Eva, was 'one of those women who like women', and the couple were treated as curiosities. The landlord of the boarding house where they shared rooms said of Colonel Barker: 'He can be a man one minute and then be a woman. Christ knows how he does it. They should lock up that sort of person, they're no use to anybody.'[147] Claims that the Colonel was actually 'intersexual' and 'the first person in the world to have the now famous operation changing her sex from that of a man to a woman' entangled matters further.[148]

The comments about Colonel Barker's Blackpool show emphasize its 'freakish' nature rather than Hirschfeld's optimistic view of a post-war welcoming of sexual differences. Its spectators lacked the admiration afforded to historic female warriors who trod the boards in uniforms and embraced their masculinity. Arkell-Smith had served in the Land Army but the attraction for the crowd that circled the pit was the lurid details of Colonel Barker's life that were splashed across the tabloids. From that coverage, his audience would have known about the sexual and economic advantages a uniform had afforded him, a contrast to the presumed innocence and gentle mocking of the wartime music hall male impersonators like Vesta Tilley.[149] In Blackpool the old Amazonian fantasy was reduced to a sideshow. As the decade progressed, stories about plucky girls in military drag began to fade from the bookshops and tabloid press.[150]

As with so many of the female warriors explored in these chapters, their real lives were often far more complex, contradictory and fascinating than their mythic representations suggest. Until the twentieth century, the combined restraints of the women's lack of literacy skills alongside national mythmaking and prevailing ideas about gender made it difficult for them to control their stories. For centuries they persisted as wondrous figures of emancipation, without the ability, or even the desire, to liberate other women from the constraints of their gender. Theirs was often a deeply felt but transitory rebellion that inspired other women to reimagine their own lives. The female warrior's heroic story, where she enacts our own secret desires, remains a potent symbol of women's possibilities and the price they paid for breaking the rules. Although the adventure stories too often overlook the horrors she suffered along with her psychic and physical wounds, it is her transformation that holds our fascination.

Chapter 8

Daughters of Warriors

Who are the descendants of the female warriors then? Why do women still enlist in the armed services, often risking their physical and mental health, and even their lives? And how do they endure resistance from their fellow soldiers and commanding officers to enter the masculine inner-sanctum of combat? After the twenty-first-century conflicts in Iraq and Afghanistan, has the presence of high-ranking female officers in Western forces changed their military cultures? What role will women play in new forms of warfare that rely less on physical strength and more on technical skills and strong psychological defences?

These are wide-ranging questions whose answers could fill many volumes. The final chapters of this book will focus on the continuities between the historical and contemporary female warriors by contextualizing women's integration in the American, British and Russian armed forces through examples drawn from the conflicts of the twentieth and twenty-first centuries. Women in these services share concerns about how attitudes towards gender equality determine their assigned roles, their advances within the military hierarchy, how to deal with intimate relationships, parenting, fears about sexual assault from their comrades and the enemy, and public perceptions about combat. Still relevant is the battle for equality where both genders are actively involved in the creation of a body politic, and in its defence. The relationship between defending one's home and country and a citizen's right to political representation are revealed as powerful and enduring themes for female warriors.

By the new millennium, women had entered front-line services in unprecedented numbers. In 2016, they were finally integrated into combat arms in the United States, a unique departure for American women. Following recent wars, women now comprise 15 per cent of active US duty military personnel,[1] and in 2016 the United Kingdom joined sixteen nations across the globe in fully opening front-line roles. Female combatants have now fought alongside men in conflicts in El Salvador, Colombia, Eritrea, Guatemala, Nicaragua, Sierra Leone, Sri Lanka and Uganda. In the Middle East, women currently make up a third of the Kurdish Peshmerga's fighters which include European female volunteers.[2] It would seem that no further evidence is needed to prove the case for women's abilities in a range of military services.

And yet women's integration into combat services remains controversial. Military historian Martin van Creveld still regards combat as 'the supreme assertion of masculinity', and war 'the highest proof of manhood'.[3] In a 2019 opinion piece for *The Wall Street Journal* Heather MacDonald, a member of the free market think tank The Manhattan Institute, dismissed the Obama-era's policy of combat integration as 'a misguided social experiment that threatens military readiness and wastes resources in the service of a political agenda'.[4] Even war veterans such as US Army Infantry Officer Andrew Exum mourn women's presence in the infantry, where, as Exum writes in his memoir of fighting in Afghanistan, 'that most endangered of species, the alpha male, can feel at home'.[5]

But as we'll see in this chapter, whether women in American front-line services and active combat have universal public support, even critics cannot deny the significance of their presence. General Volney F. Warner, endorsing Erin Solaro's 2006 book *Women in the Line of Fire: What You Should Know About Women in the Military*, acknowledges that they 'are indeed serving with distinction in an Army that simply cannot function without them'.[6] Solaro recognizes that contemporary servicewomen owe a debt to her country's historic female warriors, writing that the integration of combat services marks the 'end point for American women's struggle for citizenship, a struggle that predates the Civil War, and that is, in fact, almost as old as the Republic itself'.[7] Their expanding role in the military is an enormous military, political and cultural achievement, according to Solaro, which may explain the phenomenon of so many retired female officers taking seats in the US Senate and Congress. And yet those who serve so often remain invisible, as a young veteran told Helen Benedict in her searing account of US women serving in Iraq: 'I was [there] getting bombed and shot at, but people won't even listen when I say I was at war because I'm a female.'[8]

This chapter will provide a brief illustration of female servicewomen in Britain and the US, their accomplishments and challenges, and suggest their wider social significance. The British armed services' expansion of military occupations for women during the Second World War, which were hugely influential for developments in America, and its opening up of military operations, will also be discussed. This chapter also explores women's participation in mixed-gender units in the Second World War, and their contribution in Vietnam, a disastrous war which led to the creation of an all-volunteer force and prepared the ground for integration. It will provide examples of high-ranking US female officers' active combat roles, their willingness to speak out about the culture of misogyny, and their hopes for future generations.

In the early twenty-first century, servicewomen have also been recruited into new forms of military conflict. Chapter 9 will return to the legacy of the Soviet Red Army's more than 800,000 women who fought during the Second World War and their influence as propaganda figures in the US and Britain. It examines the historical continuities, and discontinuities between the 'girls' of the Young Communist League or Komsomol who trained for combat throughout the 1930s and contemporary Russian servicewomen. Finally, I return to Eastern Ukraine, home of the Scythian women, the origin of the Amazonian myth, and where, in 2014, Russian-backed militias carried out a campaign around the self-proclaimed and illegal separatist republics of Donetsk and Luhansk. The conflict has been described as a 'special' war that combined espionage, subversion and even terrorism to achieve its aims. Female volunteers in the campaign for the 'Novorossiya' cause were often recruited via social media sites which appealed to women in language drawn from Maria Bochkareva's appeals of 1917. A member of the extreme-right Viking Brigade describes enlisting as an extension of mothering where maternal duty extends to raising the next generation of men who will resume their warrior's role.[9]

The deeply conservative Russian propaganda's appeal to female volunteers seems to reinforce rather than challenge traditional gender roles and thus casts doubt on the argument that military participation always leads to an expanded public role for women. This chapter interrogates whether the rich history and contemporary evidence of sisters in arms has finally answered the question of their suitability and motives for going to war.

'Aren't they lucky that they can fight': Britain's Second World War female combatants

Ancient concerns about women's participation in the organized violence of warfare involving their proximity to men and their assumption of masculine power and trades, resurfaced when, following the German invasion of Poland, Britain entered the war on 1 September 1939. The presence of female volunteers in auxiliary military services during the Second World War would erase the distinction between the 'front' where male combatants risked their lives, and the 'rear' where women worked. With so many British women actively participating in the war – at its peak in September 1943 there were nearly half a million – the government obscured their role by redefining combat itself. Military historian D'Ann Campbell's observation that women would become 'the invisible combatants of World War 2' applied equally to Britain and the US.[10]

Ironically, although individual women had been fighting alongside their male comrades in combat for centuries, the British government regarded the introduction of mixed-gender units as a risky social experiment. It would soon become apparent that once again women's labour could free up men to fight as it had during the First World War. But by 1941 severe shortages led to the conscription of single women aged twenty to thirty, arousing public anxiety about morals and masculinity when three women's military units, the Auxiliary Territorial Services (ATS), the Women's Royal Air Force (WRAF) and Women's Royal Navy Service (WRNS), were vastly expanded. The ATS (which along with the WRAF was given complete military status) introduced mixed-gender units proving that, under fire, women and men could work together effectively, blurring the lines between combatant and non-combatant, front line and rear.[11] In anti-aircraft batteries, 'officers were aware of the marked degree of unit loyalty', the result of women working hard to prove themselves, even outperforming the men at some tasks.[12] Those who joined the Air Transport Auxiliary (ATA) were equally groundbreaking as they ferried planes across the country from factories to airfields and into liberated France, often testing new models.

Socialite Diana Barnato Walker, who paid for her first flying lessons out of her pocket money, aged fifteen, joined the flight service in 1941, transporting light aircraft to the Royal Fleet Air Arm and RAF squadrons. The ATA was composed of 166 experienced pilots from nine nations who volunteered for an organization which, under private banker and British Airways director Gerard d'Erlanger, recruited those disqualified for the RAF. The circumstances and motives that led Walker to enlist carry echoes of history's warrior women. Like Jeanne Merkus, Nadhezda Durova and Princess Dadeshkeliani, Walker's privileged family background smoothed her entry into the military. Walker began the war driving a Red Cross ambulance and, while ambitious to become a pilot, had only ten flying hours to her credit, far below the ATA requirement. But friends who knew A. R. O. Macmillan, the ATA's chief flying instructor, arranged for Walker to 'accidentally' meet him at Windsor Park in 1941. Charmed and reassured, Macmillan arranged a flying test to which Diana turned up wearing a leopard skin coat to impress the instructor and, soon after, she began training at White Waltham, Berkshire, 'a drab hut on a West Country airfield, miles from anywhere'.[13]

These female pilots proved their flying skills and courage as they flew prototype jets across the country – fighter planes, twin-engined and four-engined bombers and flying boats – in all weathers without radio or navigation aids. As aircraft production increased to meet demand, so did the need for the ATA to ferry more planes which became critical during the Battle of Britain in 1941 when they operated during German attacks. This led women to fly operational aircraft, fighters, which they regarded as a significant achievement, moving them ever closer into combat. Lettice Curtis and Joan Hughes were the first women to train on four-engined bombers, and by the end of the war, eleven had been cleared to fly heavy bombers.

But while the female ATA pilots would perform the same duties as men, undertaking considerable risks as they flew in dangerous conditions and endured enemy attack, they would be paid less. 'We were still considered second-class material, even though [we] were doing exactly the same job and taking similar risks,' Walker recalls in her memoir.[14] Despite her claims that the ATA women considered the pay differential 'perfectly natural', they did resent the military authorities' initial resistance to female pilots flying certain types of aircraft.[15] Walker describes the exhilaration of her job, comparing piloting a plane to creating 'an orchestra of my own making'.[16] While joyous, it was also an enormous responsibility and the female pilots exposed the paradox of being counted as 'non-combatants' even while ferrying planes loaded with guns; fifteen of the women were killed on active duty. 'We couldn't press a button to shoot anybody, and yet we were there to be shot at,' recalled Walker.[17]

The women of the Anti-Aircraft Defence also lived out this paradox. Described as evidence of 'the most far reaching experiments ever made in the British army' they were deployed across Britain at searchlight and gun stations, and at anti-aircraft batteries, to locate targets and aim, though not fire, the guns.[18] Declared members of the Armed Forces of the Crown, by October 1941, these 200 self-assured women were fully trained, kitted out in battle dress, and ready to fight alongside the men. A *Times* reporter who visited a London battery emphasized their diversity, observing that '[t]hey were drawn from all walks of life including university and arts students, linguists, an actress, a girl who washed feathers for a living and a housemaid to a royal princess'.[19] For Joan Savage Cowey, who joined aged 18, it fulfilled a girlhood wish. 'I would have loved to have been a guerrilla fighter. I always read about them. I admired the Polish and Yugoslavian girls, and I thought, "Aren't they lucky that they can fight". The whole thing appealed to me, the training, the adventure.'[20] Winston Churchill realized that for the 'ack-ack girls' to succeed, the government needed to exorcise 'the complex against women being connected with lethal work'. His youngest daughter Mary wrote to 'darling Papa' about her desire for that connection in a letter written before reporting for duty: 'I am so much thrilled by the thought of being in action.'[21] The women received the ultimate accolade when Churchill visited Mary's crew at the battery station in Richmond Park, where she served as junior commander.

But Churchill and Sir Frederick Pile, General Officer Commanding of the Anti-Aicraft Command, in their mission to recruit women and exorcise the public's complex fears about female combatants, soon saw the public mood turn ugly. By 1942, savage rumours were circulating about the servicewomen's sexual promiscuity, with the ATS, largely drawn from the working class, known as the 'the officers' groundsheets' while members of the WRNS endured the joke, 'Up with the lark and to bed with a Wren.'[22] An official Wartime Social Survey in 1941 found that men described the ATS as 'female Tommies' and 'scum of the earth', a historic formulation of the 'slut-bitch binary', where servicewomen were suspected of 'loose morals' if they looked too glamorous in their uniforms, or if too 'manly' were regarded as either asexual or lesbians. Their situation appeared impossible as they were criticized for being either predatory or passive. However, women's ATS experiences may have been more nuanced as historians Penny

Summerfield and Nicole Crockett found when they interviewed female veterans. The women describe how they developed strategies to retain sexual control when men made unwanted advances, and actually enjoyed new sexual experiences.[23] In fact, when members of the public questioned the morals of the ATS women, the men who served with them praised their military achievements without reserve and defended their reputation.[24] So while the war opened up a range of 'masculine' military occupations and trades to women, their status remained ambiguous: they were officially members of the armed services, involved in combat, but neither recognized nor rewarded equally. During the following decades, that ambiguity would remain as military officials continued to equate combat with masculinity, reducing women's historic and future participation to the kind of amusing historical anecdote symbolized by Polly Oliver, a fictional female sailor from an eighteenth-century ballad.[25]

American women enter the war

Following the United States' entry into the war on 8 December 1941, American women would serve as Army and Navy nurse corps, Red Cross nurses, and as civilian medical personnel in 'the hottest combat zones', in Europe and the Pacific.[26] While British policy makers had anticipated recruiting women into mixed-gender military units, the US military proved more hesitant.[27] In a pragmatic move in May 1942, Congress did allow the civilian Women's Army Auxiliary Corps (WAAC) to be rebranded as the Women's Army Corps (WAC), and to gain full military status a year later. Formation of the Navy's Women Accepted for Volunteer Emergency Services (WAVES) followed along with women's admission into the Marine Corps. That year, Diana Barnato Walker's equivalents, the Women Airforce Service Pilots (WASPs), was also established, recruiting 800 volunteers to fly military planes, often on hazardous trans-Atlantic missions. The Air Force became a separate service following the war and the Women in the Air Force (WAF) was created in 1948.[28]

Altogether, more than 400,000 women served in US military actions during the war, where American women faced broadly defined combat exclusion policies which were strictly enforced.[29] The Army offered them only 185 out of 482 military occupational services and these were confined to female-only units. The Navy kept all sea-going billets closed to women and restricted female strength to less than 5 per cent. The Air Force proved no better, refusing women assignments to air crew duties regardless of the aircraft's type or mission.[30] While Churchill confronted the problem by making women's combat role opaque, the American policies grew more complex as military commanders grappled with the paradox of war as a gendered activity. Meanwhile, US servicewomen shared with their British counterparts a struggle for recognition and endured public fantasies about their wanton sexuality.

Historian Linda Grant De Pauw suggests that when large numbers of uniformed women became visible on American streets in 1943, many people believed the worst about them because the military had attracted so few members of the elite, and in peacetime, none at all.[31] The FBI found that 'plainly vicious rumours' were circulating among the armed services that 'large numbers of pregnant WAACs were being shipped home from overseas' and a syndicated newspaper column suggested they had been issued with 'contraceptives and prophylactic equipment'. Although the rumours were later exposed as false, the reputational damage had been done.[32] While in reality the military kept women under extremely strict discipline, the slander continued with women of colour facing both accusations of promiscuity and racial discrimination. There was a casual assumption within the services, for example, that African American women were there to act as 'clean prostitutes' and 'afford companionship to soldiers'.[33] Despite the wartime contribution by women of colour, racially discriminatory policies in the US armed services only ended with affirmative action programmes.

When the Korean police action began in 1950, American servicewomen fared little better than they had in previous conflicts even though fifty-seven American nurses arrived in Pusan, Korea less than 72 hours after the first US troops had landed. Seventeen military women were killed during the Korean War, mostly in aircraft accidents.[34] No military service, however, came near fulfilling its recruitment targets, as the services struggled to attract and retain high-quality volunteers while ensuring their roles were socially appropriate. During the Korean action, American servicewomen had fewer occupations and overseas postings open to them than they did during the Second World War. They felt 'they were not really needed or appreciated' and 'stuck in dead-end jobs' and their presence 'a dispensable vestige'.[35] Perhaps fittingly their participation is best remembered in dramatic form as head nurse Major Margaret 'Hot Lips Houlihan' played by Loretta Swit in *M*A*S*H*, the long-running TV series that spoke to the absurdities of Vietnam.

During that war, more than 7,000 American women served and eight were killed, while their participation which ranged from 'caring from orphans to decoding body counts' has, until recently, received little appreciation.[36] Lynda Van Devanter, an Army nurse and author of the memoir *Home Before Morning* (1983) about her Vietnam experiences, describes how servicewomen negotiated being nurturing and stoic. 'Staying feminine became an impossible task', she said in a 1980 interview. 'There's a toughness you take on. It's thought of as a masculine, macho characteristic. It's not masculine, but an attitude of strength and trying to survive.'[37] Troops made sense of the nurses and WAC personnel being in this exclusively male zone of combat by regarding the women as surrogate wives, girlfriends, sisters and mothers. While playing this role, the consequences of the women's exposure to combat shaped their lives whether they were nurses caring for wounded soldiers or WAC personnel writing up killed-in-action reports.[38] Their highly visible presence would prove a turning point in a broader social transformation as restrictions on women's integration were reconsidered when the draft was scrapped in 1973. The introduction of an all-volunteer army, where women operated as 'temporary dirty workers', coincided with second wave feminism which exerted political pressure to update women's inclusion in all Military Occupational Specialties (MOSs) as a civil rights issue.[39]

The Pentagon's change of heart about expanding female personnel may have been a response to social pressure but, as it was during the Second World War, it was also a strategic response to projected demographic trends. As the pool of draft-age men shrank, women filled the gap when the all-volunteer force was implemented and, in the longer-term, supplied a stable, reliable source of labour.[40] From an overall rate of 1.6 per cent, which largely represented women in medical services, the percentage of female military personnel rose to 8.5 in 1980 and 10.8 per cent in 1989.[41] Women's active participation in warfare was increasingly recognized with the WASPs, who would inspire Martha McSally, America's first female commander of an Air Force fighter squadron, finally being granted veterans' status in 1978.[42] Over the next decades, women's participation would increase by nearly one-third, as they rose up the ranks to senior positions, took up new military occupations and, from within, demanded to be recognized for their contributions, to be paid equally, and to work without fear of sexual harassment.

Contemporary conflicts bust the myths of women in combat

In March 2003 the Bush administration launched its unilateral and controversial invasion of Iraq which the Obama administration would finish by withdrawing American troops in December 2011, ending one of America's longest wars. It had a significant impact on the discussion of women's rights, as they engaged in combat on an unprecedented scale. The first military adventure in the Persian Gulf in 1991, involving thirty-five nations in a coalition following the Iraqi invasion of Kuwait, had already tested the elaborate and restrictive system of direct-combat-probability coding (DCPC) when 86 per cent of MOSs were opened to servicewomen. However, policy insisted that once assigned to an area, female soldiers 'in the event of hostilities will remain with their assigned units and continue to perform their assigned tasks'.[43] Technological changes inevitably disrupted any clear demarcation between the front line and the rear as servicewomen experienced attacks from rocket-propelled grenades or improvised explosive devices wherever they happened to be working.

These artificial boundaries between combat and non-combat roles began to dissolve as the Gulf conflict wore on. On the ground, 41,000 women served in transport, communications, supply and even medical units, risking their lives as they crossed into combat zones to perform their jobs. But without official recognition as combatants, women struggled to move up the ranks, creating a source of deep resentment. Brian Green, congressional editor of the official magazine of the USAF, described how men keenly guarded their professional interests: 'Those with combat assignments have the inside track on promotional opportunity. Women cannot compete.'[44] This was equally true in the Marines where a soldier's status increased in proportion to their number of enemy 'kills'.[45] Nonetheless, during the Persian Gulf War a total of thirteen US servicewomen were near enough to the combat zone to be killed, four from enemy fire, including three killed by an Iraqi Scud missile attack, while twenty-one were wounded in action.[46]

Despite the military's resistance, women combatants were suddenly visible on the ground and in the media. An Army specialist from Michigan, Melissa Rathburn-Nealy, was assigned to the 233rd Transport Company when she and Specialist David Lockett were taken prisoner by Iraqi forces at Khafji on 30 January 1991. Rathburn-Nealy, aged twenty, was held until 12 March but claimed that throughout her captivity (much of it spent in solitary confinement), she had been well treated. She was the first American servicewoman to be reported missing in action since the Second World War.[47] In Britain, the tabloid newspaper *Today* reflected the media's confusion about women in combat, relying on antiquated concepts of female vulnerability. It reported Rathburn-Nealy's capture on the front page under the banner headline, 'The Unthinkable of War: Girl GI Taken by Iraqi Snatch Squad.' A senior American officer was quoted as saying, 'a woman POW is the ultimate nightmare' under the subhead: 'Allied military chiefs think the Iraqis – who treat their OWN women appallingly – might abuse or even rape the captive.' Although the newspaper had earlier carried an article urging British women to knit 'willy-warmers' for the cause (another echo of women in the home front in previous European conflicts), it now suggested readers pray for 'the girl Marine, may God protect her'.[48] Throughout the conflict, Iraqi women, portrayed as oppressed and passive, were juxtaposed against the 'girl GIs' sent to protect them.

Later, Iraqi troops captured American servicewoman Major Rhonda Cornum, a thirty-seven-year-old flight surgeon and biochemist, who was held for a week and who would testify before a presidential commission about her experience. When Cornum's helicopter had crashed, she had broken both arms, smashed her knee and been wounded in her right shoulder. As she screamed in pain, an Iraqi soldier ripped off her flight suit and she was 'violated manually – vaginally and rectally'.[49] But Cornum, who would become an expert on the psychology of combat resilience and a brigadier-general, downplayed the assault's significance. In a 1991 *New York Times* interview she said, '[it] ranks as unpleasant; that's all it ranks ... everyone's made such a big deal about this indecent assault, but the only thing that makes it indecent is that it was non-consensual.' Despite the 'phenomenal amount of focus' on her assault, Cornum diminished its significance, explaining that it was neither life threatening nor permanently disabling, disfiguring or excruciating.[50] She worried that servicewomen's experience of sexual assault as prisoners of war might be used as an argument to prevent them from entering combat-related specialisms, an articulation of the tabloid's allusion to the 'ultimate nightmare'.

Ironically, testimony from male and female veterans, as well as the Pentagon's own internal surveys would later confirm that female prisoners of war were more likely to have experienced sexual assault by their fellow soldiers. Research from September 1990, released a month after Operation *Desert Shield* had begun, reported that the majority of US servicewomen were subjected to sexual harassment. Of the 9,497 surveyed from the previous year, 64 per cent had experienced some form of harassment while 5 per cent reported sexual assault. The survey followed scathing reports that nearly all of the 220,000 women in the US armed services had been subject to discrimination and harassment.[51] Not until July 1992 during a veterans' affairs committee hearing was the extent of the problem revealed.

With depressing familiarity servicewomen described being assaulted by their superior officers, the very men charged with investigating such crimes. Army specialist Jacqueline Ortiz's sergeant 'forcibly sodomized' her in broad daylight on 19 January 1991. An army mechanic and the only woman in Delta Company of the 52nd Engineer Battalion, Oritz said she immediately reported the attack to her superiors but 'unfortunately it fell upon deaf ears'.[52] Army specialist Barbara Franco told the veterans' affairs committee about being raped at knifepoint during basic training while two other women described how male superior officers had dismissed their reports of sexual assault. As Senator Dennis DeConcini commented after the hearings, 'American women serving in the Gulf were in greater danger of being sexually assaulted by their own troops than by the enemy.'[53] According to Susan Brownmiller, author of *Against Our Will: Men, Women and Rape*, while there was extensive press and television coverage of the female prisoners of war, the US public were 'very reluctant to believe our guys would ever rape a woman'.[54]

Despite these appalling pressures, servicewomen proved their resilience in combat and swept aside anachronistic arguments that barred them from certain occupations; in Iraq and Afghanistan they were trained as intelligence collectors, linguists, interrogators and other specialties on the front lines. 'We found no evidence that female soldiers are less able than male soldiers to cope with the stressors and challenges of serving in combat', a team of military mental health experts concluded in a 2007 Pentagon report based on extensive surveys of troops in Iraq. 'When discussing the role of the female soldier in combat, the focus needs to move away from one of weakness and vulnerability, to one of strength and accomplishment.'[55] By 2008, US servicewomen were participating in battlefield missions and made up 10 per cent of the forces in Iraq and in Afghanistan during Operation *Enduring Freedom* where 160 were killed in action. An officer at the time summed up their contribution to the military as '[we] can't accomplish the mission without women'.[56] Desma Brooks, who operated a Humvee and provided security for a supply convoy, put the situation more bluntly. 'Bush was still saying women were not in combat, but what else would you call being a gunner on a highway in Iraq in the spring of 2008?'[57]

American servicemen during the Iraq war, however, continued to express through bullying, harassment and abuse their profound opposition to female combatants, who were present in unprecedented numbers. According to military sociologist Anthony King, 'For women attempting to integrate into the armed forces, it is the latter sexual categories, and above all, the slut-bitch binary, which have been particularly obstructive.'[58] Joseph Moreno, who deployed with the US military during Operation *Iraqi Freedom*, where servicewomen comprised about 10 per cent of the force, confirmed that female soldiers working in intelligence, transportation and supply operations in the theatre of war were subjected to sexual assault.[59] A brutal reminder of the difficulties servicewomen continued to face in reporting these crimes came in 2013 when the head of the Air Force's Sexual Assault and Prevention and Response Unit was charged with sexually assaulting a civilian woman in a parking lot in Arlington, Virginia.[60]

As women gained combat experience, they moved up the ranks and into positions of political power. An example of the shift in public perceptions about the military's responsibility towards the women in its ranks came in March 2019 when Republican senator Martha McSally, who commanded the Air Force's first fighter squadron with twenty-six years of military experience, disclosed her own experience of sexual abuse. At an armed services committee hearing, she directed her comments towards three fellow witnesses. 'Like you,' McSally told the servicewomen in measured tones, 'I am also a military sexual assault survivor. But unlike so many brave survivors, I didn't report the sexual assault.' The combat pilot who flew a single-seated A-10 Warthog enforcing the no-fly zone over southern Iraq after the 1991 Persian Gulf War, who was deployed in Kuwait in January

1995, and who commanded the 354th Fighter Squadron in July 2004, described its psychological consequences. 'Like so many women and men I didn't trust the system at the time. I blamed myself. I was ashamed and confused. I thought I was strong but felt powerless.' Reporting the crime to her superiors at the time would have risked ending her career.

McSally then elaborated on the servicewomen's collective experience as their reports of sexual assault either as victims or subjects of criminal investigations has risen by 10 per cent from the previous year. 'The perpetrators abused their position of power in profound ways,' she said. 'In one case I was preyed upon and raped by a superior officer.' McSally, speaking as both a survivor of rape and betrayal, and as a military commander who led pilots into combat, explained that she refused to quit and chose instead 'to be a voice within the ranks for women, and then the house, and now in the senate.' Democratic Senator Kirsten Gillibrand of New York, who sits on the subcommittee and has campaigned for better legal protection against sexual assault for servicewomen, expressed gratitude for McSally's testimony. While the senators disagreed over, among other things, Gillibrand's 2013 motion to remove such prosecutions from the military chain of command, she appreciated that McSally 'spoke that truth'. [61]

Follow McSally's revelations, many other senior servicewomen came forward to support her and to expose their own experiences of sexual assault. An investigation into Army colonel Kathryn A. Spletstoser's alleged assault by her boss, Air Force general John E. Hyten, is the most recent and high-profile case. The implications of Spletstoser's allegations are profound since General Hyten, as of August 2019, had yet to be confirmed as the vice chairman of the Joint Chiefs of Staff.[62] Democrat congresswoman Tulsi Gabbard agreed that servicewomen dreaded demotion or disbelief and so the American public remained unaware of 'how rampant [it is] in the military'. Gabbard, who served two tours as a major in the Hawaii Army National Guard, suggested the military must implement serious changes before victims could be served justice.[63]

The #MeToo movement and raised public awareness of the ubiquity of sexual harassment suggest a transformative moment. War stories where women's presence is so often marginalized, have long needed updating to reflect the immensity of their contribution and to critique the military's hyper-masculine values. Major McNulty's 2010 study of servicewomen's attitudes towards their combat roles highlights the importance of owning their narratives. 'The only way that policy makers can determine appropriate regulations for today's military is to hear from today's military members,' she wrote. 'Female service members need to write more notes, responses, articles, and books about their experiences and perspectives – to ensure that their contributions and points of view are accurately portrayed.'[64] By testifying at senator hearings, speaking in public, or writing blogs or memoirs, these women are finding venues to express their reality, even offering counter-narratives which chronicle their struggle for acceptance. Former servicewomen are continuing the Amazons' difficult and complex conversation. In commenting openly about her military sexual trauma, testimony which McSally would later describe as 'agonising' to prepare, she let slip her mask of invulnerability to reveal the painful reality of her career.[65] For McSally to enter combat – the only means by which women can rise through to the upper ranks – she ran the gauntlet of sexual harassment, exposure to ubiquitous pornography, and lewd singalongs. To survive she locked down her emotions.

But since her retirement, McSally has advocated for women's right to enter combat, a necessary means by which they can rise up through the ranks. As she wrote in 2007, 'If you want to have the best fighting force, why would you exclude 51 per cent of your population from being considered for any particular job?'[66] More than a decade later, with the barriers to MOSs now lifted, the issue of women's combat readiness may have been largely resolved. Major McNulty's study found that, 'If you ask them, most soldiers and Marines that have fought alongside their male counterparts while under fire will tell you that gender on the battlefield just doesn't matter anymore; it is the least of their worries.'[67] The revulsion at ordering women in combat, expressed by General Merrill McPeak, chief of staff of the US armed forces in 1991, was overtaken by the reality of twenty-first-century combat roles.[68] A decade after General McPeak's public reservations, American women were serving in ground troops under fire, even if unofficially acknowledged.

Despite the older generation's reservations, Major McNulty's study found that the American public also supported women in combat. By 2005, whatever the perceptions in Washington or on the home front, female troops in Iraq were already playing a unique role in the 'war on terror'. Servicewomen were employed as 'Lionesses' and as 'Marine Lionesses' in Afghanistan, accompanying all-male combat teams to search, and stay with, local women during military operations. In effect, these servicewomen were working in counter-insurgency or human intelligence operations, persuading the local populations to end terror attacks.[69] They often found themselves in the direct line of fire.

Their motives for risking their lives as combatants carry reminders of women warriors down the generations who saw participation in warfare as a civic duty that might open women's access to the public sphere. As one American servicewoman described her eagerness for battle in 2007: 'I wanted to do something important – it was my duty as a Marine.'[70] McSally, celebrated as the first woman to climb into an A-10 Warthog, known as a 'gun with an airplane attached', acknowledged the female military pilots whose work had inspired her. Armed with the knowledge that women had flown during the Second World War as WASPs, McSally told her first flight instructor about her ambition to become a fighter pilot. 'He just laughed but after Congress repealed the prohibition law in 1991, and I was named one of seven women who would be put through fighter training, he looked me up and said he was amazed I had accomplished my goal.'[71] For the American servicewomen, it was back to the future again.

From the 'ack-ack girls' to front-line combatants

Despite the success of mixed-gender units during the Second World War, British women would wait until 1973 before the army and navy opened flight training to them, with the Air Force following three years later. Enlisted women then became eligible to operate trucks, work in chemical warfare units and conduct ship repairs. The army selected its first general officers and admission standards were modified to apply equally to men and women. A 1976 report on the future employment of the Women's Royal Army Corps (WRAC) suggested that if women were to be an integral part of the army they should undergo weapons training and even be considered for duties within the Special Air Service or the Intelligence Corps. The WRAC was dissolved in 1980 and its officers were integrated into other services, making women eligible to command while new female recruits were admitted into officer candidate schools. Moreover, the bar on pregnant women and those with dependent children was lifted. But as historian Antony Beevor found, sexism seemed deeply engrained in British military culture into the 1990s: '[M]ore depressing than the often infantile sexuality which the army seems to engender in men is the day-to-day professional prejudice [with] which both servicewomen and officers have to contend ... To have a woman promoted over [a man] is seen as a humiliation.'[72] Despite changes within the British armed forces, servicewomen in the United States and the United Kingdom were still struggling for equality within higher ranks. But that was about to change.

British servicewomen in the twenty-first-century conflicts in Iraq and Afghanistan were legally barred from positions where they could 'engage and potentially kill' the enemy.[73] But technological changes and the need for personnel to operate within religious boundaries expanded their role. Although formally defined as 'attached' rather than 'assigned' to combat units, women endured the same risks as men and engaged with the enemy at close quarters. However, when four servicewomen were killed in Iraq in 2006 the British media focused on their gender, ignoring their professional identity.[74] Yet again news reports reduced these women to exceptions, novelties amidst the masculine sphere of war, their long history of participation forgotten. Like their American counterparts, however, their significant presence forced military authorities to recognize their capabilities in combat arms which marked a profound historical transformation.[75]

The changes were swift: women were serving in submarines by 2015, joining the British Army armoured corps the following year, and by 2019, they made up 10 per cent of military strength and could apply for all roles, including in front-line infantry and specialist units in the Royal Marines, in the Special Air Service and the Special Boat Service.[76] A far cry from the days of the ATS volunteers who were dismissed when pregnant, British servicewomen are now allowed maternity leave of six months with full pay, and an option of six further months on minimum pay. The policy has probably ensured that more than 90 per cent return to service after their maternity leave.[77] As a recent Royal Air Force campaign affirmed, every role is open to women, 'from spare time to the front line', reinforcing the message that 'women should be defined by actions, not clichés'. But a sample of comments beneath the video illustrates the resistance that remains: 'RIP the British military', 'women in the army so damn pathetic', and 'stop ramming feminism down people's throats'.[78]

Offline and in real life that anger is expressed as sexual harassment, with a recent survey finding that for British servicewomen this ranged from generalized sexualized behaviours to targeted sexual behaviours and particularly upsetting experiences such as sexual assault. The Royal Navy and Royal Marines showed similar findings and 15 per cent reported sexual assault, with a rate of 10 per cent in the army. Even when women filed complaints, the majority were dissatisfied with the process as many found, like their American sisters, that their superiors exacted retribution for speaking out.[79] As one woman reported on the Everyday Sexism Project website: 'I endured three years of sexual harassment from my superior in the British Army. He was awarded an MBE despite being under investigation (and found guilty) while I was medically discharged due to the mental breakdown he inflicted.'[80] Rebecca Crookshank, a former RAF member, described women's experience as, 'there's already a battle line in terms of inequality'.[81]

If there is to be real progress for servicewomen, perhaps it lies in their ability to educate the public about their job and the challenges they face in doing it. The Everyday Sexism website features testimonies from dozens of military women about how they negotiate the 'slut-bitch binary', arguments about their physical and psychological inferiority, the sexist jokes, the denigration of their skills, the lack of respect for their authority, intimidation by superior officers and the expectation that they must patrol the sexual behaviour of their male colleagues. 'MIDN' describes the gaslighting women faced at the US Naval Academy where she studied: 'A common phrase here is DUB: Dumb Ugly Bitch ... Girls here, in an effort to fit in with the male attitude of the school, just laugh it off and readily admit they are DUBS.' Jenn writes that, 'I am in the military and I have been told ... – Get back in the kitchen. – Why doesn't your husband control you. – If you were my women I would take you behind the wood shed. – I was told I needed a "good man" to fix me ... as in teach me not to disagree with a man.'[82] The website is full of such reports from women who endure the institutions' misogyny but realize the damage it does to their sense of self-worth and opportunities for developing their careers.

The ancient narratives of war are being rewritten by female fighters across the globe, including those who have risen to the highest ranks and entered politics, and their effects are being felt. But progress will never be straightforward, especially in an era when, as the complex narratives of Diana Walker, Brigadier-General Rhonda Cornum, senator Martha McSally or the chorus of voices from the Everyday Sexism website remind us, war stories are intimately bound to concepts of ideology and ultimately belong to the victors of those conflicts.

Chapter 9

Komsomol Girls to Facebook Icons

Russian women soldiers

*'Soviet literature talks about children as pioneer heroes or sons
of the regiment. There is a male culture which legitimises war.
My idea was to write a book in such a way that even generals
would feel disgusted by the idea of war. War is a monstrosity,
a form of cannibalism.'*[1]
SVETLANA ALEXIEVICH, 2019

In 1942, Lyudmila Pavlichenko, following in Maria Bochkareva's
footsteps, became Russia's latest 'Guerrilla queen' to encounter
the West. Wearing a spanking-new uniform, she was feted in
Britain, Canada and the US, at sites of bomb damage, factories
and shipyards, entertained at the White House and at Whitehall,
and addressed thousands at public events. But while Bochkareva
had been privately sponsored by women's rights activists such
as Florence Harriman and Emmeline Pankhurst, Lieutenant
Pavlichenko, a twenty-six-year-old front-line sniper, represented
the Soviet state. Although the press had long forgotten the Women's
Battalion of Death, Pavlichenko's arrival in Washington, DC
coincided with a historic moment of American-Soviet friendship.[2]
Her audiences, although curious and affectionate towards her
motherland, found the female sniper, with her tally of 309 German
kills, rather shocking. She sneered at questions about make-up and
clothes, questioned why women factory workers were paid less than

men, and protested when barred from boarding a British naval warship. This was the new model of liberated Soviet womanhood whose front-line experience had earned her the right to such plain speaking.

Pavlichenko, along with Nikolai Krasavchenko, the propaganda secretary of the Moscow Young Communist League, and fellow sniper Vladimir Pchelintsev, were first lady Eleanor Roosevelt's guests at the White House in August 1942 as delegates to an International Student Assembly.[3] The American press were fascinated by the Soviet soldiers, especially Pavlichenko who one reporter described as 'the first Amazon of the Red Army to visit the capital of the United States'. Her two-month tour coincided with the British and American military's conundrum about allowing women into combat: while in reality women were moving closer to the front line, the military strained to reassure the public that traditional roles would be preserved. The journalists laboured over how to reconcile the young, well-scrubbed Russian woman with the expert killer who bristled at questions about whether 'girls wear lipstick at the front line and what colour do they prefer', and 'what colour does Lady Pavlichenko prefer and what colour does she like?'[4] Equally objectionable to the Red Army officer were descriptions of her appearance: her 'high Russian boots', 'scarlet-trimmed khaki uniform' and figure which was considered 'a little plump, like most Russian women'. Was this the future if their women were allowed to take up arms?

Pavlichenko objected to the trivialization of her military career, and by implication, the Soviet women who had enlisted en masse to defend their country. When asked in Chicago why she had chosen such a profession, Pavlichenko retorted, 'Gentlemen, I am twenty-five years old and I have already managed to kill 309 of the fascist invaders. Do you not think, gentlemen, that you have been hiding behind my back for rather too long?'[5] Like Bochkareva, she argued that women were taking men's natural role as combatants, a situation which would be remedied when more of them enlisted. In reality, Pavlichenko's weapons training had begun before the war, along with thousands of other Soviet school girls, through the paramilitary sports organization Osoaviakhim.[6] When the Germans invaded in June 1941, Pavlichenko 'resorted to all kinds of tricks to get [into the army]', and served first in a 'destroyer squad' to 'dispose of German paratroopers' with the Red Army's 25th rifle Division.[7] She opened her sniper's tally during the Defence of Odessa which was fought in the early phase of Operation *Barbarossa* and, despite being wounded, she upped her tally to 187. After Odessa had fallen, she spent a further eight months defending Sevastopol where, with her partner (a crucial relationship as snipers trained and operated together), she destroyed an enemy observation point, and regularly fought duels with German snipers. While her division was decimated, she survived, albeit wounded, to be evacuated by submarine to Novorossiysk before being posted to a sniper school.[8]

Lieutenant Pavlichenko's dauntingly impressive military career seemed such a pure form of female patriotic sacrifice that it won her Eleanor Roosevelt's friendship and attracted many celebrities. Paul Robeson sang for the Soviet delegates and at a reception, Charlie Chaplin remarked as he kissed Pavlichenko's fingers: 'It's just incredible that this little hand has killed Nazis, has scythed them down by the hundred, without missing, at close range.'[9] She was featured on the cover of the American Communist Party magazine, *Soviet Union Today*, with biographical details that fitted neatly the female warrior trope. As a child she was, 'a tomboy and rather unruly in the classroom ... I was keen on sports of all kinds, and played all the boys' games and would not allow myself to be outdone by boys in anything. That was how I turned to sharpshooting.'[10] The article urged Americans to support a military 'Second Front' against the German forces, appealing to a sense of international friendship that she hoped would outlast the war. When folk singer Woody Guthrie's 1946 song 'Miss Pavlichenko' praised her Nazi body count, he was reminding post-war listeners that the US was indebted to the Soviet Union and should remain a trusted ally.[11]

Lieutenant Pavlichenko would make an equally deep impression in Britain when she arrived with the Soviet delegation after a few days in Canada where the Ontario premier, Mitchell Hepburn, presented her with a rifle, saying, 'I hope your present record of slaying 309 Nazis is a mere rehearsal.'[12] Even before the delegates arrived in London in November, British journalists were following the story and were as ready for this 'Red Army girl sniper' as she was for them. At a press event where she reviewed a Home Guard detachment on 5 November, she anticipated the same 'silly questions' she suffered in America[13] so warned the assembled journalists: 'I wear my uniform with honour ... It has been covered with blood in battle. It is plain to see that with American women what is important is whether they wear silk underwear under their uniforms. What the uniform stands for they have yet to learn.'[14] She hoped that British women would prove more sensible.

While the press reports did not identify Pavlichenko as part of a historic tradition of female fighters, she made her own comparison. 'We [women] have a tradition, too, to live up to,' she wrote in *Soviet Russia Today*. 'There was [Nadezhda] Durova, the Russian women guerrilla who fought against Napoleon's invading armies in 1812, and Dasha Sevastopolskya who fought in the heroic defence of Sevastapol in 1854–55. So in today's war our women have carried on these traditions – and added something.'[15] Pavlichenko insisted that women and men served with complete equality, before observing that, while most female soldiers were kept to the rear, many were serving on the front line and 'feel no limitations because of our sex'.[16] In fact, women would serve in the Red Army as junior commanding officers in male, mixed and female units and were trained in specialist institutes such as the Central Women's School for Sniper Training.[17]

An earlier generation of British readers would have found the Russian women soldiers readily identifiable from popular and specialist magazines such as *Jus Suffragii*, and from news stories.[18] But rather than treated as a novelty, British women were encouraged to emulate the Red Army's female soldiers and, as historian Chloe Ward has identified, images of Soviet women appeared in British propaganda posters, documentary shorts, theatrical features, radio broadcasts and books, supporting institutional calls for women's self-sacrifice to the war effort.[19] A film heroine based on Pavlichenko even appeared as Lieutenant Olga Bocolova in the 1944 British comedy *Tawny Pit*, where she sings the Internationale alongside

Nancy, a member of the Women's Land Army, in the idealized English village of Lipsbury Lea. It was a clever device since British women already seemed enamoured of the Soviet sniper.

On tour, Pavlichenko attracted throngs of curious women, who, like ATS volunteer Joan Savage Cowey, envied Eastern Europe's female soldiers their combat training and military 'adventure'.[20] When Pavlichenko reviewed the London Home Guard, the *Northern Daily Mail* noted that 'every window in the Ministry [of Information] was crowded with girl clerks anxious to catch sight of the Russian woman soldier'.[21] Propaganda had primed them to admire this liberated Soviet woman, who, on factory visits, supported women workers receiving equal pay with men. While the ATS pilot Diana Barnato Walker might regard such differential pay rates as 'natural', as the *Daily Record*'s reporter observed, 'Lyudmila does not approve.' Neither did she approve of being barred from a naval ship in Liverpool,[22] and in Manchester said she hoped the ban on training women in arms would be lifted. After reviewing a crew at the London Bridge fire station, she suggested that Britain's women 'will, if necessary, fight shoulder to shoulder with the men as the women of Russia have done.'[23]

However critical the Soviet delegate might be of British attitudes, female readers of the *Daily Record* were invited to draw parallels between Pavlichenko and their own wartime contribution. Typical was an RAF recruitment ad that ran alongside the coverage of her factory visit in December 1942. Under a photo of a female mechanic, the strapline read: 'these girls know their aircraft backwards after a few month's training. And they all love the work … It's a grand job, responsible and fascinating: and you get *plenty of chances to fly*.'[24] British women now had opportunities to emulate their allied heroines, despite the unequal pay.

Although journalists covering Pavlichenko's British visit fielded fewer questions about clothes and make-up, her 'feminine' qualities were still featured in their reports. *The Manchester Evening News* complimented her for 'smok[ing] a cigarette more gracefully than a Mayfair debutante as she walked amid cheering crowds of girl workers to her car.'[25] The *Yorkshire and Leeds Intelligencer* described her as 'no strapping giantess', but 'a little plump, like most Russian women, good-looking with aquiline features and a flashing smile'[26] while a *Liverpool Daily Post* columnist noted that 'she is ... undoubtedly attractive in her khaki uniform with its red to the collar and her shiny Russian boots.'[27] Pavlichenko struggled against the media's reductive attitude, writing that she realized, 'I am looked upon a little as a curiosity, a subject of newspaper headlines, for anecdotes.'[28]

However often the press evoked debutantes, playful smiles and those shiny Russian boots, many remained profoundly unsettled by Pavlichenko's attitude towards killing. Elizabeth Tenney was a student at the University of Washington, Seattle in 1942 when she hosted at her sorority house the Soviet sniper who had studied history at Kiev University. Although Pavlichenko was travelling with Eleanor Roosevelt and a 'band of foreign students' with equally incredible experiences of war, it was the Russian sniper's testimony that haunted Tenney.

> The Germans had killed her husband and young children and wiped out the rest of her family. She had picked up a rifle and taken to the woods to stalk Nazi soldiers. One by one she killed some 257, sometimes hiding in the woods all night to get a good shot. By now she had killed more enemy soldiers than any other individual Russian and had received the highest medal for bravery from the Soviet government.[29]

At a White House reception, Pavlichenko told a similar story when Mrs Roosevelt asked how, as a woman, she could shoot Germans whose faces she had seen in her rifle sight. She replied, 'I have seen with my own eyes my husband and children killed. I was next to them.'[30] *The New York Times* quoted Pavlichenko's cool explanation about her lack of 'complicated emotions' in combat: 'The only feeling I have is the great satisfaction a hunter feels who has killed a beast of prey.'[31] It was an experience shared by other female snipers such as Anya Mulatova who overcame her initial squeamishness to happily bayonet bloated German corpses 'to let the gas out'.[32]

But perhaps, for a Western audience, the detail of avenging her husband and child's death served to soften what seemed a ruthless quality that women rarely exposed in public.

Soviet military authorities most likely chose Pavlichenko to tour the West because she satisfied their specific propaganda requirements: she was a sniper, an authentic representative of Communist youth, and an articulate university student with links to the security services, the NKVD, through her father. But her biography would need massaging. Although she had been a student, in 1941 she was also a single mother with a son, Rostislav, born in 1932, when she was aged 15, and married to a fellow student. The couple soon divorced and Rostislav was raised by his grandmother which allowed Lyudmila to work, study, and eventually to become a sniper.[33] So Pavlichenko, in 1941, had lost neither child (nor children), nor husband to the Nazis when she volunteered for the Red Army, only two of many details altered for public consumption.

Russian historian Oleg Kaminsky discovered, among other discrepancies about her military record, that Pavlichenko, who claimed to have 'shot 187 fascists' while serving with the Independent Maritime Army during the siege of Odessa, had, unusually, not been decorated. In order to raise morale, anyone who distinguished themselves during the battle, whether they were cooks, clerks, artists or front-line combatants, had been awarded a medal.[34] Author Lyuba Vinogradova suggests that since the Independent Maritime Army had been annihilated at Sevastapol, there was no one left to dispute Pavlichenko's kill count which may have been much lower. She was well placed to play the role of self-sacrificing heroine with military expertise just as the USSR embarked on its mass conscription of women and her 1942 tour was as heavily covered by the Soviet media as it was in the West.[35]

While Pavlichenko's Nazi tally remains questionable, there were hundreds of thousands of Russian women who obeyed the Soviet propaganda to 'Kill the German!' and who 'saw no other way of saving their country and getting back their normal lives'.[36] During the Soviet-German war of 1941–45, when more than 20 million

Soviet citizens died, 520,000 women served in the Red Army's regular troops, and 300,000 in combat.[37] Some were motivated to realize their 'hidden female talents' while others accompanied friends, or were moved by a desire to protect their homeland.[38] Women were employed in traditional roles as medics but also operated in every area of combat, in logistics, as gunners, pilots, photographers, radio operators, mechanics, drivers as well as cooks, laundry workers and labourers who cleared the wounded and corpses from the battlefields. When given office jobs, they objected and demanded posts at the front.[39] Some formed relationships as a 'war wife' while others fought off sexual assaults, or witnessed their comrades raping enemy women.[40] If captured by the Wehrmacht, they endured many forms of sexual violence: 'coerced disrobement, sexual torture, sexual assault, sexual blackmail, rape, gang-rape, and sexual enslavement'.[41] They missed their children, their mothers, their men and their homes. As Sofya Mironovna Vereschchak, an underground fighter, describes it: 'Our time made us the way we were. We proved ourselves ... Our idea was young and we were young then.'[42]

Soviet women did indeed prove to be stoic, dedicated to their cause, and professional in their military roles. 'There probably will never again be such people as we were then. Never! So naïve and so sincere. With such faith!' said one veteran. 'We were brought up that we and the Motherland were one and the same.'[43] This fusion between individual and state identity inspired the Young Communist League Central Committee's seventy-three mobilization campaigns that recruited 400,000 young women.[44] These young women regarded their right to participate in combat violence and to acquire the specialized and technical knowledge of the modern soldier as an expression of their new, liberated Soviet womanhood.[45] Despite the intensity of their experience and the enormity of their sacrifice, however, most would be bitterly disappointed after the peace.

Post-war alienation

When the Nobel Prize-winning author Svetlana Alexievich began interviewing female veterans in the 1970s, they had endured decades of alienation from male veterans, from non-combatants and from younger generations of women, all of whom regarded them with suspicion. Historian Anna Krylova found that popular narratives reduced the women combatants' role in winning the Soviet-German war to a supporting cast who provided 'dashes of colour' while the soldiers and commanders were turned into 'self-sacrificing non-combatant nurses'.[46] As one veteran described this collective forgetting, 'What wounds us most is that we have been driven from a great past into an unbearably small present. No one invites us anymore to appear at schools, in museums, we are not needed anymore.'[47]

The female veterans agreed that while there was little public recognition of their military role, the Soviet public were quick to assume they had been hunting for husbands at the Eastern Front.[48] Klavdia S -va, a sniper, described how civilians greeted her group after the war: 'The men said nothing, but the women ... They shouted to us, "We know what you did there! You lured our men with your young c***! Army whores ... Military bitches ..." They insulted us in all possible ways.'[49] When sergeant and sniper Ekaterina Nikitchna Sannikova returned, her neighbours scoffed, 'Ha-ha-ha ... Tell us how you whored around there with the men'[50] and Tamara Stepanovna Umnyagina, a medical assistant who married an officer, also remembers wounding insults. 'After the war we had another war. Also terrible. For some reason, men abandoned us. They didn't shield us.'[51] Vinogradova summed up the quiet rage many female snipers felt: 'Male veterans were treated with a degree of respect, but women continued to be regarded with suspicion or hostility; but never with respect.'[52]

Perestroika and the development of hybrid warfare

Despite such private difficulties, between 1965 and perestroika, female veterans were highly visible at the 9 May Victory Day celebrations that marked the anniversary of Odessa's defence. But following the break-up of the Soviet Union in 1991, according to J. G. Mathers, Russian women yearned for a more conservative concept of gender. They preferred to emphasize their femininity, associating 'equality' between the sexes with the Soviet woman's 'double burden' of performing masculine work while still responsible for childcare and domestic chores. As British and American women of the 1990s struggled for equality in the workplace, Russians strove to become full-time wives and mothers. The military symbolized a place better suited to 'real men', a sentiment paradoxically endorsed by almost half of servicewomen in a contemporary poll.[53] By the new millennium, women in the contemporary Russian military remain visible on International Women's Day, which marks the Soviet Union's granting of suffrage to female voters on 8 March 1917. But women soldiers quoted in the media suggest that the incompatibility between being a 'woman' and a 'soldier' remains. Only in exceptional and transient circumstances are they fused.

A sample of Russian media interviews suggest that Russian military women believe their power resides in their role as mothers, possessed of a moral superiority over men. They seem eager to emphasize their femininity, far from Pavlichenko's disdain for media questions about clothes, hair or make-up. Kora, a female commander, explains in an interview from 2014, the year in which Russia had illegally occupied Eastern Ukraine, that International Women's Day is about women embracing their weaker, vulnerable and softer sides. To mark the day, she urged her sisters in arms to 'drop their rifles and to hold a bouquet of roses'.[54] Angela, commander of a sixteen-woman training squad at the Ryazan Higher Airborne Command School, says that 'while a woman might physically be weaker than a man, morally she is stronger.'[55] Svetlana, in her fifties, compares commanding her men to child-rearing where she punishes disobedience with push-ups or withholding lunch until their work is completed.[56]

Female volunteers for the conflict in Eastern Ukraine who featured in regular news reports from 2014 expressed similar sentiments. Stanislava, a slight, blonde twenty-four-year-old former model and florist from Ukraine, enlisted with the now-disbanded Donetsk People's Republic Army after a friend died in the conflict.

Motivated to 'get up and protect my soil, my loved ones, my mother who I really love', she had been involved in fire fights and witnessed civilian deaths 'in front of my eyes'. But she admits that 'no one wanted this war, really no one'. And yet, Stanislava describes the benefits of her military life where, with her Russian comrades, she has formed 'a new family', bonded through the common cause of 'protecting our territory'.[57]

Stanislava is alluding to Russia's annexation of Crimea when far-right organizations recruited thousands for a 'Novorossiya' army around the self-proclaimed (now illegal) separatist republics of Donetsk and Luhansk. 'Novorossiya', inspired by the historical region of the Russian Empire, legitimized the separatists and aimed to consolidate territorial divisions in the breakaway regions. Initially the Kremlin's official position supported neither the nationalist websites that recruited volunteers, nor their paramilitary camps (where they trained in firearms, survival techniques, first aid and basic discipline).[58] However, in 2015 Vladimir Putin admitted that the 'green men' without country insignia seen in Crimea were Russian soldiers and that Russian military forces were 'resolving various issues' in Eastern Ukraine.[59]

The resolution of those issues fell to young soldiers like Stanislava who, despite their front-line experience, would still be asked about feminine grooming. In her interview, Stanislava shrugs when asked if she would rather model a Kevlar vest than wear one, and says:

> Actually, we don't wear them much, it's impractical and it's very heavy, and whatever hits you isn't life-threatening. War is a terrible thing. It's dirt, dust. It's awful; we girls who are used to doing our manicures and hair, we forget that now of course. It was hard to get used to it at first – but we have. We are doing this so that in the future we can live in acceptable conditions and relive our female pleasures.[60]

Plans to marry and have a family, the epitome of such 'female pleasures' she says, had been postponed.

While Stanislava describes personal reasons for enlisting, other women joined the rebels from political commitment. Victoria, a medical student, volunteered for the extreme-right Viking Brigade after witnessing women civilians injured in the military conflict near her home of Gorlovka (Horlivka). 'Novorossiya', she hoped, would re-establish traditional gender roles and galvanize men, spoiled by Western living standards, to take up arms rather than relying on women soldiers. 'Our duty as women is to raise a new generation of male fighters so that in the future this will not repeat itself, so that men in the future will be defending us and our territories.'[61] The return to a conservative idealization of women as spiritual and moral guides, that would be compatible with Bochkareva's Women's Battalion, simultaneously made them responsible for solving the military's labour shortage in ongoing 'hybrid' conflicts.

Russian women volunteers for Eastern Ukraine fought in combat and through more contemporary forms of warfare. The case of Yulia Kharlamova-Tselinskaya, a twenty-nine-year-old from Ukraine, typifies a generation who are combining soldiering with a strange intersection of reportage, celebrity and propaganda. Yulia served in a communications unit with the Russian Airborne Forces (VDV) in 2012, before transferring to an all-male paratrooper regiment. While her body weight, at just over 100 pounds, restricted her combat training[62] she allegedly excelled at online recruitment, co-ordinating volunteers for the illegal war in Eastern Ukraine of 2014.[63] But when the military authorities discovered her online presence, Yulia claims she left to join the Novorossiyan fighters. She developed a substantial domestic and international following, curating images that eerily blend the ultra-feminine with the hyper-masculine.[64]

A trawl through her Russian Facebook page obscures rather than reveals her biographical details. In her most feminine shots Yulia poses, voluptuous in floor-length ball gowns, with her wide, blue eyes, suspiciously large lips (and breasts) and long auburn tresses. Her photo gallery offers summer shots of her peeking out from behind a broad sun hat, while dangling her slim muscular legs in a wading pool at a Mitteleuropean palace. As she frolics barefoot across lawns and through gardens, her bright cotton or sateen frocks show off her figure, her eyes shaded behind heart-shaped pink lenses. Further along, Yulia appears in overalls and crash helmet, driving an indoor go-cart, chilling with her girlfriends dressed in a parka on winter camping, scaling an indoor climbing wall or sprawled across her bed, cuddling her cats.

In masculine mode she wears the VDV's bright blue beret, a striped t-shirt, and green uniform, about to execute a parachute jump. In a sun-dappled orchard, she poses with a doll resting on her shoulder, held close, less a toy than a talisman. 'Natalia' is the American manufacturer DAMTOYS' blonde replica doll of the Russian Airborne Troops who clutches her own mini assault rifle within her plastic hands. Fans on the action figure site onesixthwarriors were quick to see a connection between 'Natalia', the DAMTOYS 2016 product (listed at $142 US), and the VDV soldier. Amidst questions about the details of 'Natalia's' parachute and radio, the fans comment on Yulia's 'hot body', that she 'is so popular there are tons of anime versions of her'. But then the tone shades into something altogether darker. As one contributor writes, 'This figure actually has its roots in reality. There's a controversial FSB [Foreign Intelligence Service] agent that has links to the Russian Fascist movement and has undertaken parachute training and the like. Her name is Yulia Kharlamova.'[65]

Born in Odessa, site of the siege in which Pavlichenko fought, Yulia claims that she became a passionate Russian patriot in her teens and studied history.[66] Rather than the past leading her to the rich heritage of female soldiers of the Soviet-German war, she cultivated an interest in fascism, seeking out 'alternative' narratives for Russia's loss of empire in 1991. Rejecting 'Russophobic propaganda' and growing more nationalistic, she left Odessa for Nizhny Novgorod to study at Lobachevsky University, where she claims she gave up her links to Ukranian fascism to become a good Russian patriot.[67] While still in her teens Yulia met a group of like-minded young men who 'radicalized' her, even photographing her in Moscow giving a Nazi salute. In a 2015 interview with Anna News (AN), the state-operated broadcaster for whom she produced packages,

Yulia explains that patriotism and the 'romance' of soldiering led her to enlist.[68]

Yulia's recruitment reveals how propaganda networks operated in Eastern Ukraine and Russia where young women and men were first radicalized online before signing up for military training. A Ukrainian news website in 2014 exposed her far-right links, posting photos of her with Alexei Milchakov,[69] notorious leader of the now-disbanded far-right paramilitary unit Rusich, which has been charged with killing soldiers of the Aydar Battaltion and the 80th Air Assault Brigade in Donbas.[70] The website included shots of Yulia in her VDV uniform with Milchakov who also recruited through his social media networks. According to news reports, his online videos document such military conquests as Milchakov cutting the ears from the corpses of Ukrainian soldiers, scratching swastikas on their faces and making selfies against the backdrop of their burned remains.[71] The Rusich separatists are alleged to have attacked the Ukrainian government forces in the village of Shchastya, Luhansk, killing eleven soldiers in 2014.

During the war in Eastern Ukraine, Yulia presented packages for AN, blending journalism and propaganda. Typical is a report aired on 28 December 2015 (although shot during the summer) from Donetsk. Although in military fatigues, Yulia appears on camera with polished fingernails, earrings, and stroking a cat while she interviews a masked, middle-aged Cossack volunteer about attacks on the Ukrainian army. Described as an educated working-class local, he dismisses Ukrainian media's reports of an official Russian military presence in the area. Despite his comments about the rebels' well-stocked armoury and military strength, the Cossack with his grey-streaked beard and t-shirt straining hard across his belly seems more a weekend than a professional warrior.[72]

A second, more recent AN report reveals how Yulia's propaganda as a female combatant not only resurrected Bochkareva's tactic of shaming men into enlisting, but fits into a wider campaign supported by Russian celebrities. From a winter camp, Yulia interviews a group of heavily armed soldiers who thank Russian contributors to the fundraising 'Save Donbas' campaign.[73] Musician Gleb Kornilov was a major sponsor, and leader of the Russian patriotic band 'Dangerous' which regularly performs at Kremlin-sponsored Night Wolves' bikers' concerts.[74] Kornilov's brand of propaganda includes a Ukrainian war ballad, 'I am Hungry', which features a Yulia lookalike for whom the conflict interrupts a budding romance. But the young woman rather than her boyfriend enlists and she snarls with contempt when he tries to dissuade her.[75] According to political scientists Alexandra Yatsyk and Andrey Makarychev, such propaganda scripts operate to win viewers' psychological and physical support for the motherland and to fill a vacuum in post-1991 Russian identity.[76]

Yulia's AN reports seem to promote this post-perestroika view of Russian women exercising their right to participate in combat and defend the Motherland, only because their men had lost their masculine power. The alliance with the far-right Novorossiyan cause, with its hyper-masculine imagery, enables them to reclaim their proper role as warriors. In a 2014 report from the specialist 'Varyag' (Viking) unit, Yulia appears alongside another unidentified young woman, in a package about combat training. Behind the women sit a group of male soldiers whose faces are hidden but who wear the Novorossiyan flag on their uniforms. The report follows the women's training in different weapons and closes with a shot of Yulia firing a rocket launcher across a field into a nearby farm building which billows with black smoke. Yulia, the presenter of this report which blends 'news' with military recruitment and propaganda, demonstrates that women can acquire specialized, technical knowledge in defending the Motherland.[77]

Yulia's role in the 2014 conflict has been strongly criticized in Ukraine where journalists exposed her links to the far-right and the FSB, charges she dismissed as 'Ukrainian rumours' in two AN reports. Despite 'people saying all kinds of horrible things about [Milchakov] online', she defends him as an impressive 'guy [who] was actually fighting the war'. She refers to her YouTube video of 18 October 2014 where she records a monologue in a strapless burgundy dress, from an anonymous hallway, to reassure her viewers: 'I am not a fake' before comparing Milchakov – who she defends as a selfless warrior, protecting the people of Luhansk, who funded his mission in Ukraine – to armchair critics who 'write nasty things about him'.[78]

In a 2014 AN report Yulia, described as a twenty-four-year-old 'beauty from Moscow', denied her role as an FSB provocateur in the violent Kiev National Guard's protest at Ukraine's parliament.[79] According to Ukrainian media, Yulia, who appears in footage of the protest wearing a blonde wig and dark glasses, had allegedly threatened conscripts' wives and families into forcing them to revolt against their government.[80] Yulia claims that Ukraine's National Guard wanted to demobilize because the soldiers were fed up with risking their lives in fighting the war, and the Ukrainian media, 'need to find someone to blame and they found me'.[81] Despite online videos which place her in Luhansk in 2014, she claimed her last visit to the country was in 2012.[82]

Kremlin critics have identified such tactics as part of Putin's 'hybrid' or 'special' war against Ukraine which has happened alongside an assault on Russian civil society which includes anonymous physical attacks, threats and intimidation, attempts at co-optation and outright disinformation.[83] American security expert John R. Schindler describes it as 'an amalgam of espionage, subversion, even forms of terrorism to attain political ends without actually going to war in any conventional sense.'[84] While Yulia Kharlamova-Tselinskaya seems to occupy an exceptional crossing point of propaganda, militarism, reportage and celebrity, other Russian servicewomen appear in the media pledging allegiance to the Motherland. The struggle to negotiate their role within the masculine sphere of the armed forces remains unresolved, even echoing sentiments from the early twentieth century. Yulia's carefully curated images of ball gowns, dolls and assault rifles are just the most recent demonstration of the military's paradoxical need for female recruits and its need to preserve traditional gender roles.

Despite the centuries-long history of Russian women's involvement in the military, the current rhetoric seems regressive and remains highly gendered. Women are still regarded, and publicly present themselves as care-givers, morally superior, spiritual beings who enter combat only as proxies for inadequate men. The young servicewomen on Russian media express a yearning for the past and their country's lost empire without reference to their foremothers' experiences fighting the fascists. Yulia's online media presence may represent a terrifying new form of warfare in which women engage in espionage, subversion, even terrorism to attain their leader's political ends. Rather than actively participating in civic life or going adventuring like the earlier Amazons, these women seem trapped in hyper-feminine roles where they must remain attractive, available and good with a gun.

Final thoughts

Whatever the future holds for women in the military, their rich history which has been chronicled over the past few decades has begun to seep into the public consciousness and inspire contemporary recruits. Just as Nadezhda Dherova, Sarah Edmonds or Flora Sandes offered heroic narratives for earlier female readers, today's servicewomen seek them out for comfort and support. On the Everday Sexism website 'Lindsey' describes how she must 'constantly defend my right to be in the military', but knows that '[h]istorically, there are some cultures who allowed, even encouraged women to fight alongside men. Also, women secretly fought in the civil war, disguising themselves as men to protect their rights, and none were ever the wiser.' Elizabeth, who describes herself as 'working full time in the military', is aware that 'women have served for hundreds of years, and yet men of all ages still won't accept it!' And 'M', who serves in the US navy on active duty while her husband does the childcare, states, 'About 20% of the US military is female. One in five. There are women serving on ships whose mothers served on ships.'[85]

The female warriors' collective stories gathered together within this volume are beginning to change how we think about women's historic participation in warfare, shattering its firmly held illusions of masculinity. As women's legacy of their experience has told us over and over again, they have been present, they have fought alongside men, risked their lives, shattered their bodies and then been excluded from the spoils. Militaries need their services but dance around definitions of combat to justify their presence while appeasing concerns about women's unfitness for combat, or lax morals or disruption of unit cohesion.

Their willingness to enlist alongside their men has so often been produced as the ultimate expression of femininity, offered in the service of nation, familial duty or romantic love. Their own words about occupying the battlefield's strange, horrifying and liminal space are rare, and in peacetime most female warriors have, as the former Komsomol girl described it, remained 'as silent as fish'[86]. Their claim to a veteran's status has been far too often ignored or rendered shameful.

But there are so many more questions to ask of these women. As we've seen, they have only just begun to describe their experiences; their attitudes towards killing; their feelings about being mothers, sexual beings and sexual objects; how combat changes them; or how it might prepare them for political power. This volume has attempted to bring together as many of these voices as possible and to identity patterns in their lives and attitudes. Sometimes they sing as a chorus and sometimes their experiences diverge. There are recurring themes but also highly specific situations which can only be explained through an understanding of particular historic and social contexts. They have, I hope, aroused your curiosity, your sympathy, your awe and your wonder. Whatever else we can say of these sisters in arms, they were, and are, remarkable. They have much to teach us about how women's negotiation for their right to equality is as ancient as the tombs in which the Scythian warriors lie buried along the shores of the Black Sea.

Endnotes

Introduction

1 De Pauw, L. G. (1998), *Battlecries and Lullabies: Women in War from Prehistory to the Present*, Norman: University of Oklahoma Press, pp. xiii, 12.
2 Fazio, T. (2018), 'Let Women be Warriors', https://www.nytimes.com/2018/11/22/opinion/let-women-be-warriors.html [accessed 7 August 2019].
3 Stock, K. (2019), https://quillette.com/2019/04/11/ignoring-differences-between-men-and-women-is-the-wrong-way-to-address-gender-dysphoria/ [accessed 7 August 2019].

Chapter 1

1 MEPO 3/439 National Archives.
2 Arkell-Smith, V., 'My Amazing Masquerade ... A Wife Confesses', *Empire News and Sunday Chronicle*, 19 February 1956.
3 'Colonel Barker Prosecuted', *The Times*, 28 March 1929.
4 MEPO 3/439. Brisby statement, 9 March 1929.
5 A letter from New Scotland Yard to the Director of Public Prosecutions in relation to the case of 'Captain H. Victor Barker DSO' revealed that: 'this man ... had been seen wearing the DSO 1914 Star, Coronation Medal, and some Foreign Order, probably French, but the War Office are unable to trace him as having served during the War and no person named Victor Barker is entitled to wear the DSO', MEPO 3/439.
6 'Colonel Barker in the Dock at the Old Bailey', *Daily Herald*, 25 April 1929.

7 Sir Ernest Wild had been a prominent supporter of the Criminal Law Amendment Bill in August 1921 which aimed to outlaw 'any act of gross indecency between female persons'. Sexual contact between women, he described as a 'very real evil', that might produce 'insanity' and threaten 'the fundamental institutions of society'. Quoted in Collis, R. (2002), *Colonel Barker's Monstrous Regiment: A Tale of Female Husbandry*, London: Virago, p. 67.

8 Houlbrook, M. (2005), *Queer London: Perils and Pleasures in the Sexual Metropolis, 1918–1957*, Chicago: The University of Chicago Press, p. 252; 'Old Bailey Acquittals', *The Times*, 15 July 1927.

9 'Woman's Strange Life as a Man', *Daily Express*, 6 March 1929.

10 'Colonel Barker Prosecuted', *The Times*, 28 March 1929.

11 Arkell-Smith, V., 'I Posed as a Man for 30 Years!' *Empire News and Sunday Chronicle*, 19 February 1956, p. 2. Collis, op. cit., pp. 46, 54.

12 'How the Colonel's Secret was Revealed', *Daily Sketch*, 6 March 1929.

13 Barker, E., 'The Other Woman Who "Stole" My "Husband"', *Sunday Express*, nd, 1929, MEPO 3/439.

14 Radclyffe Hall to Audrey Heath, 19 March 1929, quoted in Baker, M. (1985), *Our Three Selves: The Life of Radclyffe Hall*, London: Hamish Hamilton, p. 254.

15 Ibid., p. 254.

16 Derry. C. (2018), 'Lesbianism and Feminist Legislation in 1921: The age of consent and "gross indecency" between women', *History Workshop Journal*, pp. 245–63.

17 I am grateful to Julian Walker for the following references. For examples of eroticized women in uniform see 'Oh What a Surprise', *New Fun*, 2 January 1915, p. 24; 'How the Girls of England would Like to Treat the Scarborough Baby Killers if they Could Catch Them', *New Fun*, 16 January 1915, p. 5; Cartoon, *New Fun*, 16 February 1915, p. 18; 'Ready? Aye, Ready!' *Photo Bits*, 26 September 1914, p. 6; 'A Servian Joan of Arc', *Photo Bits*, 24 October 1914, p. 18. See, Walker, Julian (2018), 'Thinking Sex after the Great War', unpublished lecture, Royal Library of Brussels, 17–19 October.

18 'Colonel Barker in the Dock at the Old Bailey', *Daily Herald*, 25 April 1929.

19 Ibid.

20 'Perjury Charge', *The Times*, 26 April 1929.

21 'My Amazing Masquerade'.

22 'Colonel Barker Sent for Trial', *Daily Sketch*, 28 March 1929.

23 'Old Bailey Trial for Colonel Barker', *Daily Express*, 28 March 1929.

24 Ibid.

25 Ibid.

26 'Colonel Barker Sentenced', *The Times*, 26 April 1929.

27 'Pop' cartoon strip, *Daily Sketch*, 16 May 1929.

28 Oram, A. (2007), *Her Husband Was a Woman! Women's Gender-crossing in Modern British Popular Culture*, London: Routledge. Oram's survey of female gender-crossing in two mass circulation British Sunday newspapers found more than 200 separate reports appearing between 1910 and 1960. She argues that 'there was a huge surge of interest between 1928 and the late 1930s, with 11 reports in 1929, the year of the Colonel Barker case, and up to 9 or 10 in some subsequent years'. However, in the twenty years from 1940 to 1960, there were only thirty-five stories, an average of just one or two a year, suggesting that Colonel Barker's trial was not only hugely influential in alerting the press to this phenomenon but that it may have been superseded by other categories and understandings of sexuality and gender. (Oram, p. 3).

29 'My Amazing Masquerade'.

30 In recent scholarship see Cleves, R. H. (2015), '"What, Another Female Husband?" The prehistory of same sex marriage in America', *The Journal of American History*, 101 (4), p. 1005; Derry, C. (2017), '"The Female Husbands", Community and Courts in the Eighteenth Century,' *The Journal of Legal History*, 38 (1), pp. 54–79. Easton, F. (2003), 'Gender's Two Bodies: Women warriors, female husbands and plebeian life', *Past & Present*, 180 (8), pp. 131–74.

31 Walker, p. 6.

Chapter 2

1 Nicolaas Witsen, quoted in Dekker, R. M. and van de Pol, L. (1989), *The Tradition of Female Transvestism in Early Modern Europe*, London: Macmillan Press, p. xv.

2 Keuning, J. (1954), 'Nicholas Witsen as a Cartographer', *Imago Mundi*, 11 (1), pp. 95–110.

3 Mayor, A. (2014), *The Amazons: Lives and Legends of Warrior Women Across the Ancient World*, Princeton and Oxford: Princeton University Press.

4 Ibid., p. 30.
5 Ibid., p. 29. Mayor also points to the 2013 discovery of Etruscan women warriors by Weingarten.
6 Ibid., p. 12.
7 Ibid., pp. 19, 28.
8 Webster Wilde, L. (2016), *A Brief History of the Amazons: Women Warriors in Myth and History*, London: Robinson.
9 Mayor, p. 63.
10 Ibid., p. 20.
11 Ibid., p. 45.
12 Ibid., p. 338.
13 De Pauw, L. G. (1998), *Battlecries and Lullabies: Women in War from Prehistory to the Present*, Norman: University of Oklahoma Press, p. 84.
14 Ibid., p. 84.
15 De Pizan, Christine (2003), translated by Sarah Lawson, *Treasure of the City of Ladies, or The Book of the Three Virtues*, London: Penguin, p. 185.
16 Bradley Warren, N. (2012), 'Christine de Pizan and Joan of Arc', in L. H. McAvoy and D. Watt (eds), *The History of British Women's Writing, 700–1500*, London: Palgrave Macmillan.
17 Llewellyn Barstow, A. (1985), 'Mystical Experience as a Feminist Weapon', *Women's Studies Quarterly*, 8 (2), pp. 26–29.
18 Ibid., p. 26.
19 Pinzino, J. M. (2003), 'Joan of Arc', in R. Pennington (ed.) and R. Highnam (advisory ed.), *Amazons to Fighter Pilots: A Biographical Dictionary of Military Women*, Westport, Connecticut: Greenwood Press, Vol. 1 (A–Q), p. 236.
20 Ibid., p. 237.
21 Ibid., p. 237.
22 Bennett, J. M and McSheffrey, S. (2014), 'Early, Erotic and Alien', *History Workshop Journal*, 77 (1), pp. 1–25 and p. 3.
23 Stoyle, M. (2018), '"Give Mee a Souldier's Coat": Female cross-dressing during the English Civil War', *History: The Journal of the Historical Association*, 103 (1), pp. 5–26.
24 Quoted in Stoyle, p.14.
25 Ibid., p. 16.
26 Ibid., p. 19.
27 Stoyle, p. 20.
28 Ibid., p. 24.

29 Wilson, J. H., quoted in P. Rogers (1982), 'The Breeches Part', in P. G. Boucé (ed.), *Sexuality in Eighteenth-Century Britain*, Manchester: Manchester University Press, p. 249.

30 Shepherd, S. (1983), *Amazons and Warrior Women: Varieties of Feminism in Seventeenth Century Drama*, Brighton: Harvester, p. 69; Jardine, L. (1983), *Still Harping on Daughters: Drama in the Age of Shakespeare*, Brighton: Harvester.

31 Friedl, L. (1985), 'Women Who Dressed as Men', *Trouble and Strife: A Radical Feminist Magazine*, (6), pp. 24–29; Clark, A. (1995), *The Struggle for the Breeches: Gender and the Making of the British Working Class*, Berkley, California: California University Press; Easton, F. (2003), 'Gender's Two Bodies: Women warriors, female husbands and plebeian life', *Past & Present*, 180 (8), pp. 131–174; Easton, F. (2006), 'Covering Sexual Disguise: Passing Women and Generic Constraint', *Studies in Eighteenth-Century Culture*, 35, pp. 95–125.

32 Dugaw, D. (1989), *Warrior Women and Popular Balladry, 1650–1850*, Cambridge: Cambridge University Press.

33 Dekker and van de Pol, pp. 1, 14. §

34 Ibid., pp.101–02 for an explanation of why the phenomenon of female cross-dressing died out in the Netherlands in the nineteenth century.

35 Durova, N. (1989), *The Cavalry Maiden: Journals of Russian Officer in the Napoleonic Wars*, with translation, introduction, and notes by Mary Fleming, Bloomington and Indianapolis: Indiana University Press, p. xvii.

36 Ibid., p. 5.

37 Ibid., pp. xx, 17.

38 Zirin, M. F. (2003), 'Durova, Nadezhda Andreevna', in Pennington and Highnam, p. 129.

39 Durova, p. x.

40 Elting, J. R. (1988), *Swords Around a Throne: Napoleon's Grande Armée*, New York: Free Press, p. 612.

41 https://historycooperative.org/journal/my-death-for-the-motherland-is-happiness-women-patriotism-and-soldiering-in-russias-great-war-1914-1917/ [accessed 14 December 2018].

42 Baynes, T. S. (ed.) (1878), 'Fredrika Bremer', *Encyclopaedia Britannica*, 4 (9th edn), New York: Charles Scribner's Sons, pp. 257–58.

43 Ibid.

44 Bremer, C. (1868), *Life, Letters and Posthumous Works of Fredrika Bremer*, New York: Hurd and Houghton, p. 31.

45 Ziegler, P. (1965), *Addington: A Life of Henry Addington, First Viscount Sidmouth*, London: Collins, p. 114.

46 'Women in Red Cloaks as Soldiers', *Notes and Queries*, 7 (3), 4 June 1887, p. 452.

47 Hacker, B. (1981), 'Women and Military Institutions in Early Modern Europe: A reconnaissance', *Signs*, 6 (4), pp. 643–71.

48 Cotton, E. (1849), *A Voice from Waterloo*, London: B. L. Green, p. 55.

49 Trustram, M. (1984), *Women of the Regiment: Marriage and the Victorian Army*, Cambridge: Cambridge University Press, pp. 14–22.

50 Ibid., p. 28.

51 Dowie, M. M. (ed.) (1893), *Women Adventurers: The Adventure Series*, 15, London: Unwin Brothers, p. xvii.

52 See diverse entries in Hudson, D. (1974), *Munby: A Man of Two Worlds: The Life and Diaries of Arthur J. Munby 1828–1910*, London: Abacus.

53 'Female Pugilist', *Weekly Dispatch*, 6 October 1813.

54 A. J. Munby diaries, Vol. 34, 18 February 1866 and 24 March 1866, Trinity College Library, Cambridge (MUNB).

55 Walker, Julian (2018), 'Thinking Sex after the Great War', unpublished lecture, Royal Library of Brussels, 17–19 October, pp. 1–2.

56 'Women's Fitness for Soldiering', *The Times*, 9 October 1917.

Chapter 3

1 Quoted in Lacy, M. (2008), *The History of the Female Shipwright*, with an introduction by M. Lincoln, London: National Maritime Museum, p. 22.

2 Staats, Evers (1859), *Criminal Justice in Gelderland or Important Criminal Cases which have occurred there from 1811–1859*, Arnhem: D. A. Thieme. My thanks to Hendrick van Kerkwijk for the translation from the Dutch.

3 Dekker, R. M. and van de Pol, L. (1989), *The Tradition of Female Transvestism in Early Modern Europe*, London: Macmillan Press, pp. 31–32.

4 Lacy, p. 11.

5 Ibid., p. 11.

6 Ibid., p. 19.

7 Ibid., p. 29.

8 Ibid., p. 32.

9 'A Female Sailor'; 'Extract of a letter from an officer of the "Robert Small" off the Cape of Good Hope, October 20, 1839', *The Times*, 28 December 1839, p. 7.

10 Gunn, George (1768–1852) (fl.1791–1799); JHB 05/2000. I am grateful to Warren Sinclair for this reference.

11 'Tale of 1807: Orkney Woman's Trials', *The Orcadian*, 28 December 1922, p. 3. Hudson's Bay Company archives, A.30/9 fo.33. I am grateful to Warren Sinclair for this reference.

12 Easton, F. (2003), 'Gender's Two Bodies: Women warriors, female husbands and plebeian life', *Past & Present*, 180 (8), pp. 131–74.

13 De Foe, D. (1840), *The Novels and Miscellaneous Works of Daniel De Foe … Vol. viii. Memoirs of Captain Carleton. Life and Adventures of Mrs. Christian Davies*, London: Thomas Tegg, pp. 239–40.

14 Dugaw, D. (1989), *Warrior Women and Popular Balladry, 1600–1850*, Cambridge: Cambridge University Press, pp. 148–49.

15 Anon. (1741), *The Life and Adventures of Mrs. Christian Davies the British Amazon, Commonly Call'd Mother Ross*, London: Richard Montagu, pp. 1–2.

16 Easton (2003), op. cit., p. 133.

17 Anon. (1741), op. cit., p. 2.

18 Corfield, P. J. (1987), 'Class by Name and Number in Eighteenth-Century Britain', *History: The Journal of the Historical Association*, 72, (234), pp. 38–61, 42.

19 De Pauw, L. G. (1998), *Battlecries and Lullabies: Women in War from Prehistory to the Present*, Norman: University of Oklahoma Press, p. 116.

20 Ibid., p. 117.

21 Hagist, D. N. (2002), 'The Women of the British Army in America', http://www.revwar75.com/library/hagist/britwomen.htm#120 [accessed 18 September 2018]

22 Ibid.

23 Quoted in Hagist.

24 Quoted in Kingsley, R. F. and Clerke, F. C. (1998), 'Letters to Lord Polwarth from Sir Francis-Carr Clerke, Aide-De-Camp to General John Burgoyne', *New York History*, 79 (4), pp. 393–424; p. 413.

25 'Phoebe Hessel', *The Circulator of Useful Knowledge, Literature, Amusement and General Information*, 5 March 1825, pp. 1, 147.

26 Dugaw, D. (2004), 'Hessel [née Smith], Phoebe' (1713–1821), *Oxford Dictionary of National Biography*, https://www.oxforddnb.com/

search?q=Phoebe+Hessel&searchBtn=Search&isQuickSearch=true
[accessed 18 September 2018].

27 'Phoebe Hessel'.

28 Stark, S. J. (1996), *Female Tars: Women Aboard Ship in the Age of Sail*, London: Constable, pp. 107–10.

29 Stark points out that the 82nd Regiment did not exist in 1792, the year Talbot claimed to have enlisted, and was not sent to the West Indies until 1795, three years after she allegedly set sail. 'Furthermore, the *Crown* transport, in which Bowen and Talbot claimed to have sailed, did exist but in 1792 was sailing back to England from India', p. 109.

30 'Female Sailor', *The Times*, 12 November 1807.

31 Ibid.

32 Ibid.

33 Quoted in Stark, p. 5.

34 Quoted in Stark, p. 7.

35 Quoted in Stark, p. 47.

36 De Pauw, pp. 104–05.

37 Wheelwright, J. (1995), 'Tars, Tarts and Swashbucklers', in J. Stanley (ed.), *Bold in Her Breeches: Women Pirates Across the Ages*, London: Pandora Press.

38 Ibid., p. 179.

39 A note about the spelling of Anne Bonny's name: Daniel Defoe in *A General History of the Pyrates* records it as 'Anne Bonny, alias Bonn' (p. 130). However, in the transcript of her trial on 28 November 1720, it is recorded as 'Ann Bonny, alias Bonn' which may have been a misprint as Anne is the correct Irish spelling of the name. National Archives CO137/14.

40 Defoe, D. (1972), edited by M. Schonhorn, *A General History of the Pyrates*, London: J. M. Dent & Sons, p. 139.

41 Ibid., p. 140.

42 Ibid., p. 140.

43 Ibid., p. 130.

44 Ibid., p. 131.

45 Ibid., p. 131.

46 Ibid., p. 132.

47 Ibid., p. 132.

48 Wheelwright, p. 187.

49 *The Middlesex Journal and Evening Advertiser*, quoted in Hagist, D. N. (2002), 'The Women of the British Army in America',

http://www.revwar75.com/library/hagist/britwomen.htm#120
[accessed 18 September 2018].

50 Hagist.

51 Cuthbertson, B. (1768), *Cuthbertson's System for the Complete Interior Management and Economy of a Battalion of Infantry*, London: W. Cavel, et al., pp. 54–67. The reference to recruits sleeping naked comes from Shaw, J.R. and Teagarden, O. M. (1807), *John Robert Shaw: an autobiography of thirty years, 1777–1807*, Athens Ohio: Ohio University Press, p. 9.

52 Young, A. F. (2004), *Masquerade: The Life and Times of Deborah Sampson, Continental Soldier*, New York: Alfred Knopf, p. 79.

53 Ibid., p. 75.

54 Ibid., p. 90.

55 Ibid., p. 75.

56 Ibid., p. 21.

57 Cohen, D. A. (ed.) (1997), *The Female Marine and Related Works: Narratives of Cross-Dressing and Urban Vice in America's Early Republic*, Amherst: University of Massachusetts Press, p. 3.

58 Anon (1815), *The Female Marine; or, The Adventures of Miss Lucy Brewer*, Boston: Nathaniel Coverly, Jr.; reprinted 1966, New York: Da Capo Press, p. 50.

59 Cohen, p. 5.

60 Clarke, J. S. and McArthur, J. (eds) (2010), *The Naval Chronicle: Containing A General and Biographical History of the Royal Navy of the United Kingdom with a Variety of Original Papers on Nautical Subjects*, 28, July–December 1812, Cambridge: Cambridge University Press, p. 196.

61 Ibid.

62 Ibid.

63 Anon. (1840), *The Surprising Adventures of Almira Paul*, New York: C. E. Daniels, pp. 13–14.

64 Blanton, D. and Cook, L. M. (2002), *They Fought Like Demons: Women Soldiers in the American Civil War*, Baton Rouge, Louisiana: Louisiana State University, p. 3401.

65 Guerin, E. J. (1968), *Mountain Charley or the Adventures of Mrs. E. J. Guerin, Who Was Thirteen Years in Male Attire*, with an introduction by F. W. Mazzulla & William Kostka, Norman: University of Oklahoma Press, p. 18.

66 Ibid., p. 29.

67 Ibid., p. 22.

68 Blanton and Cook, pp. 3401–02.

69 Edmonds, S. E. E. (1865), *Nurse and Spy in the Union Army*, Philadelphia: Philadelphia Publishing, p. 6.

70 Schneider, F., 'Sarah Emma Edmonds-Seeley [sic] (Alias Franklin Thompson) The Female Soldier', *The State Republican*, 19 June 1900, p. 7.

71 Ibid.

72 Ibid.

73 Ibid.

74 Leonard, E. D. (1999), *All the Daring of the Soldier: Women of the Civil War Armies*, London: W. W. Norton and Company, p. 170.

75 *The Unsexing of Emma Edmonds* (2004) [VHS], Pepita Ferrari: Montreal, Films Piché Ferrari.

76 Schneider.

77 Edmonds, p. 18.

78 Ibid.

79 Schneider.

80 Ibid.

81 Fladeland, B (1958), 'Alias Frank Thompson', *Michigan History Magazine*, 42 (3), pp. 435–62; p. 439.

82 Ibid.

83 Danette, S. G. L. (1959), *Noble Women of the North*, New York: Thomas Yoseloff.

84 Blanton and Cook, loc. 149.

85 Dugaw, D. (1985), 'Balladry's Female Warriors: Women, warfare and disguise in the eighteenth century', *Eighteenth Century Life*, 9 (1), pp. 1–20.

86 Schneider, p. 3.

87 Blanton and Cook, loc. 615.

88 Blanton, D. (1992), *Minerva: Quarterly Report on Women and the Military*, Vol. X, Nos. 3. & 4, Fall/Winter, pp. 1–12, http://www.buffalosoldier.net/CathayWilliamsFemaleBuffaloSoldierWith Documents.htm [accessed 29 May 2019].

89 Ibid.

90 Livermore, M. (1888), *My Story of the War*, Hartford, Connecticut: A. D. Worthington & Co, p. 120.

91 Velazquez, L. J. (1876), edited by C. J. Worthington, *The Woman in Battle: A Narrative of the Exploits, Adventures, and Travels of Madame Loreta Janeta Velazquez*; reprinted 1972, New York: Arno Press.

92 Ibid., p. 16.

93 Ibid., p. 6.

94 Leonard, p. 252.

95 Livermore, p. 120; McPherson, J., 'Foreword', in L. Cook Burgess
    (1994), *An Uncommon Solider: The Civil War Letters of Sarah Rosetta
    Wakeman, alias Pvt. Lyons Wakeman, 153rd Regiment, New York State
    Volunteers, 1862–1864*, Oxford: Oxford University Press, p. xi. See
    Blanton and Cook for details of the cases of the 240 combatants, and
    Leonard, pp. 220–21.

96 Livermore, p. 120.

97 Sheridan, P. H. (1888), *Personal Memoirs of P.H. Sheridan, United
    States Army*, New York: C. L. Webster, pp. 1, 254.

98 Quoted in Blanton and Cook, loc. 1021.

99 Schneider.

100 Davis, D. T. (1917), 'Saw Active Service as a Man', Clarke Historical
    Library, Central Michigan University.

101 'Interesting Scrapbook is Discovered', *Concord News*, 1937, nd;
    'Pvt. Frank Thompson', file #943, Clarke Historical Library, Central
    Michigan University.

102 Moore, M. (1862), *The Lady Lieutenant, or the Strange and Thrilling
    Adventures of Miss Madeline Moore*, Philadelphia: Barclay and Co,
    p. 17.

103 Ibid.

104 Botchkareva, M. (1919), *Yashka: My Life as Peasant, Exile and Soldier*,
    as set down by Isaac Don Levine, New York: Frederick A. Stokes,
    pp. 18 and 27. Although she is referenced here as 'Botchkareva',
    'Bochkareva' is the most commonly used English-language spelling of
    her name.

105 Ibid., p. 28.

106 Ibid., p. 28.

107 Ibid., p. 33. Maria and Yakov (or Yankel) Buk, 'a handsome young
    man aged 24', were married by a civil agreement without the sanction
    of the church (Yakov was Jewish), which was a common practice in
    pre-revolutionary Russia where divorce was difficult to obtain.

108 Ibid., p. 66.

109 Ibid., p. ix.

110 Drieu, C. (2016), 'Maria Botchkareva, Yaska: Journal d'une femme
    combattante, Russie 1914-1917', *The Journal of Power Institutions
    in Post-Soviet Societies*, https://journals.openedition.org/pipss/4217
    [accessed 25 July 2018], p. 17. Hutton, M. (2015), *Resilient Russian
    Women in the 1920s & 1930s*, Lincoln New Brunswick: Zea Books,
    p. 33.

111 Bochkareva, p. ix.

112 Stoff, L. S. (2006), *They Fought for The Motherland: Russia's Women Soldiers in World War 1 and the Revolution*, Lawrence, Kansas: University Press of Kansas, p. 88.

113 Harriman, F. J. (1923), *From Pinafores to Politics*, New York: Henry Holt and Co., pp. 278–85.

114 Fitzgerald, Lt. Col. R. F. (1920), 'Women's Work in the Great War', unidentified Sydney newspaper, 13 March, Flora Sandes Collection in the possession of Arthur and Nan Baker [hereafter FS Coll].

115 Beatty, B. (1918), *The Red Heart of Russia*, New York: The Century Co., p. 92.

116 Bochkareva, p. 76.

117 Ibid., pp. 76 and 80.

118 Beatty, p. 100.

119 Ibid., p. 102.

120 Ibid., p. 102.

121 Bryant, L. (1918), *Six Red Months in Russia: An Observer's Account of Russia Before and During the Proletarian Dictatorship*, London: Heinemann, p. 212; Stites, R. (1978), *The Women's Liberation Movement in Russia: Feminism, Nihilism and Bolshevism, 1860–1930*, Princeton, Guilford: Princeton University Press, p. 280.

122 McDermid, J. and Hillyar, A. (1999), *Midwives of the Revolution: Female Bolsheviks and Women Workers in 1917*, London: University College London Press, p. 181.

123 A twenty-one-year-old woman who did actually follow her brother into the conflict tried at first to be enlisted as a nurse. She was so worried about her sibling, who was only thirteen years old, that she, and another woman who had also been rejected by the nursing services, borrowed money to travel to a larger city (Tiflis) where they hoped to enlist as privates in the army. Cited in McDermid, J. and Hillyar, A. (1999), *Midwives of the Revolution: Female Bolsheviks and Women Workers in 1917*, London: University College London Press. p. 117.

124 The military historian Linda Grant De Pauw defines a 'camp follower' as a woman who provides combat support which can range from nursing, to sourcing and preparing food, to proving emotional comfort and sexual services (De Pauw, p. 17).

125 Yurlova, M. (1934), *Cossack Girl*, London: Cassell and Co, pp. 18–19.

126 Ibid., p. 36.

127 Griesse, A. and Stites, R. (1982), 'Russia: Revolution and War', in Nancy Loring Goldman (ed.), *Female Soldiers – Combatants or*

Non-Combatants: Historical Perspectives, London: Greenwood Press, p. 65.

128 'Warrior Women', *Literary Digest*, 19 June 1915, p. 1,460.

129 Forbes, R. (1935), *Women Called Wild*, London: Grayson & Grayson, p. 65.

130 Alexinsky, T. (1916), *With the Russian Wounded*, London: T. Fisher Unwin, pp. 84–85.

131 Russia: 'Women Share in the War', *Jus Suffragii*, 1 November 1914, Vol. 9, (2), p. 190.

132 'Women and the War', *Jus Suffragii*, 1 May 1915, Vol. 9, (8), p. 290.

133 Russia : *Jus Suffragii*, 1 June 1915. Vol. 9, (9), p. 300.

134 Ibid.

135 'Women and War', *Jus Suffragii*, 1 February 1917, Vol. 11, (5), p. 74.

136 Quoted in Griesse and Stites, who mention that particular historical and social circumstances in Russia during the First World War facilitated the presence of female combatants: 'The front was so vast and mobile (from Riga to the Carpathians to the Black Sea), the situation so desperate, and the scene so chaotic that resistance to the presence of women was perhaps considered not worthy of the time required', p. 67.

137 Ibid., p. 63.

138 Bryant, p. 216.

139 Ibid., p. 218.

140 Griesse and Stites, p. 67.

141 'Baby Day at 69th Bazaar', *New York Times*, 4 November 1916, p. 15.

142 Quoted in Weiss, E. F. (2008), *Fruits of Victory: The Woman's Land Army of America in the Great War*, Washington, DC: Potomac Books, p. 13.

143 'Baby Day at 69th Bazaar'.

144 Weiss, pp. 16–18.

145 Sandes, F. (1927), *The Autobiography of a Woman Soldier: A Brief Record of Adventure with the Serbian Army, 1916–1919*, London: Witherby, p. 9.

146 Arkell-Smith V. (1956), 'For 30 Years I posed as a Man', *Empire News and Sunday Chronicle*, 20 February 1956, p. 2.

147 Sigerson Shorter, D. (1907), 'The Vagrant's Heart', in *The Troubadour and Other Poems*, London: Hodder and Stoughton.

148 Miller, L. (2012), *A Fine Brother: The Life of Captain Flora Sandes*, London: Alma Books, p. 29.

149 Personal scrapbook, FS Coll.

150 Miller, p. 30.

151 Ibid., p. 31.

152 Popham, H. (2003), *The FANY in Peace and War: The Story of the First Aid Nursing Yeomanry, 1907–2003*, Barnsley: Leo Cooper, p. 4.

153 London, P. (2015), 'Dorset's Wartime Heroine Mable St. Claire Stobart', *Dorset Life*, January, http://www.dorsetlife.co.uk/2015/01/dorsets-wartime-heroine-mabel-st-clair-stobart/ [accessed 27 July 2018].

154 Popham, p. 4.

155 Flora Sandes, notes for her 1920 Australian tour, FS Coll.

156 Flora Sandes, diary, 17 August, 24 August 1917, FS Coll.

157 Flora Sandes, notes for her 1920 Australian tour, FS Coll.

158 Ibid.

159 Ibid.

160 Flora Sandes, notes for her 1920 Australian tour, FS Coll.

161 Ibid.

162 Krippner, M. (1980), *The Quality of Mercy: Women at War, Serbia 1915–1918*, London: David and Charles, p. 110.

163 Flora Sandes, notes for her 1920 Australian tour, FS Coll.

164 Quoted in Miller, p. 61.

165 Miller, p. 65.

166 Miller notes that Flora's diary records the date of Cooke's death as 19 February 1915 but he had, in fact, died on 10 February, p. 377n.

167 Flora Sandes, diary 20 February 1915, FS Coll.

168 Flora Sandes, diary 22 February 1915, FS Coll.

169 Flora Sandes, notes for her 1920 Australian tour and diary 22 February 1915, FS Coll.

170 Flora Sandes, notes for her 1920 Australian tour, FS Coll.

171 Flora Sandes, diary 1 and 3 March 1915, FS Coll.

172 Flora Sandes, diary 16–21 March 1915, FS Coll.

173 Flora Sandes, diary 29 July 1915, FS Coll.

174 Hutton, I. E. (1928), *With a Woman's Unit in Serbia, Salonika, and Sebastopol*, London: Williams and Norgate, pp. 37–38.

175 Flora Sandes, diary 3 November 1915, FS Coll.

176 Hutton, pp. 65–67.

177 Sandes (1927), p. 13.

178 Flora Sandes, diary 20 November 1915.

179 Sandes, F. (1916), *An English Woman-Sergeant in the Serbian Army*, London: Hodder & Stoughton, pp. 13–15.

180 Flora Sandes, diary 28 November 1915.

181 Flora Sandes to Sophia Sandes, 21 November 1915, FS Coll.

182 Flora Sandes, diary 20 November 1915.
183 Sandes (1927), p. 12.
184 Ibid., p. 12.
185 Flora Sandes, diary 28 November 1915.
186 Sandes (1927), p. 13.
187 Ibid.
188 Sandes (1916), p. 47.
189 Sandes (1927), p. 77.
190 Ibid., pp. 76–77.
191 'The Autobiography of a Woman Soldier', *Times Literary Supplement*, 20 May 1927, p. 378.
192 Grémaux, R. (2017), 'Alone of All Her Sex? The Dutch Jeanne Merkus and the hitherto hidden other viragos in the Balkans during the Great Eastern Crisis (1875–1878)', *Balcanica*, Vol. XL VIII, (94), pp. 67–106.
193 Ibid., pp. 69–70.
194 Ibid., p. 70.
195 'Jeanne Merkus', Algemeen Ryksarchief, Collection Koopstra, 1030/63.5.
196 Grémaux, pp. 74–83. Grémaux also cites several other cases of unnamed and less well-documented female combatants in the Serbo-Turkish War of 1876–78.
197 Wright, A. and Farquhar-Bernard, A. C. (eds) (1884), *Adventures in Servia: Or, The Experiences of a Medical Free Lance Among the Bashi-Bazou, etc.*, London: W. Swan Sonnenschein & Co, pp. 51–52.
198 Ibid., p. 53.
199 See for example, Cardoza, T. (2013), '"Habits Appropriate to Her Sex": The female military experience in France during the Age of Revolution', in K. Hagemann, G. Mettele and J. Rendall (eds), *Gender, War and Politics: Transatlantic Perspectives, 1775–1830*, Basingstoke: Pan Macmillan, p. 196.
200 Lawrence, D. (1919), *Sapper Dorothy Lawrence: The Only English Woman Soldier, Late Royal Engineers, 51st Division, 179th Tunnelling Company, BEF*, London: John Lance, pp. 41–42.
201 Ibid., p. 40.
202 Mack, L. (1915), *A Woman's Experience in the Great War*, London: Mills and Boon; St. John, Lady I. (1915), *A Journey in Wartime*, London: Allen Lane; Mary Wilkinson is mentioned in Dr Katherine MacPhail to her mother, from Bellevue Samoensa, 9 October 1916, Women's Work Collection, Imperial War Museum.

203 Lawrence, p. 48.
204 Ibid., p. 58.
205 'Woman's Attempt to Join the Army', *Hornsey Journal*, 18 August 1917.
206 Ibid.
207 Oram, A. (2007), *Her Husband Was a Woman! Women's Gender-crossing in Modern British Popular Culture*, London: Routledge, p. 32.
208 Ibid.
209 *News of the World*, 20 August 1916, p. 7.
210 Ruck, B., 'Why Women Masquerade as Men: The craving they endure in this day of big things', *Illustrated Sunday Herald*, 27 August 1916.
211 Beddoe, D. (1989), *Back to Home and Duty: Women Between the Wars, 1918–1939*, London: Pandora, p. 10.
212 Howard Chandler Christy, First World War American recruiting poster, Imperial War Museum, Cat No. 0246.
213 'Woman's Attempt to Join the Army'.

Chapter 4

1 Valerie Arkell-Smith, *The Sunday Dispatch*, 31 March 1929.
2 Bratton, J. (1987), 'King of the Boys', *Women's Review*, 20, p. 12.
3 On the image of the military nurse in Britain pre-1914 see Summers, A. (1988), *Angels and Citizens: British Women as Military Nurses, 1854–1914*, London: Routledge.
4 Anon. (1750), 'Some Account of Hannah Snell: the female soldier', *The Scots Magazine*, Vol. 12, pp. 330–32.
5 Snell, H. (1750), *The Female Soldier: The Surprising Life and Adventures of Hannah Snell*, London: R. Walker, p. 30. Snell is cited as the author in the British Library catalogue even though Walker operated as both publisher and editor. Snell biographer Matthew Stephens perhaps most appropriately identifies him as 'the creator'. Stephens, M. (2004), *Hannah Snell: The Secret Life of a Female Marine*, Sutton, Surrey: Ship Street Press, digital edn, loc. 1093.
6 Snell., p. 72.
7 Dickens, C. (1872), 'British Amazons', *All the Year Round*, 7 (175), 6 April, pp. 448–52.
8 Ibid.
9 Annual Register, 1815, p. 64.
10 Davies, W. H. (1986), *The Autobiography of a Super-Tramp*, Oxford: Oxford University Press, p. 84.

11 Ibid.

12 Ibid., pp. 86 and 84.

13 Quoted in Holmes, R. (2002), *Scanty Particulars: The Life of Dr. James Barry*, London: Viking, p. 85.

14 For more details on Barry's life, see Du Preez, M. and Dronfield, J. (2016), *Dr. James Barry: A Woman Ahead of her Time*, London: OneWorld Publications.

15 Vinton, J. A. (1916), 'The Female Review: Life of Deborah Sampson, the Female Soldier in the War of the Revolution, with an Introduction and Notes', *Notes and Queries*, (47), p. 131. Young, A. F. (2004), *Masquerade: The Life and Times of Deborah Sampson, Continental Soldier*, New York: Alfred Knopf. Young notes the inconsistency in the spelling of Robert Shurtliff, citing a receipt for a bounty for 'the sum of sixty pounds' to serve in the Continental Army for a three-year term, which could also be read as 'Shurtlieff', pp. 86–87.

16 Young, pp. 48–49.

17 Jerome Robbins' diary, 1 and 11 November 1861, Michigan Historical Collections, Bentley Historical Library, University of Michigan (hereafter BHLUM).

18 Ibid., 7 November 1861.

19 Burg, B. R. (ed.) (2002), *Gay Warriors: A Documentary History from the Ancient World to the Present*, New York and London: New York University Press, p. 172.

20 Jerome Robbins, diary, 11 November 1861, BHLUM.

21 Ibid., 16 November 1861.

22 Ibid., 17 November 1861.

23 Ibid., 19 November 1861.

24 Ibid., 6 December 1861.

25 Ibid., 20 December 1861.

26 Ibid., 22 and 23 December 1861.

27 Ibid., 20 December 1861.

28 Ibid., 23 December 1861.

29 Ibid., 3 March 1861.

30 Ibid., 20 December 20 1861.

31 Ibid., 4 April 1863.

32 Franklin Thompson muster roll for March–April 1863, 2nd Regiment Michigan Infantry. Military Service Records of Franklin Thompson, Co. F. 2nd Michigan Infantry, in RG94, Records of the Adjutant General's Office, Compiled Military Service Records, National Archives, Washington, DC.

33 Jerome Robbins, diary 20 April 1863, BHLUM.
34 Sarah Emma Edmonds to Jerome Robbins, Washington, DC, 10 May 1863, BHLUM.
35 Ibid.
36 Sarah Emma Edmonds to Jerome Robbins, Falmouth, Virginia, 16 January 1865, BHLUM.
37 Jerome Robbins, diary 20 April 1861.
38 Fladeland, B. (1958), 'Alias Franklin Thompson', *Michigan History*, Vol 42 (3), pp. 435–62, p. 455.
39 Ibid., p. 457.
40 Leonard, E. D. (1999), *All the Daring of the Soldier: Women of the Civil War Armies*, London: W. W. Norton and Company, p. 171.
41 RG 15 Records of the Veterans Administration, Sarah Emma Edmonds Seelye Pension File, application #526889.
42 Quoted in Anon. (1741), *The Life and Adventures of Mrs. Christian Davies the British Amazon, Commonly Call'd Mother Ross*, London: Richard Montagu, Part 1, p. 20.
43 Ibid., p. 27.
44 Ibid., p. 27.
45 Anon. (1810?), *The Life and Extraordinary Adventures of Susanna Cope: The British Female Soldier*. Banbury: Cherney, np.
46 Stephens, M. (2014), *Hannah Snell: The Secret Life of a Female Marine*, Sutton, Surrey: Ship Street Press, digital edn, loc. 411.
47 Anon. (1750), p. 87.
48 Stark discusses the lack of veracity of Snell's account by comparing ship's muster books and pension records against the 'welter of misinformation' in subsequent biographical accounts. See Stark, S. J. (1996), *Female Tars: Women Aboard Ship in the Age of Sail*, London: Constable, pp. 102–07, n. 39, p. 187.
49 Quoted in Stark, p. 157. It is ironic that when Lacy, who went to sea to escape domestic service, lodges with her master, Mr Acquiler in Gosport, his wife demands that she 'clean shoes, knives and forks, and do all the drudgery of the house': Lacy, M. (2008), *The History of the Female Shipwright*, with an introduction by M. Lincoln, London: National Maritime Museum, p. 147.
50 Lacy, op. cit., p. 153.
51 Ibid., p. 62.
52 Ibid., p. 96.
53 Ibid., p. 103.
54 Ibid., p. 131.

55 Ibid., p. 154.

56 Hitchcock, T. (2012), 'The Reformulation of Sexual Knowledge in Eighteenth-Century England', *Signs*, 37 (4), pp. 823–32; p. 826.

57 Lanser. S. (2001), 'Sapphic Picaresque, Sexual Difference and the Challenges of Homo-adventuring', *Textual Practice*, 15 (2), pp. 251–68.

58 Ibid.

59 Vinton, J. A. (1916), 'The Female Review: Life of Deborah Sampson, the Female Soldier in the War of Revolution', *The Magazine of History, Notes and Queries*, extra no.

60 Ibid., p. 150. See also Young who provides evidence that Sampson made a few questionable claims about her service, namely that she served not three years on active service but a three-year *term* and was discharged after seventeen months, p. 5.

61 Ibid.

62 Vinton, p. 150.

63 Ibid., p. 153 n.

64 Young, p. 154.

65 Ibid., p. 155.

66 Ibid., p. 303.

67 Dekker, R. M. and van de Pol, L. (1989), *The Tradition of Female Transvestism in Early Modern Europe*, London: Macmillan Press, p. 48.

68 Trumbach, R. (1994), 'London's Sapphists: From three sexes to four genders in the making of modern culture', in G. Herdt (ed.), *Third Sex Third Gender: Beyond Sexual Dimorphism in Culture and History*, New York: Zone Books, pp. 111–36; p. 121.

69 Stoff, L. S. (2006), *They Fought for the Motherland: Russia's Women Soldiers in World War 1 and the Revolution*, Lawrence, Kansas: University Press of Kansas, p. 39.

70 Dadeshkeliani, K. (1934), *Princess in Uniform*, translated by A. J. Ashton, London: Bell, p. 108.

71 Ibid., p. 108.

72 Ibid., p. 110.

73 Ibid., pp. 118–19.

74 Ibid., pp. 119–20.

75 Gardo, L. (1938), *Cossack Fury: The Experiences of a Woman Soldier with the White Russians*, London: Hutchinson and Co, p. 103. Lul Gardo was the stage name of Varvara Kassovskaia, who claimed to have written under a pseudonym to protect her family, then living in the Soviet Union. However, according to historian Jonathan D. Smele, her experiences as a soldier in the White Army had not

been authenticated. See Jonathan D. Smele in *Historical Dictionary of the Russian Civil War: 1916–1926*, London: Rowan & Littlefield, p. 391. Nevertheless, even by 1924 Varvara was giving press interviews: 'Madame Kassovskaia's Thrilling Story', *Adelaide Register*, 7 April 1924, p. 12.

For a reference to her singing career and marriages, see 'Madame Varvara Kassovskaia, http://luingahg.blogspot.com/p/scottish-friendship-brought-world-fame_7.html [accessed 8 August 2018]; 'Varvara K – a woman with many names,' by Tana, 19 August 2015; http://www.findrussianheritage.com/destination-australia/varvara-k-a-woman-with-many-names/ notes the popularity of her story, with more than 200 articles about it published in the Australian press, mostly in 1924 when she arrived in the country [accessed 8 August 2018]. 'Traditional Songs: National Programme Daventry', *The Radio Times*, 782, 26 September 1938, p. 26.

76 Yurlova, M. (1934), *Cossack Girl*, London: Cassell and Co, p. 44.
77 Ibid., p. 45.
78 Ibid., p. 47.
79 Ibid., p. 53.
80 Sandes, F. (1927), *The Autobiography of a Woman Soldier: A Brief Record of Adventure with the Serbian Army, 1916–1919*, London: Witherby, p. 149.
81 Ibid., p. 138.
82 Botchkareva, M. (1919), *Yashka: My Life as Peasant, Exile and Soldier*, as set down by Isaac Don Levine, New York: Frederick A. Stokes, p. 76.
83 Ibid., p. 78.
84 Ibid., p. 78.
85 Ibid., p. 82.
86 Titunik, R. F. (2009), 'Are We all Torturers Now? A reconsideration of women's violence at Abu Ghraib', *Cambridge Review of International Affairs*, 22 (2), pp. 257–77; p. 269.
87 Botchkareva, p.102.
88 Titunik, p. 269.
89 Quoted in Titunik, p. 274.
90 Botchkareva, p. 88.
91 Ibid., p. 88.
92 Sandes, pp. 85–86.
93 Hopfl, H. (2003), 'Becoming a (Virile) Member: Women and the military body', *Body and Society*, 9 (4), pp. 13–30.
94 Ibid., p. 25.

95 Sandes, p. 84.

96 Ibid., p. 82.

97 Ibid., p. 212.

98 Ibid., p. 85.

99 Lawrence, D. (1919), *Sapper Dorothy Lawrence: The Only English Woman Soldier, Late Royal Engineers, 51st Division, 179th Tunnelling Company, BEF*, London: John Lance, p. 93.

100 Ibid., p. 110.

101 Dadeshkeliani, p. 97.

102 'At the Mansion House', *Weekly Dispatch*, 5 July 1840.

103 Velazquez, p. 6.

104 Arkell-Smith, V. (1956), 'My Amazing Masquerade ... A Wife Confesses', *Empire News and Chronicle*, 19 February 1956.

105 'Woman's Strange Life as a Man', *Daily Express*, 6 March 1929.

106 'How the Colonel's Secret Was Revealed', *Daily Sketch*, 6 March 1929.

107 Benewick, R. (1972), *The Fascist Movement in Britain*, London: Penguin, p. 37.

108 Jane, E. A. (2017), 'Dude ... Stop the Spread': Antagonism, agonism, and #manspreading on social media, *International Journal of Cultural Studies*, 20 (5), pp. 459–75.

109 Sandes, p. 210.

110 Ibid., pp. 125–26.

111 Ibid., p. 68.

112 Ibid., p. 68.

113 Ibid., p. 87.

114 Flora Sandes to unknown, 14 October 1916, FS Coll.

115 Yurlova, p. 66.

116 Ibid., p.126.

117 Ibid., pp.126–27.

118 Ibid., p. 120.

119 Bochkareva, p. 163.

120 Stites, p. 298.

121 Stockdale, M. (2004), '"My Death for the Motherland is Happiness": Women, patriotism, and soldiering in Russia's Great War, 1914–1917', *American Historical Review*, 109 (1), pp. 78–116.

122 Ibid., p. 102.

123 Griesse and Stites, p. 64.

124 Farmborough, pp. 306–07.

125 Flora Sandes to Fanny Sandes, 'In the Trench', 24 July 1917, FS Coll.

126 Yurlova, p. 79.

127 Ibid., p. 79.
128 Ibid., p. 94.
129 Ibid., p. 155.
130 Lawrence, p. 93.
131 Mundell, F. (1898), *Heroines of History*, London: The Sunday School Union, p. 40.
132 Botchkareva, p. 116.
133 Sandes, p. 31.
134 Flora Sandes to Sophia Sandes, 21 November 1915, FS Coll.
135 Sandes, p. 176.
136 Flora Sandes to Sophia Sandes, 14 October 1916, FS Coll.
137 Sandes, p. 141.

Chapter 5

1 '"Gleanings from Dark Annals": Modern Amazons', *Chambers's Journal*, 30 May 1863, Vol. 419, pp. 348–51.
2 Mayor, A. (2014), *The Amazons: Lives and Legends of Warrior Women Across the Ancient World*, Princeton and Oxford: Princeton University Press, p. 321.
3 Winston Churchill quoted in Spencer, C. (2005), *Blenheim: Battle for Europe*, Phoenix: London, p. 136.
4 Anon. (1741), *The Life and Adventures of Mrs. Christian Davies the British Amazon, Commonly Call'd Mother Ross*, London, 2nd ed, 2 parts and appendix, p. 53.
5 Ibid., p. 77.
6 Ibid., Part 2, p. 45.
7 Ibid., p. 15.
8 Ibid., p. 31.
9 Anon. (1750), *The Female Soldier; or, The Suprising Life and Adventures of Hannah Snell*, London: Robert Walker.
10 Ibid., p. 31.
11 Ibid., p. 58.
12 Stephens, M. (2014), *Hannah Snell: The Secret Life of a Female Marine*, Sutton, Surrey: Ship Street Press, digital edn, loc. 529–30.
13 Ibid., p. 586. For details of Belchier, see Love, H. D. (1996), *Vestiges of Old Madras*, 1640–1800, Vol. 2, 27 January 1747 [1748], New Delhi: Mittal Publications, p. 386.
14 Stephens, loc. 599.
15 Ibid., loc. 660.

16 Dowie, M. M. (ed.) (1893), *Women Adventurers: The Adventure Series*, 15, London: T. Fisher Unwin, p. 115.

17 Ibid., p. 116.

18 Ibid., p. 116.

19 Stephens, loc. 690.

20 Young, A. (2004), *Masquerade: The Life and Times of Deborah Sampson, Continental Soldier*, New York: Alfred A. Knopf, p. 94.

21 Mann, H. (1797), *The Female Review*, Dedham, Massachusetts: Nathaniel and Benjamin Heaton, p. 173.

22 Ibid., p. 175. Young identified Cron Pond as Compond, approximately nine miles east of Peekskill, New York, p. 127.

23 Mann, p. 254.

24 Young, pp. 129–30.

25 Young, p. 130.

26 Quoted in Vinton, J. A. (1916), 'The Female Review: Life of Deborah Sampson, the Female Soldier in the War of Revolution', *Notes and Queries*, extra no. 47, p. 123.

27 Mann, p. 191.

28 Ibid., p. 194. Young's biography clarifies the identity of Dr Binney and Mary Parker, op. cit., pp. 149–50.

29 Mann, p. 195.

30 Young, op. cit., p. 155.

31 'Another Female Sailor', *Weekly Dispatch*, 17 December 1843.

32 'Police Intelligence, Mansion House', *Morning Post*, 31 March 1868, p. 7.

33 'At Mansion House', *Weekly Dispatch*, 5 July 1840.

34 'A Female Sailor; Extract of a letter from an officer of the "Robert Small" off the Cape of Good Hope, October 20, 1839', *The Times*, 28 December 1839, p. 7.

35 Ibid.

36 'At Mansion House'.

37 Ibid.

38 Ibid.

39 Ibid.

40 'Female Sailor', *The Times*, 12 November 1807.

41 'Another Female Sailor', *Weekly Dispatch*, 25 July 1841.

42 'Flogging Female Prisoners', *Weekly Dispatch*, 10 June 1838.

43 Ibid.

44 Quoted in Coues, E. (ed.) (1965), *New Light on the Early History of the Greater Northwest: The Manuscript Journals of Alexander Henry*

and of David Thompson, 1799–1814: Official Geographer of the Same Company 1799–1814: Exploration and Adventure Among the Indians on the Red, Saskatchewan, Missouri and Columbia Rivers, Minneapolis: Ross and Haines, p. 426.

45 Fidler, Peter, *Journal of a Journey from Swan to the Red River*, Ref:3/3 fo. 58. Provincial Archives of Manitoba. Hudson's Bay Company archives, Winnipeg, Massachusetts.

46 William Harper to William Watt, Albany Fort, 5 September 1808, Earnest Marwick Collection, Orkney Parish Archives, Kirkwall, Orkney.

47 I am grateful to Warren Sinclair for these references. Correspondence with W. Sinclair, 9 July 1990.

48 *Annual Register*, 1807, p. 463.

49 Ibid. I am grateful to Peter Moore for his insight on this case.

50 *Naval Chronicle* 18 (July–December 1807), p. 342.

51 ADM 1/5383, court-martial of William Berry.

52 Annual Register, 1835, pp. 24–26.

53 Ibid.

54 Ibid.

55 Ibid.

56 Godineau, D. (1988), translated by Katherine Streip, *Women of Paris and Their French Revolution*, Berkley: University of California Press, p. 108.

57 Conner, S. P. (2003), 'French Revolution and Napoleonic Era, Women Soldiers in', in R. Pennington (ed.) and R. Highnam (advisory ed.), *Amazons to Fighter Pilots: A Biographical Dictionary of Military Women*, Vol. 1, A–Q, pp. 174–80.

58 Quoted in Lampron, E., 'French Revolution, Impact of War on Women's Protest During the', in B. Cook (ed.) (2006), *Women and War: A Historical Encyclopedia from Antiquity to the Present*, Vol. 2, Oxford: ABC Clio, p. 208.

59 Conner, p. 179.

60 Cardoza, T. (2013), '"Habits Appropriate to Her Sex": The female military experience in France during the Age of Revolution', in K. Hagemann, G. Mettele and J. Rendall (eds), *Gender, War and Politics: Transatlantic Perspectives, 1775–1830*, Basingstoke: Pan Macmillan, pp. 188–205 ; pp. 189 and 193.

61 St-Germain Leduc (1842), *Les Campagnes de Mademoiselle Thérèse Figueur, Aujourd'hui Madame Veuve Sutter etc*, Paris: Dauvin et Fontaine, Libraries, pp. 84–87.

62 Conner, S. P. (2003), 'Figueur, Thérèse', in Pennington and Higham, pp. 170–71; Anon. (1861), 'A Female Warrior', *The London*

Journal, and Weekly Record of Literature, Science, and Art, 33 (836), p. 108.

63 Vandam, A. D. (1894), 'The Real Madame Sans-Gêne', *The New Review*, 11 (62) pp. 24–34, p. 32.

64 Gilbert, O. P. (1932), *Women in Men's Guise*, translated by J. Lewis May, London: John Lane, The Bodley Head, p. 80.

65 *Éntrennes de La Vertu, pour l'année 1793; Seconde de la République*, Paris: Chez Savoye, p. 49.

66 Anon. (1850), 'The History of the Girondists. Translated from the French of Lamartine', *Reynold's Miscellany of Romance, General Literature, Science, and Art*, 4 (103), 29 June, p. 362.

67 Ibid.

68 Gilbert, p. 80. While Gilbert records the name as de Fernig, it appears as Fernig in other primary and secondary references.

69 Ibid.

70 Ibid., p. 82.

71 Anon. (1850), 'Book Thirty-Seven', *Reynolds Miscellany of Romance, General Literature, Science, and Art*, 6 July, pp. 363 and 375.

72 Ibid., p. 375.

73 Gilbert, p. 87.

74 Godineau, pp. 243–44.

75 Lampron, E. (2006), 'Fernig, Félicité (1170–1841), and Fernig, Théophile (1775–1819)', in Cook, p. 183.

76 Cardoza, p. 197.

77 Gilbert, pp. 87–88. For the Brûlon quotation, Anon. (1856), 'Madame Brûlon', *The United States Magazine*, 1, pp. 207–08.

78 Gilbert, p. 88.

79 Anon. (1856), p. 208.

80 Ibid.

81 Lady Charlotte Guest's manuscript journal, April 1851, Paris. I am indebted to Angela John for this reference.

82 Cardoza, p. 189.

83 Lawrence, D. (1919), *Sapper Dorothy Lawrence: The Only English Woman Soldier, Late Royal Engineers, 51st Division, 179th Tunnelling Company, BEF*, London: John Lance, p. 128.

84 Ibid., p. 131.

85 Ibid., p. 133.

86 Ibid., p. 133.

87 Ibid., p. 136.

88 Ibid., p. 160.

89 Ibid., p. 151.
90 Ibid., p. 149.
91 Ibid., p. 152.
92 Ibid., p. 175.
93 'Tells How She Hid on Army Transport', *The New York Times*, 17 July 1917, p. 6.
94 Ibid.
95 Stoff, L., 'Smirnova, Zoia F.', in Pennington and Higham, Vol. 2, p. 403.
96 Quoted in 'Young Girls Fighting on the Russian Front' (1916), *Current History: A Monthly Magazine of the New York Times*, May, 4 (2), pp. 365–67.
97 'German Amazons Dressed as Men Soldiers Haughty Toward Their Russian Captors', *New York Times*, 12 January 1915, p. 4.
98 'Rifles Russia Needs Now', *New York Times*, 13 November 1915, pp. 1–2.
99 Hagemann, K. (2011), 'Mobilizing Women for War: The history, historiography, and memory of German women's war service in the two world wars', *Journal of Military History*, 75, pp. 1055–93. Hagemann quotes the Prussian War Ministry from March 1917, to the 56,877 women who had already replaced 'military persons' in the military administration. Women were also deployed in the rear area of the army (Etappe), directly behind the front, p. 1069.
100 'Yarn of a Don Cossack', *New York Times*, 4 December 1914, p. 2.
101 Dadeshkeliani, K. (1934), *Princess in Uniform*, translated by A. J. Ashton, London: Bell, p. 161.
102 Sandes F. (1927), *The Autobiography of a Woman Soldier: A Brief Record of Adventure with the Serbian Army, 1916–1919*, London: Witherby, p. 158.
103 Ibid., p. 161.
104 Ibid., p. 161.
105 Ibid., p. 16.
106 Flora Sandes to Sophia Sandes, 14 October 1916, FS Coll.
107 Ibid.
108 Yurlova, M. (1934), *Cossack Girl*, London: Cassell and Co, p. 156.
109 Ibid., p. 21.

Chapter 6

1 Mayor, A. (2014), *The Amazons: Lives and Legends of Warrior Women Across the Ancient World*, Princeton and Oxford: Princeton University Press, pp. 27 and 28.

2 Ibid., p. 30.

3 De Pauw, L. G. (1998), *Battlecries and Lullabies: Women in War from Prehistory to the Present*, Norman: University of Oklahoma Press, p. 16.

4 Rogers, P. (1982), 'The Breeches Part' in Paul-Gabriel Boucé (ed.), *Sexuality in Eighteenth-Century Britain*, Manchester: Manchester University Press, pp. 244–57; p. 249. Lock, G. and Worrall, D. (2014), 'Cross-Dressed Performance at the Theatrical Margins: Hannah Snell, the Manual Exercise, and the New Wells Spa Theater, 1750', *Huntington Library Quarterly*, 77 (1), pp. 17–36. Lock and Worrall mention several other precursors to Snell's military theatrics including Charles Shadwell's Drury Lane comedy, *The Humours of the Army* (1713), and Charlotte Charke's cross-dressed appearance as the Fool in Odell's version of the Shadwell play, p. 25.

5 Stephens, M. (2014), *Hannah Snell: The Secret Life of a Female Marine*, Sutton, Surrey: Ship Street Press, digital edn, loc. 713.

6 Ibid., loc. 713 and 724.

7 Lock and Worrall, p. 18.

8 Quoted in Stephens, loc. 771.

9 Lock and Worrall, p. 32.

10 Ibid., p. 784.

11 WO 116/4, Royal Chelsea Hospital admission book, 1746–54.

12 *Annual Register*, 1782, p. 221.

13 Lacy, M. (2008), *The History of the Female Shipwright*, with an introduction by M. Lincoln, London: National Maritime Museum, p. 138.

14 Ibid., p. 152.

15 Ibid., p. 153.

16 Ibid., p. 153.

17 Ibid., pp. 153 and 154.

18 Ibid., p. 158.

19 Ibid., p. 163.

20 Ibid., p. 164.

21 Stark, S. J. (1996), *Female Tars: Women Aboard Ship in the Age of Sail*, London: Constable, pp. 164–65, quotes the Admiralty minutes report of 28 January 1772 and the Navy Board's Abstract of Letters on the determination on Lacy's pension.

22 Quoted in Young, A. (2004), *Masquerade: The Life and Times of Deborah Sampson, Continental Soldier*, New York: Alfred A. Knopf, p. 228.

23 Arundell, D. (1965), *The Story of Sadler's Wells, 1683–1977*, London: David Charles, p. 71.

24 Ibid.

25 Playbill, Royal Amphitheatre, Astleys, Gabrielle Enthoven Collection, Victoria and Albert Theatre Museum.

26 'At the Mansion House', *Weekly Dispatch*, 5 July 1840.

27 'A Female Sailor – Romantic Adventure', *Weekly Dispatch*, 8 February 1835.

28 Thornton. A. J. (1835), *The Interesting Life and Wonderful Adventures of that Extraordinary Woman Anne Jane Thornton, the Female Sailor; Disclosing Important Secrets, Unknown to the Public*, London: [no publisher].

29 Dugaw, D. (1989), *Warrior Women and Popular Balladry, 1650–1850*, Cambridge: Cambridge University Press, p. 151.

30 Edmonds, S. Emma E. (1864), *Unsexed; or, The Female Soldier: The Thrilling Adventures of a Woman, as Nurse, Spy and Scout, in Hospitals, Camps and Battlefields*, Philadelphia: Philadelphia Publishing. It was reissued in 1865 under the title, *Nurse and Spy in the Union Army*.

31 Leonard, E. D. (1999), *All the Daring of the Soldier: Women of the Civil War Armies*, London: W. W. Norton and Company, pp. 58–59.

32 Ibid.

33 Quoted in Blanton, D. and Cook, L. M. (2002), *They Fought Like Demons: Women Soldiers in the American Civil War*, Baton Rouge, Louisiana: Louisiana State University, p. 2865.

34 Edmonds, S. Emma E. (1865), *Nurse and Spy in the Union* Army, p. 33.

35 'Oh Jerome, it is pleasant to have a lady friend once more and I know one in the person of Miss Lizzie H. to whom I could trust the innermost secret of my heart.' Edmonds to Jerome Robbins, Washington, DC, 10 May 1863, Michigan Historical Collections, Bentley Historical Library, University of Michigan (BHLUM).

36 Edmonds (1865), *Nurse and Spy in the Union Army: Comprising the Adventures and Experiences of a Woman in Hospitals, camps and Battlefields*, Hartford, Conn: W. S. Williams, p. 6.

37 Schneider, F., 'Sarah Emma Edmonds-Seeley [sic] (Alias Franklin Thompson) The Female Soldier', *The State Republican*, 19 June 1900, p. 7.

38 Edmonds (1865), p. 333.

39 A. J. Munby diaries, Vol. 12, 27 January 1862, Trinity College Library, Cambridge (MUNB).

40 Hudson, D. (1974), *Munby: Man of Two Worlds: The Life and Diaries of Arthur J. Munby 1828–1910*, Abacus: London, p. 188.

41 Munby diaries, Vol. 13, 4 June 1862, MUNB.

42 Munby diaries, Vol. 11, 30 November 1861, MUNB.

43 Munby diaries, Vol. 13, 23 July 1862, MUNB.

44 Hudson, pp. 237–38.

45 'Law Intelligence: Thames', *The Morning Post*, 31 March 1868, p. 7.

46 Hindley, C. (1966), *Curiosities of Street Literature*, Vol. 2, London: Broadsheet King, p. 141.

47 Walker, J. (2018), 'Thinking Sex after the Great War', Royal Library of Brussels, 17–19 October, p. 3.

48 'The Belle of Cairo', *Edinburgh Evening Despatch*, 16 May 1903.

49 Dugaw, D. (1982), *The Female Warrior Heroine in Anglo-American Balladry*, University of California, PhD thesis, p. 92.

50 'Gleanings from the Dark Annals; Modern Amazons', *Chambers's Journal*, 30 May 1863.

51 HBCA reference: B.3/d/122 fo. 54d, 57d, 60.; B.3/a/111 fo. 23d; B.3/f/7 fos. 1d-2.

52 Hargreaves, R. (1930), *Women-at-Arms: Their Famous Exploits Throughout the Ages*, Hutchinson & Company: London, p. 262.

53 Census of Stromness, 1821, 1851, 1861. Death recorded in *The Orcadian*, 23 November 1861, p. 3.

54 *Historical and Scientific Society of Manitoba: annual report for the year 1888: Transcript 31*, Winnipeg, Manitoba: Historical and Scientific Society of Manitoba, p. 18.

55 Bell, C. N. (1934), 'First White Woman in Western Canada', *Winnipeg Free Press*, 23 June, p. 8.

56 HBCA reference: B.3/d/122 fo. 54d, 57d, 60.; B.3/a/111 fo. 23d; B.3/f/7 fos. 1d-2.

57 Dowie, M. M. (ed.) (1893), *Women Adventurers: The Adventure Series*, 15, London: T. Unwin, p. x.

58 Caulfield, J. (1819), *Portraits, Memoirs, and Characters of Remarkable Persons*, Vol. 2, London: S. Kirby, p. 112.

59 Ibid., p. 111.

60 Halberstam, J. (1998), *Female Masculinity*, Durham: Duke University Press, pp. 1–2.

61 *The Soldier's Companion; or, Martial Recorder, consisting of biography, anecdotes, poetry, and miscellaneous information peculiarly interesting to*

those connected with the military profession, etc. London: Edward Cock, 1824.

62 Ibid., p. 349.

63 Ibid., p. 346.

64 Carr, J. (1811), *Descriptive Travels in The Southern and Eastern Parts of Spain and the Balearic Isles in the Year 1809*, London: Sherwood, Neely et al., pp. 32–33.

65 Wilke, D., *The Maid of Saragossa*, London: G. Moon, p. 14, and on p. 16 Wilke identifies Saragossa as the inspiration for the 'Spanish maid' in Lord Byron's poem 'Childe Harold'.

66 Carr, op. cit., p. 33.

67 Ibid., p. 32.

68 Ibid., p. 37.

69 Trustram, M. (1984), *Women of the Regiment: Marriage and the Victorian Army*, Cambridge: Cambridge University Press, p. 28.

70 Parton, J. (1869), *Eminent Women of the Age: The Lives and Deeds of the Most Prominent Women of the Generation*, Hartford, Connecticut: S. M. Betts & Co.

71 Hacker, B. (1981), 'Women and Military Institutions in Early Modern Europe: A reconnaissance', *Signs*, 6 (4), pp. 634–71.

72 Carter, T. (1860), *Curiosities of War and Military Studies: anecdotal, descriptive and statistical*, London: Groombridge and Sons, p. 95.

73 Ibid., p. 98.

74 *The London Gazette*, 1 June 1847.

75 Rowbotham, Commander W. B. (1937), 'The Naval Service Medal, 1793–1840', *The Mariner's Mirror: The Journal of the Society for Nautical Research*, 23, July, p. 366.

76 Ibid., pp. 351–70, pp. 366–67.

77 Clayton, E. C. (1879), *Female Warriors: Memorials of Female Valour and Heroism, from the Mythological Ages to the Present Era*, Vol. 1, p. 3.

78 Ibid., Vol. 1, p. 2.

79 Dowie, M. M. (1901), 'Ethel F. Heddle, Celebrated Lady Travellers', *Good Words*, 42, p. 18.

80 Dowie (1893), op. cit., p. x.

81 Munby, A. J. (1881), 'Female Soldiers and Sailors', *Notes and Queries*, 6th series, 3, 19 February, p. 228.

82 Hiley, M. (1979), *Victorian Working Women*, Gordon Fraser: London, p. 176

83 Dowie (1893), p. xxii.

84 Stephen, L. (ed.) (1888), *Dictionary of National Biography*, Vol. 14, London, p. 133.

85 These notes appear on the British Library's copy of, J. (1742), *The British Heroine: Or An Abridgement of the Life and Adventures of Christian Davies, Commonly Call'd Mother Ross*, Reading: J. Newberry & C. Micklewright Wilson.

86 'Ultra-Centenarianism', *Notes and Queries*, 4th series, 12, 20 September 1873, pp. 221–22; 'Ultra-Centenarianism', *Notes and Queries*, 5th series, 21 March 1874, pp. 221–23.

87 Ibid.

88 'Hannah Snell', *Notes and Queries*, 8th series, 2, 3 December 1892, p. 171.

89 'Female Soldiers and Sailors', *Notes and Queries*, 6th series, 3, 19 February 1881, p. 283.

90 'What Can Women Do?' *Chambers's Journal*, 458, 5 October 1872, p. 635.

91 Leonowens, A. H. (1870), *The English Governess at the Siamese Court: Being Recollections of Six Years in the Royal Palace at Bangkok*, London: Trubner, p. 94.

92 Burton, R. F. (1864), *A Mission to Gelele, King of Dahome*, London: Tinsley Brothers; Duncan, J. (1847), *Travels in Western Africa in 1845 and 1846; Comprising a Journey through the Kingdom of Dahomey etc.*, London: Richard Bentley; Forbes, F. E. (1851), *Dahomey and the Dahomans Being the Journals of Two Missions to the King of Dahomey*, Paris: W. Galignani and Co, p. 8.

93 Munby diaries, Vol. 65, 22 June 1893, p. 174, MUNB.

94 Morton-Williams, P. (1993), 'A Yoruba Woman Remembers Servitude in a Palace of Dahomey, in the Reigns of Kings Glele and Behanzin', *Africa: Journal of the International African Institute*, 63 (1), pp. 102–17.

95 Moncrieff, A. R. H. (1913), *Heroes of the European Nations*, London: A & C Black, p. 10.

96 'Letter from an American girl in France', Miscellaneous 4, 60, Women's Work Collection, Imperial War Museum.

97 Ibid.

98 Farmborough, F. (1974), *Nurse at the Russian Front: A Diary 1914–1918*, London: Constable, pp. 299–300; pp. 304–05.

99 Dixon, J., *'The Little Grey Partridge': The Diary of Ishobel Ross, Serbia 1916–1917*, unpublished diary, pp. 18 and 25, Imperial War Museum.

100 *Nursing Times*, 19 September 1915.

101 Corbett, E. (1964), *Red Cross in Serbia 1915–1919: A Personal Diary of Experience*, Banbury: Cheney, p. 163.

102 *Coffs Harbour and Dorrigo Advocate*, 21 August 1920, FS Coll.

103 *Sydney Sun*, 18 June 1920, FS Coll.

104 'Girls Love of Adventure', *Liverpool Weekly Courier*, 13 December, 1919, p. 3.

105 Ibid.

106 Ibid.

Chapter 7

1 Gannett, D. (1802), *An Address Delivered with Applause, At the Federal Street Theatre, Boston, Successive Nights of the Different Plays, beginning March 22, 1802*, Dedham, Massachusetts, p. 6.

2 Ibid.

3 Quoted in Anon. (1905), 'Deborah Gannett', *Sharon Historical Society*, 2, Boston: C.H. Hight, p. 192.

4 Young, A. (2004), *Masquerade: The Life and Times of Deborah Sampson, Continental Soldier*, New York: Alfred A. Knopf, p. 205.

5 Quoted in Vinton, J. A. (1916), 'The Female Review: Life of Deborah Sampson, the Female Soldier in the War of the Revolution, with an Introduction and Notes', *The Magazine of History, Notes and Queries*, (47), p. 24.

6 Ibid., p. 9.

7 Ibid., p. 24.

8 Young, p. 206.

9 Gannett, p. 12.

10 Ibid., p. 14.

11 Quoted in Anon. (1905), op. cit., p. 192.

12 Gannett, p. 4.

13 Anon. (1905), p. 193.

14 Vinton, p. 18.

15 Ibid., p. 18.

16 Ibid., p. 8.

17 Ibid., p. 17.

18 De Pauw, L. G. (1981), 'Women in Combat: The Revolutionary War experience', *Armed Forces and Society*, 7 (2), pp. 209–26.

19 E. E. Seelye to Albert E. Cowles, Fort Scott, Kansas, 15 August 1883 [emphasis in original], BHLUM.

20 RG 15. Records of the Veterans Administration. Sarah Emma Edmonds Pension File. Application #526889. National Archives, Washington, DC.

21 Schneider, F., 'Sarah Emma Edmonds-Seeley [sic] (Alias Franklin Thompson) The Female Soldier', *The State Republican*, 21 June 1900, p. 7.

22 'Franklin Thompson alias Sarah E. E. Seelye', *House Reports*, No. 820, quoted in Fladeland, B. (1938), 'Alias Franklin Thompson', Vol. 42, (3), pp. 435–62

23 Schneider, F., 'Sarah Emma Edmonds-Seeley [sic] (Alias Franklin Thompson) The Female Soldier', *The State Republican*, 26 June 1900, p. 7 ; see also Fladeland, B. (1958), 'Alias Franklin Thompson', Michigan History, 42 (3), pp. 435–62.

24 E. E. Seelye to R. H. Halsted, La Porte, Texas, 21 September 1897, Clarke Historical Library. Central Michigan University.

25 Schneider, F. 'Sarah Emma Edmonds-Seeley [sic] (Alias Franklin Thompson) The Female Soldier', *The State Republican*, 21 June 1900, p. 7.

26 Seelye to Halsted, op. cit.

27 RG 15. Records of the Veterans Administration. Sarah Emma Edmonds Pension File. Application #526889. National Archives, Washington, DC.

28 E. Edmonds to J. Robbins, Washington, DC, 10 May 1863, Michigan Historical Collections, Bentley Historical Library, University of Michigan (BHLUM).

29 Fladeland, op. cit., p. 462.

30 L. J. Velazquez to General Jubal Early, 18 May 1878, Tucker Family Papers, Southern Historical Collection, University of North Carolina (hereafter SHC). On the father of Velazquez's son, see Blanton, D. and Cook, L. M. (2002), *They Fought Like Demons: Women Soldiers in the American Civil War*, Baton Rouge, Louisiana: Louisiana State University, p. 3245.

31 General Jubal Early to W. F. Slemons, 22 May 1878, Tucker Family Papers, SHC.

32 Ibid.

33 Ibid.

34 Velazquez to Early.

35 Early to Slemons.

36 Leonard, E. D. (1999), *All the Daring of the Soldier: Women of the Civil War Armies*, London: W. W. Norton and Company; Blanton and Cook, loc. 3210.

37 James Longstreet to E. W. Park, Gainsville, Georgia, 18 June 1888, William R. Perkins Library, Duke University.

38 Dowie, M. M. (ed.) (1893), *Women Adventurers: The Adventure Series*, 15, London: T. Unwin, p. 51.

39 Blanton and Cook, loc. 452.

40 Ibid., loc. 1002.

41 Ibid., loc. 3064.

42 Clausius, G. P. (1958), 'The Little Soldier of the 95th. Albert D. J. Cashier', *Journal of Illinois State Historical Society*, 51 (4), pp. 380–87.

43 Ibid., and Blanton and Cook, p. 3073–110.

44 Clausius, p. 385.

45 Blanton and Cook, pp. 3145–54.

46 Anon. (1741), *The Life and Adventures of Mrs. Christian Davies the British Amazon, Commonly Call'd Mother Ross*, London, Part 2, p.79.

47 Ibid., p. 82.

48 Ibid., p. 91.

49 Ibid., p. 101.

50 Boyer, A. J. (1739), *The Political State of Great Britain for the Month of July 1739*, London: T. Cooper, p. 90.

51 'Phoebe Hessel', *The Gentleman's Magazine*, December 1817, p. 550.

52 Ibid., p. 550; Martin, A. (1871), *History of Brighton*, Brighton: W. J. Smith, p. 83.

53 Andrews, W. (1899), *Curious Epitaphs*, London: W. Andrews & Co, p. 3.

54 'Phoebe Hessel', *The Circulator of Useful Knowledge, Literature, Amusement, and General Information*, 5 March 1825, No. 10, p. 147.

55 Anon. (1750), 'Some Account of Hannah Snell, the female soldier', *The Scots Magazine*, Vol. 12, pp. 330–32.

56 Anon. (1750), p. 128.

57 Stephens, M. (2014), *Hannah Snell: The Secret Life of a Female Marine*, Sutton, Surrey: Ship Street Press, digital edn, loc. 901.

58 Ibid., loc. 901 on the Habgood marriage. Hannah Snell's celebrated status may also have been the source of funding for George's education. According to Reverend Daniel Lysons' *Environs of London* she continued to have some public following since, 'a lady of fortune who admired the heroism and eccentricity of her conduct, having honoured her with particular notice, became godmother to her son and contributed liberally to his education', Lysons, D. (1795), *The Environs of London: Being a Historical Account of the Towns, Villages, and Hamlets within 12 miles of the Capital*, Vol. 2, London: T. Cadell, p. 164.

59 Woodforde, J. (1999), *The Diary of a Country Parson, 1758–1802*, Canterbury Press: Norwich, p. 100.

60 Stephens, op. cit., p. 946.

61 The author and publisher of an 1804 account of Hannah Snell's life, R. S. Kirby, is quoted in Stephens's biography as the source on George selling his mother's portrait by subscription. Kirby, quoted in Stephens, loc. 949.

62 Platt, J. C. (1843), 'Medical and Surgical Hospitals and Lunatic Asylums', in Charles Knight (ed.), *London*, Vol. 5, London: C Knight & Co., p. 383.

63 Stephens, op. cit., loc. 962.

64 Lacy, M. (2008), *The History of the Female Shipwright*, with an introduction by M. Lincoln, London: National Maritime Museum, p. 170.

65 Ibid., p. 169.

66 Ibid., p. 5.

67 Guillery, P. (2000), 'The Further Adventures of Mary Lacy: "Seaman", shipwright, builder', *History Workshop Journal*, Vol. 49, pp. 212–19.

68 *Annual Register*, 1802, pp. 431–32.

69 *Annual Register*, 1859, p. 428.

70 Conner, S. P. (2003), 'French Revolution and Napoleonic Era, Women Soldiers', in R. Pennington (ed.) and R. Higham (advisory ed.), *Amazons to Fighter Pilots: A Biographical Dictionary of Military Women*, Vol. 1: A–Q, pp. 174–80; Figueur ref. p. 171.

71 Vandam, A. D., *The New Review*, July 1894, Vol. 11 (62), pp. 24–34 and p. 34.

72 Cardoza, T. (2013), '"Habits Appropriate to Her Sex": The female military experience in France during the Age of Revolution', in K. Hagemann, G. Mettele and J. Rendall (eds), *Gender, War and Politics: Transatlantic Perspectives, 1775–1830*, Basingstoke: Pan Macmillan, pp. 196–97.

73 Hagemann, K. (2015), *Revisiting Prussia's War Against Napoleon: History, Culture, and Memory*, Cambridge: Cambridge University Press, p. 301.

74 Ibid., p. 334.

75 Conner, S. P. (2003), 'Engle, Regula', in Pennington and Higham, p. 153.

76 Conner, S. P. (2003), 'Xaintrailles, Marie-Henriette Heiniken', in Pennington and Higham, pp. 493–94

77 Quoted in Wright, D. (1922), *Women and FreeMasonry*, Rider: London, p. 82.

78 Conner, 'Xaintrailles, Marie-Henriette Heiniken', pp. 493–94.

79 Jeanne Merkus, Algemeen Rijksarchief (hereafter AR), Collection Koopstra, 1030/63, (5).

80 Ibid.

81 Ibid.

82 Quoted in Zirin, M. F. (1989), 'Translator's introduction', in N. Durova, *The Cavalry Maiden: Journals of a Russian Officer in the Napoleonic Wars*, Bloomington and Indianapolis: Indiana University Press, p. xxiv.

83 Ibid., p. xxv.

84 Ibid., p. xxv.

85 Holmgren, B. (1995), 'Why Russian Girls Loved Charskaia', *The Russian Review*, 54 (1), pp. 91–106; p. 97.

86 Ibid., p. 101. Stoff claims that a biography of Durova published in the years just before the First World War 'probably influenced young women to join the fighting. Durova's story was resurrected, although hurriedly and with many errors, during the Second World War in an effort to attract women to military service during the conflict.' Stoff, L. S. (2006), *They Fought for the Motherland: Russia's Women Soldiers in World War I and the Revolution*, Lawrence, Kansas: University Press of Kansas, p. 20.

87 Quoted in Stoff, p. 31.

88 Ibid., p. 21.

89 Zirin, p. xxiv.

90 Sandes, F. (1927), *The Autobiography of a Woman Soldier: A Brief Record of Adventure with the Serbian Army, 1916–1919*, London: Witherby, p. 221..

91 Bray, J., *Biography of Dr. Katherine Stuart MacPhail*, unpublished ms. Imperial War Museum, p. 48.

92 Sandes (1927), p. 221.

93 Ibid., p. 221.

94 Documents from FS Coll.

95 'The Autobiography of a Woman Soldier', *Times Literary Supplement*, 20 May 1927, p. 378.

96 Sandes, p. 200.

97 Ibid., p. 220.

98 Miller, L. (2012), *A Fine Brother: The Life of Captain Flora Sandes*, London: Alma Books, p. 296.

99 Flora Sandes, diary 5 July 1941, FS Coll.

100 Flora Sandes, diary 11 September 1941, FS Coll.

101 Flora Sandes Yudenitch to Colonel L. R. Smellie, Wickham Market, Suffolk, 4 January 1950, Women's Work Collection, Imperial War Museum.

102 Ibid.

103 *Woman's Sunday Mirror*, 1956, FS Coll.

104 Sandes, op. cit., p. 38.

105 Flora Sandes to Smellie, 10 September 1950, Women's Work Collection, Imperial War Museum.

106 Lucas, J. G. (1946), 'Nostalgia for War', *Readers' Digest*, np. FS Coll.

107 In conversation with Mira Harding, Dittisham, Devon, April 1987, who, as a child in Belgrade, knew Flora Sandes as a family friend. 'She was wearing a skirt and she was Mrs. Yudenitch but I knew that she was a soldier.'

108 Serbian National Invalid Fund to Flora Sandes Yudenitch, 28 December 1939 and Invalid's Certificate, 20 February 1930.

109 'Jeanne Merkus', op. cit. (6).

110 Farmborough, F. (1974), *Nurse at the Russian Front: A Diary 1914–1918*, London: Constable, p. 368. Maria Bochkareva's departure from Russia is further complicated by claims that she appealed to Lenin and Trotsky who granted her permission to travel home to Siberia and then to the United States. 'The Battalion of Death', *Times Literary Supplement*, 31 July 1919, p. 407.

111 Dorr, R. C. (1924), *A Woman of Fifty*, New York: Funk and Wagnalls, p. 367.

112 Stoff, pp. 211–12.

113 Harriman, F. J. (1923), *From Pinafores to Politics*, New York: Henry Holt and Co: p. 279.

114 Ibid., p. 280.

115 Ibid., p. 281.

116 Ibid., pp. 284–85.

117 Stoff, pp. 212–13.

118 Stockdale, op. cit.

119 Lawrence, D. (1919), *Sapper Dorothy Lawrence: The Only English Woman Soldier, Late Royal Engineers, 51st Division, 179th Tunnelling Company, BEF*, London: John Lance, p. 189.

120 Oliver, S., 'She Fought on the Somme Disguised as Tommy. So Why did Dorothy die Unloved and Unlauded in a Lunatic Asylum?' *Mail on Sunday*, 12 January 2014.

121 Transcript of notes for Dorothy Lawrence. Box H11/HLL/B/37/035 West London NHS Trust.

122 Ibid.

123 Ibid.; Marzouk, L., 'Girl Who Fought Like a Man', *Hendon and Finchley Times*, 20 November 2003, https://www.times-series.co.uk/

news/432132.Girl_who_fought_like_a_man/ [accessed 14 December 2018].

124 Newton, E. (1984), 'The Mythic Mannish Lesbian: Radclyffe Hall and the New Woman', *Signs*, 9 (4), pp. 558–75.

125 Hirschfeld, M. (1910), *Transvestites: The Erotic Drive to Cross Dress*, translated by Michael A. Lombardi-Nash, Buffalo: Prometheus.

126 Krafft-Ebing, R. von (1965), *Psychopathia Sexualis: With Special Reference to the Antipathetic Sexual Instinct*, London: Staplis Press, p. 265.

127 Ibid., p. 97.

128 Ibid., p. 264.

129 Ibid., p. 280.

130 Ibid., p. 287.

131 Ibid., p. ix.

132 Hirschfeld, p. 111.

133 Oram, A. (2007), *Her Husband Was a Woman! Women's Gender-crossing in Modern British Popular Culture*, London: Routledge, for an in-depth exploration of female husbands and other representations of passing women in early twentieth-century British newspapers.

134 Wren, P. C. (ed.) (1931), *Sowing Glory: The Memoirs of 'Mary Ambree', the English Woman-Legionary*, London: John Murray; 'Paris Day-by-Day – Woman in the Foreign Legion', *Daily Telegraph*, 19 June 1931, p. 11.

135 Forbes, R. (1938), *Women of All Lands: Their Charm, Culture and Characteristics*, London: Amalgamated Press.

136 Ibid., p. 38.

137 Ibid., pp. 132, 9 and 189.

138 Forbes, R. (1935), *Women Called Wild*, London: Grayson & Grayson, p. 172.

139 Ibid., p. 174.

140 'The Turkish Joan of Arc', *New York Times*, 22 September 1917, p. 97.

141 Arkell-Smith, V. (1956), *Empire News and Sunday Chronicle*. 1 April.

142 Collis, pp. 199–201.

143 'Mystery identity in theft charge' (1934), *Western Mail*, 5 September, p. 7.

144 'Woman who posed as Colonel Barker' (1937), *Gloucester Citizen*, 22 March, p. 1.

145 Arkell-Smith, V. (1956), *Empire News and Sunday Chronicle*, 8 April.

146 Indoor entertainment 2, Freak Shows, Box 59-D, Mass Observation Archive, University of Sussex.

147 Ibid. Interview with Blackpool landlord Jack Gallimore about Colonel Barker's seven-week stay.

148 Ibid. See also Meyerowitz, J. (2002), *How Sex Changed: A History of Transsexuality in the United States*, Cambridge, Harvard University Press, who quotes 'Miss R. R.' writing to *Your Body* magazine, inquiring about a change of sex in 1937, p. 14.

149 Bratton, J. (1987), 'King of the Boys', *Women's Review*, Vol. 20, pp. 12–14.

150 Oram, p. 131: 'The classic trickster cross-dressing story dramatically declined as a popular genre during the 1940s and 50s.'

Chapter 8

1 Mattocks, K. M. et al. (2012), 'Women at War: Understanding how women veterans cope with combat and military sexual trauma', *Social Science and Medicine*, 74 (4), pp. 537–45.

2 Darden, J. T. (2015), 'Assessing the Significance of Women in Combat Roles', *International Journal*, 70 (3), pp. 454–62. For examples of European volunteers see Turner, J. (2018), 'She Killed 100 fighters in Syria. Back Home she fears for her life', *The Times*, 28 December, pp. 30–33. https://www.channel4.com/news/the-german-woman-who-says-she-went-to-syria-to-fight-isis [accessed 13 June 2019].

3 Quoted in MacKenzie, M. (2015), *Myths, Men and Policy Making*, Cambridge: Cambridge University Press, p. 1.

4 MacDonald, H. (2019), 'Opinion: Women Don't Belong in Combat Units', *Wall Street Journal*, 16 January.

5 Exum, A. (2004), *This Man's Army: A Soldier's Story from the Frontlines of the War on Terrorism*, New York: Penguin, digital edn, loc. 515.

6 Solaro, E. (2006), *Women in the Line of Fire: What You Should Know About Women in the Military*, New York: Seal, p. 6.

7 Ibid., p. 7.

8 Benedict, H. (2009), *The Lonely Soldier: The Private War of Women Serving in Iraq*, Boston: Beacon Press, p. 2.

9 https://www.youtube.com/watch?v=scKM7eS_JVY [accessed 13.3.2019].

10 Campbell, D. (2003), 'Women in Combat: The World War ll Experience in the United States, Britain, Germany and the Soviet Union' , in Walter L. Hixson (ed.), *The American Experience in World*

War ll: The American People at War: Minorities and Women in the Second World War, London: Routledge, pp. 95–117, p. 95.

11 Griesse, A. and Stites, R. (1982), 'Russia: Revolution and War', in Nancy Loring Goldman (ed.), *Female Soldiers – Combatants or Non-Combatants: Historical Perspectives*, London: Greenwood Press, p. 31.

12 Schwarzkopf, J. (2013), '"Combatant or Non-Combatant?" The Ambiguous Status of Women in British Anti-Aircraft Batteries during the Second World War', *War and Society*, 28 (2), pp. 105–31, p. 121, p. 124.

13 Walker, D. B. (2003), *Spreading My Wings*, London: Grub Street. loc. 880, 942. 'Drab hut' quote in 'Forgotten Pilots' https://www.youtube.com/watch?v=Nx4rSlUlaCo [accessed 24 July 2019].

14 Ibid., loc. 1057.

15 Ibid., loc. 1057. Schwarzkopf quotes Helen Gwynne-Vaughan, Chief Controller of the ATS on the subject of differential pay where she argues that 'because of women's non-combatant status, the principle of equal pay for equal work, which she highly cherished, was not infringed'. Schwarzkopf, p. 128.

16 Walker, loc. 2597.

17 Saywell, S. (1985), *Women in War: From World War II to El Salvador*, Harmondsworth: Penguin, pp. 22 and 19.

18 'Our Special Correspondent With The Army, "A.T.S. Girls" Work On Gun Site', *Times*, 11 October 1941, p. 4. *The Times* Digital Archive, http://tinyurl.galegroup.com/tinyurl/BPoNu7 [accessed 22 July 2019].

19 Ibid.

20 Saywell, p. 11.

21 Churchill quote in Schwarzkopf, p. 111. Soames, M. (2012), *A Daughter's Tale: The Memoir of Winston and Clementine Churchill's Youngest Child*, London: Black Swan, p. 289

22 Schwarzkopf, p. 113; Summerfield, P. and Crockett, N. (1992), '"You Weren't Taught that with the Welding": lessons in sexuality in the Second World War', *Women's History Review*, 1 (3), pp. 437–438 and 442.

23 Summerfield & Crockett, p. 442.

24 Schwarzkopf, p. 126–27.

25 Crawley. S. M. (1950), 'The Use of Woman-Power in the Army', *The Army Quarterly*, 56 (2), pp. 217–25. 'Sweet Polly Oliver' is an English broadside ballad that dates from 1840 and is typical of the

eighteenth- and nineteenth-century heroines who pass as men to follow their lovers to war. https://en.wikipedia.org/wiki/Sweet_Polly_Oliver [accessed 25 September 2019].

26 De Pauw, Linda Grant (1998), *Battle Cries and Lullabies: Women in War from Prehistory to the Present*, Norman: University of Oklahoma Press, p. 248.

27 Campbell, D. (2003), 'Women in Combat: The World War ll Experience in the United States, Britain, Germany and the Soviet Union', in Walter L. Hixson (ed.), *The American Experience in World War ll: The American People at War: Minorities and Women in the Second World War*, London: Routledge, pp. 95–117.

28 De Pauw, op. cit., pp. 250–51; Moskos, C. (1990), 'Army Women', *The Atlantic Monthly*, Vol. 226, (2), pp. 71–78 and p. 72.

29 Rogan, H. (1981), *Mixed Company: Women in the Modern Army*, Boston MA: Beacon Press, p. 147.

30 Tuten, J. M. (1982), 'The argument against female combatants', in Nancy Loring Goldman (ed.), *Female Soldiers – Combatants or Noncombatants? Historical and Contemporary Perspectives*, Westport, CT: Greenwood Press, pp. 237–65.

31 De Pauw, p. 251.

32 Ibid., p. 253.

33 Ibid., p. 256.

34 *Women in the Military: Where They Stand* (2019), 10th edition, Service Women's Action Network, Washington, DC, p. 3.

35 Witt, L. et al. (2005), '*A Defensive Weapon, Known to be of Value*': *Servicewomen of the Korean War*, London: University Press of New England, p. 245.

36 See for example Heather Marie Stur (2012), *Beyond Combat: Women and Gender in the Vietnam War Era*, Cambridge: Cambridge University Press; Marshall, K. (1987), *In the Combat Zone: An Oral History of American Women in Vietnam, 1966–1975*, Boston: Little, Brown and Company.

37 Quoted in Stur, p. 105.

38 Ibid., p. 107.

39 Quoted in DeFleur L. (1984), 'Women in Khaki: The American Enlisted Woman', *American Journal of Sociology*. 89 (6), pp. 1472–73: https://www.jstor.org/stable/2779208 [accessed on 25 July 2019].

40 Steihm, J. H. (1989), *Arms and the Enlisted Woman*, Philadelphia, PA: Temple University Press, pp. 34–41.

41 Women's Research and Education Institute (1990), *Facts About Women in the Military: 1980–1990*, Washington, DC: WREI, p. 1.

42 *Women in the Military: Where They Stand*, pp. 2 and 8.

43 Moskos, p. 73

44 Green, B. (1990), 'Women in Combat', *Air Force Magazine* (June).

45 Quoted in Wright, G. (2018), '"I am a Soldier, not a Gender": Iraq War Literature and the Double Bind of Being a Woman in Combat', *Women's Studies: An interdisciplinary journal*, 47 (6), p. 666.

46 https://abcnews.go.com/International/story?id=79646&page=1 [accessed 22 March 2019].

47 https://www.pownetwork.org/gulf/rd035.htm [accessed 22 March 2019].

48 Quoted in Wheelwright, J. (1990), '"It Was Exactly Like the Movies!" The Media's Use of the Feminine During the Gulf War', in E. Addis, V.E. Russo and L. Sebesta (eds), *Women Soldiers: Images and Realities*, London: The Macmillan Press, pp. 111–36.

49 https://www.nytimes.com/1992/06/29/us/female-pow-is-abused-kindling-debate.htm [accessed 22 March 2019].

50 Ibid.

51 *Washington Times*, 12 September 1990.

52 Sciolino, E., Military Women Report Pattern of Sexual Abuse by Servicemen' *The New York Times*, 1 July, 1992; Loubet, S. T., 'A Soldier's Story'. *Ms.* November/December, 1992, p. 88.

53 Quoted in Walker, M., 'Sex Attacks "rife" on US Servicewomen', *The Guardian*, 2 July 1992.

54 Conversation with the author, 1 February 1991.

55 *Women in the Military: Where They Stand*, pp. 9 and 10.

56 Leavenworth, J. (2008), 'War Over Women in Combat', *Hartford Courant*, 18 March , p. A1.

57 Quoted in Thorpe, H. (2014), *Soldier Girls: The Battles of Three Women at Home and at War*, New York: Scribner, p. 301.

58 King, A. C. (2015), 'Women Warriors: Female Accession to Ground Combat', *Armed Forces & Society*, 41 (2), pp. 379–87.

59 https://thehill.com/opinion/civil-rights/433458-military-commanders-must-take-the-lead-in-battle-against-sexual-assault [accessed 18 March 2019].

60 *Women in the Military: Where They Stand*, p. 26.

61 https://www.nytimes.com/2019/03/06/us/politics/martha-mcsally-sexual-assault.html [accessed 25 March 2019].

62 https://www.nytimes.com/2019/07/26/us/politics/hyten-assault-joint-chiefs [accessed 5 August 2019].

63 https://thehill.com/homenews/campaign/433437-gabbard-says-there-is-still-a-fear-of-retaliation-in-the-military-about [accessed 18 March 2019]. Gabbard has been criticized recently for her public support for President Assad, for meeting with president-elect Trump at Trump Tower and for possible Kremlin links. https://www.nbcnews.com/news/amp/ncna964261? [accessed 5 August 2019].

64 McNulty, Major Shelly S. (2012), 'Myth Busted: Women Are Serving in Ground Combat Positions', *Air Force Review*, 68, pp. 119–65, p. 165.

65 https://www.nytimes.com/2019/03/07/us/politics/mcsally-assault-military.html [accessed 29 March 2019]. Women in other branches of the military services have also come forward with claims of sexual assault such as nuclear guard Jennifer Glover, https://www.nytimes.com/2019/02/14/opinion/nuclear-site-guard-sexual-assault.html [accessed 5 August 2019].

66 Quoted in McNulty, p. 159.

67 Ibid., p. 160.

68 McSally, M. E. (2011), 'Defending America in Mixed Company: Gender in the US Armed Forces', *Daedalus*, 140 (3), The Modern American Military, pp. 148–64, p. 150.

69 McNulty, pp. 124, 125, 130, 152 and 162.

70 McNulty, p. 135.

71 Carl Bergquist, '1st Air Force female pilot in combat reflects on career', *US Air Force*, 6 December 2006.

72 Wheelwright, J. (1992), '"A Brother in Arms, a Sister in Peace": Contemporary issues of gender and military technology', in G. Kirkup and L. Smith Keller (eds), *Inventing Women: Science, Technology and Gender*, Milton Keynes: Open University/Polity Press, pp. 213–23.

73 Ette, M. (2013), 'Gendered Frontlines: British press coverage of women soldiers killed in Iraq', *Media, War and Conflict*, 6 (3), pp. 249–62.

74 Ibid.

75 King, A. (2015), 'The Female Combat Soldier', *European Journal of International Relations*, 22 (1), pp. 122–43.

76 https://www.theguardian.com/uk-news/2018/oct/25/all-roles-in-uk-military-to-be-open-to-women-williamson-announces [accessed 8 April 2019].

77 Sasson-Levy, O. and Lapid, E. (2017), 'Women in the British Army – Everywhere, But Few', *Israeli Defense*, 30 March. http://imgs.syndigate.info/589/1674/82/149087100940 [accessed 26 July 2019].

78 https://www.youtube.com/watch?v=lLXKxe5yv3Y [accessed 25 July 2019].

79 https://girltalkhq.com/metoo-the-military-new-data-examines-how-service-women-deal-with-sexual-harassment [accessed 8 April 2019].

80 https://www.boltburdonkemp.co.uk/military-claims/sexual-harassment-armed-forces/#panel-5 [accessed 8 April 2019].

81 Ibid.

82 https://everydaysexism.com/page/2?s=women+in+the+military [accessed 7 April 2019].

Chapter 9

1 Svetlana Alexievich, quoted in Luke Harding, 'Books Interview', *The Guardian*, 12 October 2019.

2 'Russian Women Sniper', *Yorkshire and Leeds Intelligencer*, 7 November 1942, p. 4.

3 Vinogradova, L. (2017), *Avenging Angels: Women Snipers on the Eastern Front*, translated from the Russian by Arch Tait, London: MacLehose Press, digital edn, loc. 390.

4 Quoted in Vinogradova, loc. 415.

5 Ibid., loc. 444; Vinogradova points out that Pavlichenko had just turned 26.

6 Krylova writes that women formed 10 to 20 per cent of OSOAVIAKHIM members. Krylova, A. (2010), *Soviet Women in Combat: A History of Violence on the Eastern Front*, Cambridge: Cambridge University Press, p. 55.

7 Smith, J. (1942), 'Lieutenant Liudmila Pavlichenko to the American People', *Soviet Russia Today*, October edition, p. 10.

8 Vinogradova, loc. 453–61.

9 Quoted in Vinogradova, loc. 470 from her memoir: Pavlichenko, Liudmila (1958), *Geroicheskaia byl*, Moscow: Politizdat.

10 Smith, p. 10.

11 https://www.woodyguthrie.org/Lyrics/Miss_Pavilichenko.htm [accessed 29 July 2019].

12 'Mr. Hepburn Says More Must Be Done', *Belfast News-letter*, 23 September 1942, p. 2.

13 'No Frills about Lyudmila', *Aberdeen Press and Journal*, 7 November 1942, p. 4.

14 'Russian Girl Sniper in London', *Birmingham Mail*, 5 November 1942, p. 4.

15 Smith, p. 33.

16 'Soviet Snipers in London', *The Times*, 7 November 1942, p. 2.

17 Krylova, p. 164.

18 One example of many can be found in *The Sphere*, 8 September 1917, whose cover features under the strapline, 'For the Honour of Russia – the Women Who Stepped Into the Breach', an image of a wounded woman soldier. I am grateful to Julian Walker for this reference.

19 Ward, C. (2014), '"Something of the Spirit of Stalingrad": British women, their Soviet sisters, propaganda and politics in the Second World War', *Twentieth Century British History*, 25 (3), pp. 435–60.

20 Saywell S. (1985), *Women in War: From World War II to El Salvador*, Harmondsworth: Penguin, p. 11.

21 'Soviet Woman Sniper's Visit', *Northern Daily Mail*, 6 November 1942, p. 8.

22 'Why Pay Women Less Than Men? – Asks Lyudmila', *Daily Record*, 5 December 1942, p. 3.

23 'Red Army Girl, Calls the London Fire Brigade As Test', *Liverpool Echo*, 7 November 1942, p. 3.

24 'Soviet Woman Sniper's Visit', *Northern Daily Mail*, 6 November 1942, p. 8, emphasis in original.

25 'British Women Should be Trained to Arms', *Manchester Evening News*, 25 November 1942, p. 8.

26 'Russian women sniper', *Yorkshire and Leeds Intelligencer*, 7 November 1942, p. 4.

27 'Our London Letter: Good Shot', *Liverpool Daily Post*, 7 November 1942, p. 2.

28 Smith, p. 33.

29 Tenney, E. M. (1992), 'Mrs. Roosevelt, the Russian Sniper, and Me', *American Heritage*, 43 (2), p. 28.

30 Vinogradova, loc. 485. The author quoted from Jesse Storey's article in the Canadian magazine, *New Advance*, which Vladamir Pchelintsev quotes in his memoir, 'Osobaia missia', Internet version.

31 'Girl Sniper Calm over Killing Nazis', *The New York Times*, 29 August 1942, p. 17.

32 Vinogradova, loc. 4768.

33 Ibid., loc. 496.

34 Ibid., loc. 531.

35 Ibid., loc. 357.

36 Ibid., loc. 616.

37 Krylova, p. 3.

38 Ibid., p. 14.

39 Alexievich, S. (2017), *The Unwomanly Face of War*, London: Penguin Classics, digital edn, loc. 177, 181, 212, 323.

40 Ibid., pp. 235–36; 'war wife' and sexual assault, rape, p. 307.

41 Mulhauser, R. (2017), 'Reframing Sexual Violence as a Weapon and Strategy of War: The case of the German Wehrmacht during the war and genocide in the Soviet Union, 1941–1944', *Journals of the History of Sexuality*, 26 (3), pp. 366–401 and 382.

42 Alexievich, p. 273.

43 Ibid., pp. 27 and 36.

44 Vinogradova, loc. 4749.

45 Krylova, p. 14.

46 Krylova, p. 5; Krylova. A. (2010), 'Neither erased nor remembered: Soviet "Women Combatants" and Cultural Strategies of Forgetting in Soviet Russia, 1940s–1980s', in F. Biess, F. and R. G. Moeller (eds), *Histories of the Aftermath: Legacies of the Second World War in Europe*, Oxford: Berghahn Books, p. 86.

47 Alexievich, p. xxx.

48 Ibid., p. 223.

49 Ibid., p. 272.

50 Ibid., pp. 76, 96 & 237.

51 Ibid., p. 328.

52 Vinogradova, loc. 4104.

53 Mathers, J. G. (2006) in S. L. Webber, and J. G. Mathers (eds), *Military and Society in Post-Soviet Russia*, Manchester: Manchester University Press, p. 212.

54 https://www.youtube.com/watch?v=GIPSxzmAWiQ [accessed 12 October 2019].

55 https://www.youtube.com/watch?v=PiZbVOr_hno
http://vmeste-rf.tv/news/95942/
https://rg.ru/2013/06/24/reg-cfo/vdv-anons.html
[accessed 13 March 2019].

56 https://www.youtube.com/watch?v=ehnk9MufrSc [accessed 13 March 2019].

57 https://www.youtube.com/watch?v=__2Atv-QUI4 [accessed 13 March 2019].

58 Tim Whewell, BBC News Magazine, 18 December 2014, https://
    www.bbc.co.uk/news/magazine-30518054 [accessed 24 February
    2019]; https://www.bbc.com/news/world-europe-29721466 [accessed
    24 February 2019].

59 Kuzio, T. (2017), 'Ukraine between a Constrained EU and Assertive
    Russia', *Journal of Common Market Studies*, 55 (1), pp. 103–20.
    The XX Committee (2015), 'Russia's "Secret" Army in Ukraine',
    28 August. Available online at: http://20committee.com/2015/08/28/
    russias-secret-army-in-ukraine-2/ [accessed 3 March 2019].

60 https://www.youtube.com/watch?v=__2Atv-QU14 [accessed 13
    March 2019].

61 https://www.youtube.com/watch?v=scKM7eS_JVY [accessed
    13 March 2019].

62 https://www.youtube.com/watch?v=0rZFF4ZcdMw [accessed
    9 March 2019], MS translation. This interview has had almost 69,000
    views to date.

63 http://lurkmore.to/%D0%9D%D0%BE%D1%80%D0%B4%D0%B8
    %D0%BA%D0%B0 [accessed 9 March 2018].

64 https://www.youtube.com/watch?v=KKiAsLVcDLc [accessed
    22 October 2014].

65 1911 OSW member Re: DAMToys 1/6 Russian Airborne Troops
    – Natalia (78035), https://www.onesixthwarriors.com/forum/sixth-
    scale-action-figure-news-reviews-and-discussion-/851484-damtoys-
    1-6-russian-airborne-troops-natalia-78035-a-2.html [accessed 27
    October 2019].

66 Anna News, 9 March 2015, https://www.youtube.com/
    watch?v=KKiAsLVcDLc [accessed 12 October 2019].

67 Ibid.

68 Ibid.

69 https://www.unian.net/politics/996869-agenta-fsb-i-podrugu-boevika-
    sadista-harlamovu-videli-pod-ap-vovremya-bunta-natsgvardii-foto.
    html [accessed 25 September 2019].

70 https://belsat.eu/en/news/russian-neo-nazi-who-tortured-ukrainian-
    prisoners-shows-off-his-holiday-in-belarus/ [accessed 15 October
    2019].

71 https://toinformistoinfluence.com/2014/10/20/russian-gru-spetsnaz-
    photographed-sniping-in-ukraine-during-ceasefire/ [accessed 25
    September 2019].

72 https://www.youtube.com/watch?v=OoTT9jwYxTI [accessed 15
    October 2019].

73 https://www.youtube.com/watch?v=g_LB8YhLtv8 [accessed 15 October 2019].

74 Yatsyk, A. (2018), 'Russia's Anti-American Propaganda in the Euromaidan era', *PONARS Eurasia* Policy Memo No. 514, 3 March, http://www.ponarseurasia.org/memo/russias-anti-american-propaganda-euromaidan-era [accessed 16 September 2019].

75 https://www.youtube.com/watch?v=8PofBSyZpGo [accessed 12 October 2019].

76 Makarychev, A. and Yatsyk, A. (2018), 'Illiberal geographies: popular geopolitics and Russian biopolitical regionalism', *Eurasian Geography and Economics*, 59 (1), pp. 51–72.

77 https://www.youtube.com/watch?v=cyAOwSYDu2w [accessed 13 March 2019].

78 https://www.youtube.com/watch?v=ff8Ue-S3VEw [accessed 8 March 2019]. For more on Milchakov see https://belsat.eu/en/news/russian-neo-nazi-who-killed-ukrainians-trained-belarus-teens-now-fighting-in-syria/ [accessed 1 March 2019].

79 https://www.youtube.com/watch?v=odWs49QW6Ik [accessed 10 February 2019].

80 http://podrobnosti.ua/998177-organizator-bunta-natsgvardii-julija-harlamova-sluzhit-v-fsb-i-druzhits- zhivoderom-milchakovym-foto-video.html [accessed 12 October 2019]. Yulia defends against these accusations of involvement with the National Guard strike on Anna News on 22 October 2014, https://www.youtube.com/watch?v=XA4ZKUvQIMo [accessed 13 October 2019].

81 https://www.youtube.com/watch?v=2wpfzv2l4RE [accessed 12 October 2019].

82 https://www.youtube.com/watch?v=odWs49QW6Ik [accessed 2 August 2019].

83 http://www.interpretermag.com/an-invasion-by-any-other-name-the-kremlins-dirty-war-in-ukraine/ [accessed 10 March 2019].

84 https://www.nytimes.com/2014/04/21/world/europe/photos-link-masked-men-in-east-ukraine-to Russia [accessed 10 March 2019].

85 https://everydaysexism.com/page/2?s=women+in+the+military [accessed 7 March 2019].

86 Alexievich, p. 109.

Select Bibliography

Archival materials

A.J. Munby Diaries, Trinity College Library, Cambridge.
Ernest Marwick Collection, Orkney Parish Archives, Kirkwall, Orkney.
Gabrielle Enthoven Collection, Victoria and Albert Museum.
Hudsons Bay Company Archives, Winnipeg, Manitoba.
Jeanne Merkus, Collection Koopstra, Algemeen Rijksarchief, The Hague.
Jerome John Robbins Papers, Michigan Historical Collections, Bentley
    Historical Library, University of Michigan, Ann Arbor, Michigan.
MEPO files Valerie Arkell-Smith, National Archives, Kew.
National Archives, Washington, DC.
Observer accounts (1937–1966), Mass Observation Archive, University of
    Sussex, Falmer, UK.
Old Parish Register of Births, Deaths and Marriages, 1861, Kirkwall, Orkney.
Records of the Veterans Administration, RG15, Sarah Emma Edmonds
    Pension File, Washington, DC.
S. Emma E. Edmonds (Seelye) Papers, Clarke Historical Library, Central
    Michigan University, Mount Pleasant, Michigan.
Tucker Family Papers, Southern Historical Collection at the Louis Round
    Wilson Special Collections Library, University of North Carolina,
    Chapel Hill, NC.
West London NHS Trust.
Women's Work Collection, Imperial War Museum, London.

Published materials

Alexievich, S. (2017), *The Unwomanly Face of War*, London: Penguin
    Classics, digital edn.

Alexinsky, T. (1916), *With the Russian Wounded*, London: T. Fisher Unwin.

Andrews, W. (1899), *Curious Epitaphs*, London: W. Andrews & Co.

Anon. (1741), *The Life and Adventures of Mrs. Christian Davies the British Amazon, Commonly Call'd Mother Ross*, London: Richard Montagu.

Anon. (1810?), *The Life and Extraordinary Adventures of Susanna Cope: The British Female Soldier*, Banbury: Cherney.

Anon. (1815), *The Female Marine; or, The Adventures of Miss Lucy Brewer*, Boston: Nathaniel Coverly, Jr.; reprinted 1966, New York: Da Capo Press.

Anon. (1840), *The Surprising Adventures of Almira Paul*, New York: C. E. Daniels.

Arundell, D. (1965), *The Story of Sadler's Wells, 1683–1977*, London: David Charles.

Baker, M. (1985), *Our Three Selves: The Life of Radclyffe Hall*, London: Hamish Hamilton.

Beatty, B. (1918), *The Red Heart of Russia*, New York: The Century Co.

Beddoe, D. (1989), *Back to Home and Duty: Women Between the Wars, 1918–1939*, London: Pandora.

Benedict, H. (2009), *The Lonely Soldier: The Private War of Women Serving in Iraq*, Boston: Beacon Press.

Benewick, R. (1972), *The Fascist Movement in Britain*, London: Penguin.

Bennett, J. M and McSheffrey, S. (2014), 'Early, Erotic and Alien', *History Workshop Journal*, 77 (1), pp. 1–25.

Blanton, D. (1992), *Minerva: Quarterly Report on Women and the Military*, Vol. 10, Fall/Winter, pp. 1–12

Blanton, D. and Cook, L. M. (2002), *They Fought Like Demons: Women Soldiers in the American Civil War*, Baton Rouge, Louisiana: Louisiana State University.

Botchkareva, M. (1919), *Yashka: My Life as Peasant, Exile and Soldier*, as set down by Isaac Don Levine, New York: Frederick A. Stokes.

Bradley Warren, N. (2012), 'Christine de Pizan and Joan of Arc', in L. H. McAvoy and D. Watt (eds), *The History of British Women's Writing, 700–1500*, London: Palgrave Macmillan.

Bremer, C. (1868), *Life, Letters and Posthumous Works of Fredrika Bremer*, New York: Hurd and Houghton.

Bryant, L. (1918), *Six Red Months in Russia: An Observer's Account of Russia Before and During the Proletarian Dictatorship*, London: Heinemann.

Burton, R. F. (1864), *A Mission to Gelele, King of Dahome*, London: Tinsley Brothers. Duncan, J. (1847), *Travels in Western Africa in 1845 and 1846; Comprising a Journey through the Kingdom of Dahomey etc.*, London: Richard Bentley.

Campbell, D. (2003), 'Women in Combat: The World War ll Experience in the United States, Britain, Germany and the Soviet Union', in Walter L. Hixson (ed.), *The American Experience in World War ll: The American People at War: Minorities and Women in the Second World War*, London: Routledge, pp. 95–117.

Cardoza, T. (2013), '"Habits Appropriate to Her Sex": The female military experience in France during the Age of Revolution', in K. Hagemann, G. Mettele and J. Rendall (eds), *Gender, War and Politics: Transatlantic Perspectives, 1775–1830*, Basingstoke: Pan Macmillan.

Carr, J. (1811), *Descriptive Travels in The Southern and Eastern Parts of Spain and the Balearic Isles in the Year 1809*, London: Sherwood, Neely et al.

Carter, T. (1860), *Curiosities of War and Military Studies: anecdotal, descriptive and statistical*, London: Groombridge and Sons.

Caulfield, J. (1819), *Portraits, Memoirs, and Characters of Remarkable Persons*, Vol. 2, London: S. Kirby.

Clark, A. (1995), *The Struggle for the Breeches: Gender and the Making of the British Working Class*, Berkley, California: California University Press.

Clarke, J. S. and McArthur, J. (eds) (2010), *The Naval Chronicle: Containing A General and Biographical History of the Royal Navy of the United Kingdom with a Variety of Original Papers on Nautical Subjects*, 28, July–December 1812, Cambridge: Cambridge University Press.

Clausius, G. P. (1958), 'The Little Soldier of the 95th. Albert D. J. Cashier', *Journal of Illinois State Historical Society*, 51 (4), pp. 380–87.

Clayton, E. C. (1879), *Female Warriors: Memorials of Female Valour and Heroism, from the Mythological Ages to the Present Era*, Vol. 1.

Cohen, D. A. (ed.) (1997), *The Female Marine and Related Works: Narratives of Cross-Dressing and Urban Vice in America's Early Republic*, Amherst: University of Massachusetts Press.

Collis, R. (2002), *Colonel Barker's Monstrous Regiment: A Tale of Female Husbandry*, London: Virago.

Cook Burgess, L. (1994), *An Uncommon Solider: The Civil War Letters of Sarah Rosetta Wakeman, alias Pvt. Lyons Wakeman, 153rd Regiment, New York State Volunteers, 1862–1864*, Oxford: Oxford University Press

Corfield, P. J. (1987), 'Class by Name and Number in Eighteenth-Century Britain', *History: The Journal of the Historical Association*, Vol. 72, pp. 38–61.

Cotton, E. (1849), *A Voice from Waterloo*, London: B. L. Green.

Coues, E. (ed.) (1965), *New Light on the Early History of the Greater Northwest: The Manuscript Journals of Alexander Henry and of David*

Thompson, 1799–1814: Official Geographer of the Same Company 1799–1814: Exploration and Adventure Among the Indians on the Red, Saskatchewan, Missouri and Columbia Rivers, Minneapolis: Ross and Haines.

Crawley. S. M. (1950), 'The Use of Woman-Power in the Army', *The Army Quarterly*, 56 (2), pp. 217–25.

Cuthbertson, B. (1768), *Cuthbertson's System for the Complete Interior Management and Economy of a Battalion of Infantry*, London: W. Cavel et al.

Dadeshkeliani, K. (1934), *Princess in Uniform*, translated by A. J. Ashton, London: Bell.

Darden, J. T. (2015), 'Assessing the Significance of Women in Combat Roles', *International Journal*, 70 (3), pp. 454–62.

Davies, W. H. (1986), *The Autobiography of a Super-Tramp*, Oxford: Oxford University Press.

De Foe, D. (1840), *The Novels and Miscellaneous Works of Daniel De Foe... Vol. viii. Memoirs of Captain Carleton. Life and Adventures of Mrs. Christian Davies*, London: Thomas Tegg.

Defoe, D. (1972), *A General History of the Pyrates*, edited by M. Schonhorn, London: J. M. Dent & Sons.

Dekker, R. M. and van de Pol, L. (1989), *The Tradition of Female Transvestism in Early Modern Europe*, London: Macmillan Press.

De Pauw, L. G. (1981), 'Women in Combat: The Revolutionary War experience', *Armed Forces and Society*, 7 (2).

De Pauw, L. G. (1998), *Battlecries and Lullabies: Women in War from Prehistory to the Present*, Norman: University of Oklahoma Press.

De Pizan, Christine (2003), *Treasure of the City of Ladies, or The Book of the Three Virtues*, translated by Sarah Lawson, London: Penguin.

Derry, C. (2017), '"The Female Husbands", Community and Courts in the Eighteenth Century', *The Journal of Legal History*, 38 (1), pp. 54–79.

Derry. C. (2018), 'Lesbianism and Feminist Legislation in 1921: The age of consent and "gross indecency" between women', *History Workshop Journal*, Vol. 86, pp. 245–63.

Dorr, R. C. (1924), *A Woman of Fifty*, New York: Funk and Wagnalls.

Dowie, M. M. (ed.) (1893), *Women Adventurers: The Adventure Series*, 15, London: Unwin Brothers.

Dugaw, D. (1985), 'Balladry's Female Warriors: Women, warfare and disguise in the eighteenth century', *Eighteenth Century Life*, 9 (1), pp. 1–20.

Dugaw, D. (1989), *Warrior Women and Popular Balladry, 1650–1850*, Cambridge: Cambridge University Press.

Du Preez, M. and Dronfield, J. (2016), *Dr. James Barry: A Woman Ahead of her Time*, London: OneWorld Publications.

Durova, N. (1989) translation, introduction, and notes by Mary Fleming Zirin, *The Cavalry Maiden: Journals of a Russian Officer in the Napoleonic Wars*, Bloomington and Indianapolis: Indiana University Press.

Easton, F. (2003), 'Gender's Two Bodies: Women warriors, female husbands and plebeian life' *Past & Present*, Vol. 180, pp. 131–74.

Easton, F. (2006), 'Covering Sexual Disguise: Passing Women and Generic Constraint', *Studies in Eighteenth-Century Culture*, Vol. 35, pp. 95–125.

Edmonds, S. Emma E. (1864), *Unsexed; or, The Female Soldier: The Thrilling Adventures of a Woman, as Nurse, Spy and Scout, in Hospitals, Camps and Battlefields*, Philadelphia: Philadelphia Publishing.

Elting, J. R. (1988), *Swords Around a Throne: Napoleon's Grande Armée*, New York: Free Press.

Ette, M. (2013), 'Gendered Frontlines: British press coverage of women soldiers killed in Iraq', *Media, War and Conflict*, 6 (3), pp. 249–62.

Exum, A. (2004), *This Man's Army: A Soldier's Story from the Frontlines of the War on Terrorism*, New York: Penguin.

Farmborough, F. (1974), *Nurse at the Russian Front: A Diary 1914–1918.* London: Constable.

Fieseler, B., Hampf, M.M. and Schwarzkopf, J. (2014), 'Gendering combat: Military women's status in Britain, the United States and the Soviet Union during the Second World War', *Women's Studies International Forum*, 47, pp. 115–26.

Fladeland, B. (1958), 'Alias Frank Thompson', *Michigan History Magazine*, 42 (3), pp. 435–62.

Forbes, F. E. (1851), *Dahomey and the Dahomans Being the Journals of Two Missions to the King of Dahomey*, Paris: W. Galignani and Co.

Forbes, R. (1935), *Women Called Wild*, London: Grayson & Grayson.

Friedl, L. (1985), 'Women Who Dressed as Men', *Trouble and Strife: A Radical Feminist Magazine*, Vol. 6, pp. 24–29.

Gannett, D. (1802), *An Address Delivered with Applause, At the Federal Street Theatre, Boston, 4 Successive Nights of the Different Plays, beginning March 22, 1802*, Dedham, Massachusetts.

Gardo, L. (1938), *Cossack Fury: The Experiences of a Woman Soldier with the White Russians*, London: Hutchinson and Co.

Gilbert, O. P. (1932), *Women in Men's Guise*, translated by J. Lewis May, London: John Lane, The Bodley Head.

Godineau, D. (1988), translated by Katherine Streip, *Women of Paris and Their French Revolution*, Berkley: University of California Press.

Grémaux, R. (2017), 'Alone of All Her Sex? The Dutch Jeanne Merkus and the hitherto hidden other viragos in the Balkans during the Great Eastern Crisis (1875–1878)', *Balcanica* vol. XLVIII, (94), pp. 67–106.

Griesse, A. E. and Stites, R. (1982), 'Russia: Revolution and War', in Nancy Loring Goldman (ed.), *Female Soldiers – Combatants or Non-Combatants: Historical Perspectives*, London: Greenwood Press, pp. 61–84.

Guerin, E. J. (1968), *Mountain Charley or the Adventures of Mrs. E. J. Guerin, Who Was Thirteen Years in Male Attire*, introduction by F. W. Mazzulla & William Kostka, Norman: University of Oklahoma Press.

Guillery, P. (2000), 'The Further Adventures of Mary Lacy: "Seaman", shipwright, builder.' *History Workshop Journal*, Vol. 49, pp. 212–19.

Hacker, B. (1981), 'Women and Military Institutions in Early Modern Europe: A reconnaissance', *Signs*, 6 (4), pp. 634–71.

Hagemann, K. (2011), 'Mobilizing Women for War: The history, historiography, and memory of German women's war service in the two world wars', *Journal of Military History*, 75, pp. 1055–93.

Halberstam, J. (1998), *Female Masculinity*, Durham: Duke University Press.

Hargreaves, R. (1930), *Women-at-Arms: Their Famous Exploits Throughout the Ages*, London: Hutchinson & Company.

Harriman, F. J. (1923), *From Pinafores to Politics*, New York: Henry Holt and Co.

Hirschfeld, M. (1910), *Transvestites: The Erotic Drive to Cross Dress*, translated by Michael A. Lombardi-Nash, Buffalo: Prometheus.

Hitchcock, T. (2012), 'The Reformulation of Sexual Knowledge in Eighteenth-Century England', *Signs*, 37 (4), pp. 823–32.

Holmes, R. (2002), *Scanty Particulars: The Life of Dr. James Barry*, London: Viking.

Holmgren, B. (1995), 'Why Russian Girls Loved Charskaia', *The Russian Review*, 54 (1), pp. 91–106.

Hopfl, H. (2003), 'Becoming a (Virile) Member: Women and the military body', *Body and Society*, 9 (4), pp. 13–30.

Houlbrook, M. (2005), *Queer London: Perils and Pleasures in the Sexual Metropolis, 1918–1957*, Chicago: The University of Chicago Press.

Hudson, D. (1974), *Munby: A Man of Two Worlds: The Life and Diaries of Arthur J. Munby 1828–1910*, London: Abacus.

Hutton, I. E. (1928), *With a Woman's Unit in Serbia, Salonika, and Sebastopol*, London: Williams and Norgate.

Jane, E. A. (2017), 'Dude … Stop the Spread': Antagonism, agonism, and #manspreading on social media, *International Journal of Cultural Studies*, 20 (5), pp. 459–75

Jardine, L. (1983), *Still Harping on Daughters: Drama in the Age of Shakespeare*, Brighton: Harvester.

Keuning, J. (1954), 'Nicholas Witsen as a cartographer', *Imago Mundi*, Vol. 11, pp. 95–110.

King, A. C. (2015), 'The female combat soldier', *European Journal of International Relations*, 22 (1), pp. 122–43.

King, A. C. (2015), 'Women Warriors: Female Accession to Ground Combat', *Armed Forces & Society*, 41 (2), pp. 379–87.

Kingsley, R. F. and Clerke, F.-C. (1998), 'Letters to Lord Polwarth from Sir Francis-Carr Clerke, Aide-De-Camp to General John Burgoyne', *New York History*, 79 (4), pp. 393–424.

Krippner, M. (1980), *The Quality of Mercy: Women at War, Serbia 1915–1918*, London: David and Charles.

Krylova. A. (2010), 'Neither erased nor remembered: Soviet "Women Combatants" and Cultural Strategies of Forgetting in Soviet Russia, 1940s–1980s', in F. Biess & R. G. Moeller (eds), *Histories of the Aftermath: Legacies of the Second World War in Europe*, Oxford: Berghahn Books.

Krylova, A. (2010), *Soviet Women in Combat: A History of Violence on the Eastern Front*, Cambridge: Cambridge University Press.

Kuzio, T. (2017), 'Ukraine between a Constrained EU and Assertive Russia', *Journal of Common Market Studies*, 55 (1), pp. 103–20.

Lacy, M. (2008), *The History of the Female Shipwright*, with an introduction by M. Lincoln, London: National Maritime Museum.

Lanser, S. (2001), 'Sapphic Picaresque, Sexual Difference and the Challenges of Homo-adventuring', *Textual Practice*, 15 (2), pp. 251–68.

Lawrence, D. (1919), *Sapper Dorothy Lawrence: The Only English Woman Soldier, Late Royal Engineers, 51st Division, 179th Tunnelling Company, BEF*, London: John Lance.

Leonard, E. D. (1999), *All the Daring of the Soldier: Women of the Civil War Armies*, London: W. W. Norton and Company.

Leonowens, A. H. (1870), *The English Governess at the Siamese Court: Being Recollections of Six Years in the Royal Palace at Bangkok*, London: Trubner.

Llewellyn Barstow, A. (1985), 'Mystical Experience as a Feminist Weapon', *Women's Studies Quarterly*, 8 (2), pp. 26–29.

Lysons, D. (1795), *The Environs of London: Being a Historical Account of the Towns, Villages, and Hamlets within 12 miles of the Capital*, Vol. 2, London: T. Cadell.

Mack, L. (1915), *A Woman's Experience in the Great War*, London: Mills and Boon.

MacKenzie, M. (2015), *Myths, Men and Policy Making*, Cambridge: Cambridge University Press.

Mann, H. (1797), *The Female Review*, Dedham, Massachusetts: Nathaniel and Benjamin Heaton.

Martin, A. (1871), *History of Brighton*, Brighton: W.J. Smith.

Mattocks, K. M. et al. (2012), 'Women at War: Understanding how women veterans cope with combat and military sexual trauma', *Social Science and Medicine*, 74 (4), pp. 537–45.

Mayor, A. (2014), *The Amazons: Lives and Legends of Warrior Women Across the Ancient World*, Princeton and Oxford: Princeton University Press.

McDermid, J. and Hillyar, A. (1999), *Midwives of the Revolution: Female Bolsheviks and Women Workers in 1917*, London: University College London Press.

McNulty, Major Shelly S. (2012), 'Myth Busted: Women Are Serving in Ground Combat Positions', *Air Force Review*, 68, pp. 119–65.

McSally, M. M. E. (2011), 'Defending America in Mixed Company: Gender in the US Armed Forces', *Daedalus*, 140 (3), The Modern American Military, pp. 148–64.

Meyerowitz, J. (2002), *How Sex Changed: A History of Transsexuality in the United States*, Cambridge: Harvard University Press.

Miller, L. (2012), *A Fine Brother: The Life of Captain Flora Sandes*, London: Alma Books.

Moore, M. (1862), *The Lady Lieutenant, or the Strange and Thrilling Adventures of Miss Madeline Moore*, Philadelphia: Barclay and Co.

Morton-Williams, P. (1993), 'A Yoruba Woman Remembers Servitude in a Palace of Dahomey, in the Reigns of Kings Glele and Behanzin', *Africa: Journal of the International African Institute*, 63 (1), pp. 102–17.

Mulhauser, R. (2017), 'Reframing Sexual Violence as a Weapon and Strategy of War: The case of the German Wehrmacht during the war and genocide in the Soviet Union, 1941–1944', *Journals of the History of Sexuality*, 26 (3), pp. 366–401.

Newton, E. (1984), 'The Mythic Mannish Lesbian: Radclyffe Hall and the New Woman', *Signs*, 9 (4), pp. 558–75.

Oram, A. (2007), *Her Husband Was a Woman! Women's Gender-crossing in Modern British Popular Culture*, London: Routledge.

Parton, J. (1869), *Eminent Women of the Age: The Lives and Deeds of the Most Prominent Women of the Generation*, Hartford, Connecticut: S. M. Betts & Co.

Pennington, R. (ed) and Higham, R. (advisory ed), *Amazons to Fighter Pilots: A Biographical Dictionary of Military Women*, Vol. 1 & 2, Westport, Connecticut: Greenwood Press.

Platt, J. C. (1843), 'Medical and Surgical Hospitals and Lunatic Asylums', in Charles Knight (ed.), *London*, Vol. 5, London: C. Knight & Co.

Popham, H. (2003), *The FANY in Peace and War: The Story of the First Aid Nursing Yeomanry, 1907–2003*, Barnsley: Leo Cooper.

Rogan, H. (1981), *Mixed Company: Women in the Modern Army*, Boston MA: Beacon Press.

Rogers, P. (1982), 'The Breeches Part', in P. G. Boucé (ed.), *Sexuality in Eighteenth-Century Britain*, Manchester: Manchester University Press.

Sandes, F. (1916), *An English Woman-Sergeant in the Serbian Army*, London: Hodder & Stoughton.

Sandes, F. (1927), *The Autobiography of a Woman Soldier: A Brief Record of Adventure with the Serbian Army, 1916–1919*, London: Witherby.

Saywell, S. (1985), *Women in War: From World War II to El Salvador*, Harmondsworth: Penguin.

Schwarzkopf, J. (2013), 'Combatant or Non-Combatant? The Ambiguous Status of Women in the British Anti-Aircraft Batteries during the Second World War', *War and Society*, 28 (2), pp. 105–31.

Shaw, J. R. & Teagarden, O. M. (1807), *John Robert Shaw: an autobiography of thirty years, 1777–1807*, Athens, Ohio: Ohio University Press.

Shepherd, S. (1983), *Amazons and Warrior Women: Varieties of Feminism in Seventeenth Century Drama*, Brighton: Harvester.

Sheridan, P. H. (1888), *Personal Memoirs of P. H. Sheridan, United States Army*, Vol. 1, New York: C. L. Webster.

Smith, J. (1942), 'Lieutenant Liudmila Pavlichenko to the American People', *Soviet Russia Today*, October edition.

Snell, H. (1750), *The Female Soldier: The Surprising Life and Adventures of Hannah Snell*, London: R. Walker.

Soames, M. (2012), *A Daughter's Tale: The Memoir of Winston and Clementine Churchill's Youngest Child*, London: Black Swan.

Solaro, E. (2006), *Women in the Line of Fire: What You Should Know About Women in the Military*, New York: Seal.

The Soldier's Companion; or, Martial Recorder, consisting of biography, anecdotes, poetry, and miscellaneous information peculiarly interesting to those connected with the military profession, etc. (1824), London: Edward Cock.

Stark, S. J. (1996), *Female Tars: Women Aboard Ship in the Age of Sail*, London: Constable.

Steihm, J. H. (1989), *Arms and the Enlisted Woman*, Philadelphia, PA: Temple University Press.

Stephens, M. (2014), *Hannah Snell: The Secret Life of a Female Marine*, Sutton, Surrey: Ship Street Press, digital edn.

Stites, R. (1978), *The Women's Liberation Movement in Russia: Feminism, Nihilism and Bolshevism, 1860–1930*, Princeton: Princeton University Press.

St. John, Lady I. (1915), *A Journey in Wartime*, London: Allen Lane.

St-Germain Leduc (1842), *Les Campagnes de Mademoiselle Thérèse Figueur, Aujourd'hui Madame Veuve Sutter etc*, Paris: Dauvin et Fontaine, Libraries.

Stockdale, M. (2004), '"My Death for the Motherland is Happiness": Women, patriotism, and soldiering in Russia's Great War, 1914–1917, *American Historical Review*, 109 (1), pp. 78–116.

Stoff, L. S. (2006), *They Fought for The Motherland: Russia's Women Soldiers in World War 1 and the Revolution*, Lawrence, Kansas: University Press of Kansas.

Stoyle, M. (2018), 'Give Mee a Souldier's Coat': Female cross-dressing during the English Civil War', *History: The Journal of the Historical Association*, Vol. 103, pp. 5–26.

Stur, H. M. (2011), *Beyond Combat: Women and Gender in the Vietnam War Era* Cambridge: Cambridge University Press.

Summers, A. (1988), *Angels and Citizens: British Women as Military Nurses, 1854–1914*, London: Routledge.

Tenney, E. M. (1992), 'Mrs. Roosevelt, the Russian sniper, and me', *American Heritage*, 43 (2).

Thornton. A. J. (1835), *The Interesting Life and Wonderful Adventures of that Extraordinary Woman Anne Jane Thornton, the Female Sailor; Disclosing Important Secrets, Unknown to the Public*, London: [no publisher].

Titunik, R. F. (2009), 'Are we all torturers now? A reconsideration of women's violence at Abu Ghraib', *Cambridge Review of International Affairs*, 22 (2), pp. 257–77.

Trumbach, R. (1994), 'London's Sapphists: From three sexes to four genders in the making of modern culture,' in G. Herdt (ed.), *Third*

Sex Third Gender: Beyond Sexual Dimorphism in Culture and History, New York: Zone Books, pp. 111–36.

Trustram, M. (1984), *Women of the Regiment: Marriage and the Victorian Army*, Cambridge: Cambridge University Press.

Tuten, J. M. (1982), 'The argument against female combatants', in Nancy Loring Goldman (ed.), *Female Soldiers – Combatants or Non-Combatants? Historical and Contemporary Perspectives*, Westport, CT: Greenwood Press.

Velazquez, L. J. (1876), *The Woman in Battle: A Narrative of the Exploits, Adventures, and Travels of Madame Loreta Janeta Velazquez*, edited by C. J. Worthington; reprinted New York: Arno Press, 1972.

Vinogradova, L. (2017), *Avenging Angels: Women Snipers on the Eastern Front*, translated from the Russian by Arch Tait, London: MacLehose Press, digital edn.

Vinton, J. A. (1916), 'The Female Review: Life of Deborah Sampson, the Female Soldier in the War of the Revolution, with an Introduction and Notes', *The Magazine of History, Notes and Queries*, (47).

Walker, D. B. (2003), *Spreading My Wings*, London: Grub Street.

Ward, C. (2014), '"Something of the Spirit of Stalingrad": British women, their Soviet sisters, propaganda and politics in the Second World War', *Twentieth Century British History*, 25 (3), pp. 435–60.

Webber, S. L and Mathers, J. G. (eds) (2006), *Military and Society in Post-Soviet Russia*, Manchester: Manchester University Press.

Webster Wilde, L. (2016), *A Brief History of the Amazons: Women Warriors in Myth and History*, London: Robinson.

Weiss, E. F. (2008), *Fruits of Victory: The Woman's Land Army of America in the Great War*, Washington, DC: Potomac Books.

Wheelwright, J. (1990), '"It Was Exactly Like the Movies!" The Media's Use of the Feminine During the Gulf War', in E. Addis, V. E. Russo & L. Sebesta (eds), *Women Soldiers: Images and Realities*, London: The Macmillan Press.

Wheelwright, J. (1992), '"A brother in arms, a sister in peace": contemporary issues of gender and military technology', in G. Kirkup & L. Smith Keller (eds), *Inventing Women: Science, Technology and Gender*, Milton Keynes: Open University/Polity Press, pp. 213–23.

Wheelwright, J. (1995), 'Tars, Tarts and Swashbucklers', in J. Stanley (ed.), *Bold in Her Breeches: Women Pirates Across the Ages*, London: Pandora Press.

Witt, L. et al. (2005), *"A Defensive Weapon, Known to be of Value": Servicewomen of the Korean War*, London: University of New England Press.

Woodforde, J. (1999), *The Diary of a Country Parson, 1758–1802*, Norwich: Canterbury Press.

Worrall, D. (2014), 'Cross-Dressed Performance at the Theatrical Margins: Hannah Snell, the Manual Exercise, and the New Wells Spa Theatre, 1750', *Huntington Library Quarterly*, 77 (1), pp. 17–36.

Wren, P. C. (ed.) (1931), *Sowing Glory: The Memoirs of 'Mary Ambree', the English Woman-Legionary*, London: John Murray.

Wright, A. and Farquhar-Bernard, A. C. (eds) (1884), *Adventures in Servia: Or, The Experiences of a Medical Free Lance Among the Bashi-Bazou, etc.*, London: W. Swan Sonnenschein & Co.

Wright, D. (1922), *Women and FreeMasonry*, London: Rider.

Young, A. F. (2004), *Masquerade: The Life and Times of Deborah Sampson, Continental Soldier*, New York: Alfred Knopf.

Yurlova, M. (1934), *Cossack Girl*, London: Cassell and Co.

Ziegler, P. (1965), *Addington: A Life of Henry Addington, First Viscount Sidmouth*, London: Collins.

Newspapers and journals

Aberdeen Press and Journal
Air Force Magazine
Atlantic Monthly
Belfast News-letter
Birmingham Mail
Chambers's Journal
Coff's Harbour and Dorrigo Advocate
Daily Express
The Daily Herald
Daily Record
Daily Sketch
Edinburgh Evening Dispatch
Empire News and Sunday Chronicle
The Guardian
The Gentleman's Magazine
Hartford Courant
Hornsey Journal
Illustrated Sunday Herald
Jus Suffragii
Literary Digest
Liverpool Daily Post

Liverpool Echo
Liverpool Weekly Courier
The Liverpool Weekly Post
The London Gazette
The London Graphic
Magazine of History, Notes and Queries
Mail on Sunday
Manchester Evening News
Michigan History Magazine
Morning Post
Ms Magazine
New Fun
New York Times
New York Times Magazine
News of the World
Northern Daily Mail
Notes and Queries
Nursing Times
The Orcadian
Photo Bits
Post and Tribune
Reader's Digest
The Scots Magazine
The Sphere
The State Republican
Sunday Express
Sydney Sun
The Times
Trouble and Strife
Wall Street Journal
Washington Times
Weekly Dispatch
Winnipeg Free Press
Yorkshire and Leeds Intelligencer

Index